THE CHANGING OF THE GUARD

THE CHANGING OF THE GUARD

**How the Liberals Fell from Grace
and the Tories Rose to Power**

Norman Snider

LESTER
&ORPEN
DENNYS
PUBLISHERS

Canadian Cataloguing in Publication Data

Snider, Norman, 1945 –
The changing of the guard: how the Liberals fell from grace and the Tories rose to power

ISBN 0-88619-090-8.

1. Canada — Politics and government — 1980-1984.*
2. Politics, Practical — Canada.
3. Canada. Parliament — Elections, 1984.* I. Title.

FC625.S65 1985   971.064'6   C85-098173-5
F1034.2.S65 1985

Design by Thornley Design Associates Limited
Typesetting by Q Composition Incorporated
Set in 11 pt. Century Old Style

Printed and bound in Canada by
John Deyell Company for

Lester & Orpen Dennys Limited
78 Sullivan Street
Toronto, Ontario M5T 1C1

To My Mother

Parts of this book have appeared, sometimes in different form, in *Quest Magazine* and *The Globe and Mail*.

CONTENTS

Foreword

This book came about because of a suggestion from the editor of *Quest Magazine*, Michael Enright. The last piece I had done for Enright had concerned itself with the heavyweight championship fight in Las Vegas, between the Canadian title-holder, Trevor Berbick, and the estimable Larry Holmes. Enright knew I liked to cover large-scale events tinged with absurdity. Why not have a look at the Progressive Conservatives as they met in Winnipeg to review the leadership of Joe Clark?

On first glance it seemed quite a shift in gears, from heavyweights in Las Vegas to the hapless Mr Clark in Winnipeg. But when I got out west I discovered for myself the truth of Dalton Camp's observation that Canadian politics were less dull than those who wrote about them. As revealed by their Convention contortions in Winnipeg, the Tories were an unusual bunch. Moreover, politics presented an occasion to make the kind of observations about this country and its people that I had been hoarding for a lifetime.

Gradually the articles turned into a series of articles and thence into this book. The events that transpired in January of 1983 in Winnipeg unleashed a number of consequences that didn't cease until Brian Mulroney was elected Prime Minister in September of 1984. Having once engaged in political events, I found it impossible to disengage my interest until a conclusion was reached. The country could palpably be observed to be changing in a number of significant ways. Unlike the social transformations of the previous two decades, those of the 1980s were generally not the sort to inspire writers to hit the campaign trail. They were less obviously spectacular but in their own way equally dramatic. The early 1980s were hard times. There was less money around, less opportunity, but as yet there were no Depression-style soup-lines or shanty-towns. The country was coming to the end of the long reign of Pierre Trudeau. The values of the welfare state were under siege. The gulf between rich and poor was widening. The future, dimly perceived, had a jagged outline.

Accordingly, there was much that was demoralizing for writers facing the current decade; many of them turned away from the sombre contemporary scene in order to contemplate various historical pasts. Still, if a writer couldn't choose the nature of his time, he could yet choose the part he would play in it. In a gloomy era, social criticism becomes increasingly stigmatized as mere negativity. In the context of willed optimism you can do your best to preserve clear sight.

Many events transpired in the writing of this book, not the least of which was the demise of *Quest Magazine*. It is customary in the recollection of political campaigns to make obligatory obeisance to the rigours of the road. I have to say that I enjoyed every moment, or nearly every moment. If there were exhaustions, they were noble exhaustions. And in the course of these travels, I developed a rough appreciation of my country. Patriotism is, after all, one of the more uncomfortable emotions for a writer to feel, since you are hard pressed to find language unburdened by cliché or cheap sentiment in which to express it. It is, after all, the unique nature of Canada that you can go on knowing the worst about the country and still keep loving it. But then, that is a particular mixture of emotions solely reserved for whatever place you call home.

Toronto, March 1985

CHAPTER 1

THE 66 PERCENT SOLUTION

According to those technologists of the soul, the psychoanalysts, depression is introverted hate. Thus imprisoned, murderous impulses turn in on themselves, curdle the mood and sit upon the spirit with all the weight of poured concrete. Well, you don't have to be Freud to detect the depression that comes off the delegates to the general meeting of the Progressive Conservative Party of Canada as they hurry out of the freezing cold into the Winnipeg Convention Centre on a Wednesday afternoon late in January 1983. Unimproved by the tootling of a ragged trio of musicians playing "Tea for Two" sourly out of tune, their low spirits float all through the lobby and up the escalators like steam from a sewer.

But who can blame them? Instead of lolling on a beach in the Bahamas, Jamaica or Bermuda, soaking up some rays, they're in Winnipeg where the blue news on cable television keeps the citizenry informed from moment to moment on the frostbite factor — from that point where it's comfortable to ski to the one where exposed skin will freeze in less than a minute. Yes, here they are, condemned to three or four days in melancholy Winnipeg, which in three decades has gone from being Canada's third city, after Toronto and Montreal, to a ranking well behind Vancouver, Edmonton and Calgary. Unpretentious, homely Winnipeg, a small, flat, friendly place that never boomed or bust, with a decrepit inner core.

Connected to the Holiday Inn by a glass passageway, currently obscured by the posters of those running for executive positions within the party, the Winnipeg Convention Centre is a vast oblong cathedral in concrete that concedes little to the aesthetic sense. The bottom floor, which the delegates now enter, is divided into a warren of small meeting rooms where the party women and youth are to gather; the second floor, in conformity with the current architectural dogma of multi-use, sports a cinema playing *Tootsie*, a mini-mall with bookstore, florist, travel agency, two restaurants and a gift shop. The two big rooms upstairs are named with all the poetry of a telephone listing: Hall A and Hall B. The former, which will serve as the

1

convention floor, is currently closed to journalists, who are already bridling. The effect of having the two huge halls on the top floor gives the building a top-heavy feel, like a steamship with its engines and cargo up top and its bridge below. Since nobody is in a hurry to venture into frostbite country, the convention is to give a sense of being hermetically sealed, outward bound, on a bizarre voyage of its own.

Looking down at the arriving delegates searching for their luggage, you are confronted by a sea of blue pinstripes. You can see that under their military-style fawn camel-hair jobs or 1920s' raccoon coats, two male Tories out of three wear a blue suit. Now among all those high-school vice-principals, accountants, tycoons, Rotarians, advertising men, fraternity boys and professional pols that make up the host of the Conservatives, there is great and subtle variation in the blue suit, from the Tip Top Tailors number sported by small-town delegates to the Savile Row splendour of the ex-cabinet ministers. Nonetheless, there are innumerable social uses to which one can put a Conservative blue suit. It is, after all, the perfect closet in which to hide. Jews, Orientals, homosexuals — all have their place in this party, as long as they wrap themselves up in the Suit, which announces to the world: "I am for order, decorum and piety." If New Democrats and other varieties of socialists want to unionize the entire country, so that one can conceive of them endeavouring to form the Canadian Union of Venture Capitalists, the promise of Tory free enterprise is that anybody can become management. That is to say, privatize garbage collection, have the lowest of collectors go into business for himself, put him in a blue suit and call him Boss. That is the message of the Suit: "I was born to give orders."

Order, decorum and piety are stereotypically considered qualities that make for the health of a society or a political party. Not so for the Conservatives. For them, it is these very qualities that contribute to their malaise, all those chronic pathologies and complexes to which the party has been susceptible for some seventy-five years. There is the Tory Syndrome, as diagnosed by the good Dr George Perlin of Queen's University, a disease of misperception, whereby the many years out of power cause the Tories to blame all their problems on their leader, instead of on the party, and waste themselves in internecine squabbles. There is the Flora Syndrome, a neurotic tic whereby a good Tory Blue Suit announces himself loyally for the party front-runner, piously plasters himself with her buttons, and then, in the privacy of the polling booth, when nobody is looking, unburdens his secret store of resentment and votes for somebody else.

Several weeks before, I had lunched with a man who had been introduced to me as "too bright for the Tory party." He had worked with Stanfield, written speeches for Clark and Bill Davis, differed with them both and now was out of politics. He was indeed an intelligent sort of gent, with a shrewd sense of the disabling afflictions of his party. "Disraeli once said," he told me over pasta in one of Toronto's glossier bistros, "that the Conservative Party in England was an organized hypocrisy. In Canada, it's just a disorganized hypocrisy." On the plane out to Winnipeg, a delegate from Eglinton-Lawrence, the riding within whose stolid confines I grew up, offered a further definition. "A Tory," he said, "is a man who knows what he doesn't want, but doesn't know how to go about getting it."

No wonder, then, that the delegates look a touch down in the mouth as they arrive at the Convention Centre. There is a huge graph posted up on the wall at the entrance, demonstrating their enormous lead in the polls, way ahead of the abominated Liberals month after month. This, after all, is the great Conservative moment in history. Margaret Thatcher in Britain, Ronald Reagan in the United States, the dead hand of the Squeeze throttling every incautious impulse. But here in Canada, the Conservatives had fumbled away power in 1979, by their own ineptitude resurrecting Pierre Trudeau, Lord Dracula himself. Now, razor-sharp, blood-stained incisors at the ready, he still reigns supreme. Whose fault? Perlin's Syndrome always prompts Tories to believe that their leader is at fault. Unlike the Liberals, whose constitution allows for leadership review after elections, the Tories have institutionalized their disease by insisting on a leadership review every two years.

Here in Winnipeg, there is an underlying feeling that if it weren't for the poor political judgment of Joe Clark, instead of palely languishing out of power in the grip of Syndromes, the Tories would be in boisterous good health, rolling in the clover of perks, patronage and power, vigorously throwing the bums off welfare, privatizing every crown corporation and generally saving the world from socialism. Yet, at the same time, there is nothing more important to the Tory mindset than loyalty, obedience to authority, *respect for the Boss*. Nevertheless, once again, they are here to determine their chief's fitness to lead, and scarcely one of them would admit it. At the conference, there are no overt demonstrations against Clark, but

3

late at night in my hotel two pieces of paper arrive, shoved under the door within moments of each other. The first is a card depicting a red, high-heeled slipper and promising "Attractive Female Companions for Discriminating Gents, Free Transportation Provided." The other is a flyer for the pro-leadership-convention forces, saying "71 percent of Canadians want a PC Leadership Convention." Tory delegates were feeling a secret itch to depose their leader, just as they were tempted to fool around on the wife. Once again the Tory delegate is a cauldron of conflicting emotions that he has forbidden himself to express. Little wonder he's depressed.

On Thursday morning, Joe Clark makes his entrance into Hall A. There are those public personalities who improve in estimation when viewed in the flesh. Joe Clark is not one of them. Wearing a blue suit with a subtle wine-red stripe, he makes his way into the hall, awkward as a stork on stilts, accompanied by the modern panoply of power — television cameras, boom mikes and exploding flashbulbs. What a strange creature is Charles Joseph Clark! While many of the Tories seem afflicted with a bad case of jowls, a swelling ham of meat under the chin, Clark is *all* jowls and they quiver wildly as he nods and shakes hands and nods again. The eyes are disproportionately small, the ears disproportionately large. Up close, one can see a network of small veins under the skin that another ten years of passionately savaging the Grits promise to turn into the full red mottle of an apoplectic complexion. But Clark's chest is puffed up and out like a pouter pigeon's; after all, he's proud to be a genuine Canadian celebrity. Every time he goes to Cornwall or Moncton, the locals are thrilled to meet him, almost as much as if he were Bruno Gerussi or Fred Davis. Nonetheless, those television viewers and voters who think Clark is a mere wimp and pushover are wrong. A genuine sense of authority comes off the man. No mere wimp, Joe Clark is Prince of the Wimps, King of the Mugwumps.

Maureen McTeer is a shock and a surprise. Where seven years of celebrity have merely puffed up her husband, they have made her strikingly beautiful, her dark hair shiny, her violet eyes as glittering as any movie star's. Generally, Conservative women come in three varieties. The first is the old-style Rosedale Tory, who looks as if she was once head girl at Havergal College, comes out of the old money tradition of "helping those less fortunate," and serves on the boards of Children's Aid and the Humane Society. Her style is "sensible": cashmere sweaters, plaid skirts, everything unadorned and slightly dowdy, as if high fashion was the preoccupation of the feckless and irresponsible. The second sees her political activities as a useful adjunct to her career. This type often wears a strange kind of self-imposed uniform, in blue or red, that resembles an airline stewardess's get-up and is the female equivalent of the Blue Suit. You can see her joining investment clubs and taking courses on How to Manage Men on the Job.

In contrast, the third type, of which Maureen McTeer is a premier example, radiates the ultragroomed look of powerful Ottawa or Washington: Holt Renfrew and Bonwit Teller on the hoof, not hip enough for Bloomingdale's, let alone Fiorucci. If Joe Clark walked into a room in New York City, he would need an introduction and an explanation before anybody paid him the least attention. His wife could turn heads anywhere. Seen together, they make a curious couple: the Beauty and the Wimp.

Hall A is jammed with the party faithful, squirming in moulded plastic seats of red, yellow and blue. Up on the six-foot-high platform there is a backdrop depicting the nation in Tory blue, superimposed with a computer grid. As we shall see, the grid is mightily symbolic of Clark's vision. On each side of this map of Canada there is a Coke-commercial-style graphic depicting the family of man from Newfoundland to Vancouver Island. There's an Eskimo, Ukrainians folk dancing, blue-collar workers, fishermen — minorities conspicuous by their absence in Hall A. Up front there's a band in straw hats and blue-striped vests that wouldn't be out of place at a Polish wedding in Kapuskasing, playing every type of music from polkas to Dixieland except their own. On the organ, cheap lettering of the kind purchased in hardware stores announces the Ike Kelneck Band. The girl singer, a juicy little thing in poured-on jeans, is just twitching away, pounding a tambourine, the only bit of overt sex visible for miles. She sings: "Parties make the world go round, so let's have a party."

Around the room are arrayed the massed forces of the media. All of CBC, French and English, radio and television, CTV, CITY-TV from Toronto. There is all the nation's press, from *Le Devoir* to *The Globe and Mail* to *The Calgary Herald* and *The Windsor Star*. There is a celebrity convoy that contains Allan Fotheringham, Barbara Amiel and Mordecai Richler. For months and months Canadian politics have been a desert for the media. There's nothing left to write about the moribund Grits, little of interest coming out of Ottawa. Right now, the focus of interest in Canada is this Tory party, syndromes and all. Far ahead in the polls, they seem very likely to form the next government. Right now, the Tories are the story; all of Canada is watching on TV, and the convention is a hot ticket.

Just before the meeting starts, the supporters of Peter Elzinga, a candidate for the party's presidency and an ardent proponent of a return to the noose, make what passes for a demonstration on behalf of their man. Wearing white plastic cowboy hats, and carrying placards, they shuffle around, diffident, embarrassed and grim, waiting for the cameras to take notice. They look terribly uncomfortable, like unwilling family members posing for a snapshot. After all, it was the weirdos who made such public exhibitions of themselves with placards — nuclear disarmers, striking unionists, women against pornography — never Tories.

The meeting starts with all due ceremony; Conservatives believe in ritual. Everybody sings along to the national anthem, except there's one problem: the verse presents a host of conflicting and disharmonious variations — somebody keeps changing the damn thing! A parson with a bleating voice then begs God to bring down "the spirit of wisdom upon our leaders." The Deity could not be listening since the next speaker but one is Peter Blaikie, the outgoing president of the party.

Blaikie, tall, with dark, beetling eyebrows and wearing a nice grey check job that must have been the height of elegance along Sherbrooke Street circa 1947, takes upon himself the mantle of that noted statesman, Spiro T. Agnew. As far as Blaikie is concerned, there's no division about the leadership in his party, it is all "gratuitous rubbish" invented by the media. But nonetheless, in this illusory matter, he declares himself "positively neutral." Blaikie goes on to denounce the pundits by name — Gwyn, Winsor and Fotheringham — and then condemns the press as a whole as a pack of "hanging vultures." "Oh, yes," my Tory insider had said back in Toronto, "there's one other thing about Conservatives: they hate the media." There was no mystery about that. The Tories believed in order and decorum, and the media were a carnival sideshow that, so far from believing in privacy and self-restraint and shoving the unseemly under the carpet, insisted every time on hauling the bleeding guts of the party onto the table and sorting through the entrails for omens. Yet if the Tories hate the media, the media are not impressed. Throughout Blaikie's diatribe, Fotheringham ostentatiously reads from a pile of newspapers, only checking his watch periodically to see how long the party president has spoken. After Blaikie has droned on, thanking his wife, his secretary and his Aunt Betsy, Fotheringham announces,

6

"It's 20 minutes now." Blaikie certainly does like the sound of his own voice. Ten seconds before Blaikie ends, Fotheringham says, "They're going to give him a standing ovation now." As if on cue, the hall leaps to its feet, applauding.

Now it's Clark's turn. There are those devils with silver tongues who make every not so profound word sound like God's Truth. Clark is the opposite. He makes even the truthful notes he sounds resemble white noise.

When every other kid his age was idolizing somebody like Elvis Presley, Joe Clark was idolizing John Diefenbaker. His speaking style still shows it. He tucks his chin deep into his jowls, strikes a grave, self-important, grandfatherly tone, and without fail hits the selfsame note: My fellow Canadians, the country is going to the dogs. While Clark's manner is not so unattractive in a hall, it is notorious poison on television. There are his supporters in the press who curse the television age for putting such a frivolous emphasis on the visual element: hair, teeth, striking features. As far as I can see, Clark is the equivalent of a nineteenth-century politician, with every attribute and talent except that he has a bad stammer and can't address a public meeting in a hall. His supporters then damn the age for forcing politics into halls. For better than twenty years, the public life of North America has taken place on television. The fact is that anybody who isn't good in front of the cameras has little future in politics.

Clark's speech is familiar stuff. The country lies in ruins and Pierre Trudeau is to blame. The Grits are poisoning the wells, raping the virgins and barely refraining from human sacrifice. And the NDP, pinko bastards that they are, back them up. He then goes on to say that his own party has "an unparalleled opportunity to elect a national government that will quite fundamentally and quite literally change the course of Canadian history. They are weak," he says, "we are strong. Where they are weakening, we are strengthening." Then, Clark makes a remarkable slip of the tongue. "The eighteenth of February this year begins the fourth year in office of the Trudeau government. It is the last year of Pierre Trudeau's life . . . political life." The return of the repressed! With a vengeance! I'd read that Clark has a savage personal detestation for the man who has been kicking sand in his face for seven years, but now it appeared that at some level of his psyche he actually wished him dead! "It is the last year of the Liberal government," he concludes. "We together are the Canadian political movement that will not only win the next election but will save the country from the dissension and the disappointment and the disillusion and the despair that has gripped it under the Liberal years. That's our purpose, that's what we're here for." Again the crowd leaps to its feet and wildly applauds.

Getting up from my seat among the press, I privately disagree. For once, true enough, the perennial Conservative lament held true: the country was going to the dogs. But as far as I could see, nobody anywhere on the planet understood what was going on with the global economy. Conservative economic remedies had been tried across the border and they had merely resulted in pervasive unemployment. Only the Falklands and the good General Galtieri were responsible for the continued popularity of Margaret Thatcher. Just at present, though, Clark's strategy is apparently to concentrate his party's attention on the sins of the government and the proximity of power and to deflect the focus away from any consideration of his own failings.

The corridors outside the hall are lined with huge colour posters of Clark looking statesmanlike. The ubiquity of these posters around the Convention Centre becomes oppressive, almost totalitarian. Of all the Tory politicians here, his is the one personality officially recognized. Nobody else is to give a major speech. Peter Worthington, a persistent critic of Clark's, stands in the corridor, next to his ally, Elmer MacKay. "This officially isn't a leadership convention, but it is," he is saying. At this point Worthington is a journalist on the way to becoming a politician. "They can pretend what they like," Worthington continues, "but there's only one issue." "Isn't that hypocritical?" somebody asks. "Of course it is," he replies, green eyes flaring in anger. "It's ludicrous. But this is a very strange party."

MacKay then avers as how, even though they are opposed to Clark, they're all Conservatives together and there's no ill will. A delegate beside him, an elderly man with a white crew cut and festooned with buttons, disagrees. "Anybody who isn't for Joe Clark is on the side of the Liberals," he shouts. The woman beside him yells, "We're here to elect Joe Clark!" No, she realizes, they're not there to elect Joe Clark, they're here to . . . what?

Later on, in the mall, I run into Peter Blaikie. I ask him about his characterization of the media as "hanging vultures."

"I have made the point," he tells me, "that there are very, very few delegates talking publicly about the leadership. They're considering it privately as they have every right to do. Yet the coverage in the media would create the impression that the party's engaged in a huge public debate. That's just not true."

"You feel the leadership issue is concocted by the press?"

"Not at all. What I say is that the discussion is taking place privately, that what the thinking people are doing privately does not lead to the kind of sensationalism we have heard."

"Don't you think you're trying to sweep it all into a closet?"

Blaikie is losing patience. "We're not sweeping anything into a closet. People are going to vote tomorrow night. Whatever is the result of that vote, we'll live with. But that is something completely different from the sense that's being created that everybody in the party is practically on a street corner on a soapbox. That's just not the case."

"But if leadership isn't an issue, why are you here?"

"You're not listening," he explodes. "You're not listening to one word I say! Of course it's an issue. I'm saying it's a private issue. People are making a private decision and that's how it should be."

"Aren't politics public, not private?"

"It'll be public tomorrow night."

Walking away from Blaikie, it occurs to me that the Conservatives are like a certain kind of Wasp family where the daughter is going crazy upstairs, alone in her bedroom, the son is getting ready to elope with the Jamaican maid, Mother is drowning her sorrows in gin, but not a word about any of these things is mentioned at the dinner table, and the front porch stays calm. One day Father takes a shotgun to them all, and the neighbours say, "They were such a quiet, private family."

That afternoon, across the street in the Manitoba Suite of the Charter House Hotel, the overt anti-Clark forces are in full distemper, getting ready to make a move. These guys have the unlikely effect of making you sympathize with Joe Clark. As well as being a political party, the Conservatives are a kind of lifelong social club, and there are a number of longtime members who have been manoeuvred off the roster of delegates by the Clark organization. Some of them are in this room and they're festering with rancour. There's a large number of young Tories here as well. The sergeant-at-arms guarding the door wears a blue blazer, has close-set eyes and the look of a private-school bully. There's an older man, a delegate from Etobicoke Lakeshore, who twirls his mustachios like a silent-movie villain. There's a blackboard on which the room numbers of hospitality suites are listed, targeted for the proselytizers. Among themselves, the thirty or forty conspirators packed into the small room pass a flyer touting a speech by Paul Fromm, a veteran of many a far-right organization in Toronto. They wear buttons saying "Socialism is just a phase you're going through." There is even a reporter from William F. Buckley's *National Review* to lend the proper tone.

John Gamble, a right-wing MP from Toronto, who looks like a cartoon figure of a capitalist, in fur-trimmed coat, fur hat and, yes, a blue pinstriped suit, gives a speech in which he relies heavily on the accumulated wisdom of cab drivers he has known over the last couple of days: none of them likes Clark. He mentions a young Conservative who stated in *The Globe and Mail* that the NDP and Liberal supporters in his college political science course want to keep Clark as leader. "The people who are telling us 'don't vote for a convention,' " he says, "are on the side of the Liberals!"

Somebody else gets up and says, "The change from yesterday to today is amazing. They've come to this convention thinking Joe Clark is safe, and they've started to talk to people and they see he's in deep trouble. Our base vote is 40 percent, it's rock hard and we're at 50 percent." He sits down to cheers and applause.

Another of the anti-Clark conspirators gets up and cautions the eastern pro-review forces against appearing to be against the West, urging them to reassure the westerners that they would vote for Peter Lougheed. A silver-haired longtime Conservative from Calgary West, Carl Youngren, rises to address this point. "I don't think there's anything against Conservatives in the east," he says, "but one of the things that angers westerners is the Dalton Camp association. That's where the trouble starts. He's still the cross the party has to bear, the Achilles' heel." Then Youngren goes into a full, choleric denunciation, a raging tirade: "Dalton Camp is a Judas goat, another thing, a Black Angel, and unchristian. We have to get rid of that man. We have to get him off the media, we have to get rid of him, we have to get rid of Eddie Goodman and all those Red Tories; then we'll have the westerner a bit better."

Of course, the previous day, Dalton Camp had referred to those in this room as "a cashew coalition of nuts and extremists." John Morrison, one of the chief instigators of the anti-Clark movement, a jowly, self-described "freelance public relations man," who has just addressed this meeting, does not like what Camp has said. Swathed in a heavy parka, Morrison has a bristling red moustache and a florid complexion; when Camp's name is mentioned, he gets so angry that he looks as if he's going to explode. "We are the mainstream party.

We are going to prove that Friday night. If Dalton Camp doesn't like it, he can join another party or go back to the Liberals where he came from." There is little of the traditional Tory belief in keeping things bottled up in this room: the rage and frustration are out in the open here, for all to see. They think Clark's chance of getting power "damn slim"; they see him as "flip-flopping all over the place." Worst of all, they damn him in the vocabulary of free enterprise. "You can't sell him in my riding," says John Barrett, the man with the mustachios from Etobicoke-Lakeshore. "This party has to be in the business of presenting a viable product to the Canadian people. With Joe Clark we can't do that."

"Shouldn't we have some kind of march?" asks a young Tory of the fraternity-boy variety. But, enraged as they are, the anti-Clark forces feel that too overt a demonstration will work against them. They know their party.

"I think if we were to leave here at the same time," says Barrett, "and go over to the convention with our posters and stickers, it's gonna seem like that."

Once on the convention floor, the anti-Clark forces start to proselytize. Peter Millar, a farmer and small businessman from London, buttonholes a grey-haired delegate wearing a Clark button. Millar has the confidential, insinuating air of a practised salesman. The man says he's still undecided about the leadership issue, wants to talk to a few more people. "I know in my riding 80 percent of the public wants to see a leadership convention," says Millar. "That's why I want to see a review. This way we can have a more effective party and policy than the ones we have." The man declines to take a pro-convention button.

Meanwhile, another delegate from London is having a disagreement with a reporter. Vic Graat, an oily-haired man in a blue pin-striped suit, with an unpleasant rosebud mouth, believes that Pierre Trudeau is a communist. In all seriousness.

"Fidel Castro wouldn't think so."

"Three crown corporations were taken over by the government," Graat shouts incoherently. "No reason; just because they were the government. That's communism, no question."

"That's indiscreet but it's true," says Millar.

"Petro-Can!" shouts Graat. "That's communism. I go to your bank account and take it. What's that?"

The reporter shrugs.

"It's communism!"

11

Giving up on the unbelieving reporter, Graat is enraged. "These guys don't want to hear the truth," he raves. "They just want to hear garbage!"

In the background there's a workshop entitled "Fighting the Liberals," featuring freeze-frames of the cabinet, caught eyes closed, that make Trudeau and his ministers look like Al Capone and his henchmen. In the press lounge I run into a grizzled delegate from Quebec, with the appearance of a mortician from Chicoutimi, who looks like the ghost of Réal Caouette. "I'm with Joe," he tells me, "If Joe gets out, I get out. I've had enough of this bullshit." The man is exercised over the Jerusalem incident. Why did Joe get involved? "Arabs and Jews. That's like Lucifer and Satan. Let them kill each other."

The delegates I met Thursday, the right wingers, were by and large small businessmen, farmers, petite bourgeoisie, bristling with resentent at those who threatened the little bulwarks they had raised against life: the high-taxing politicians, the idlers on welfare, the city slickers and trendies, and all the rest. On Thursday morning, in the coffee shop of the Marlborough Inn, I meet the left wing of Canadian conservatism in the person of the son of this country's greatest tycoon, Charles Taylor, son of E.P. and author of a book called *Radical Tories: The Conservative Tradition in Canada*, who is in Winnipeg to be interviewed by CBC's *The Journal*.

I had grabbed Taylor's book immediately on publication. It was the age of conservatism, ideologically speaking, and while we had the testimony of innumerable Jewish ex-Trotskyists inventing the terms of American neoconservatism in New York, there had been little written in the Canadian context. Although Taylor scorned the nostalgia for Empire that characterized previous generations of anglophilic Canadian Tories, his book was suffused with a nostalgia for Canada's Victorian roots. Together with his friend and mentor, Scott Symons, Taylor professed a brand of conservative thought best characterized as Aesthetic Toryism, which liked to compare Robert Stanfield to a wonderful piece of Canadiana furniture, that doted on Stephen Leacock and old Ontario summer homes with graceful porches and balconies. Taylor's version of conservatism was the closest thing Canada had to the articulation of an aristocratic creed (unless it be found in the novels of Robertson Davies), complete with Red Tory notions about social decency and responsibilities to the poor. It was a

12

squire-like vision, anti-American, anti-urban, anti-cosmopolitan. Since I would give the entire oeuvre of Stephen Leacock for one page of Henry Miller, prefer the skyscraper to the farmhouse, and could tolerate Toronto only so far as it was coming to resemble Manhattan, I was particularly anxious to meet Taylor and talk to him.

He is tall, pale, wears severe-looking spectacles, has thinning fair hair. You can see him as a character out of Henry James, half connoisseur, half plutocrat. As a Canadian conservative, his attitude to the Progressive Conservative Party is very much *de haut en bas*. I ask him just how much George Grant and Donald Creighton he perceives in the speeches of Joe Clark. "Well," he replies, "some of his speeches recently sound like pure Reagan. He has no concept of what the country is about and what the traditions are. Now that may be pure politics on his part because of the poor position he's been in for the past three years. But I think that's true of the party as a whole; they're not aware of their past." I ask him if the PCs are moving farther to the right. "They deny that," he says. "They say that the Liberals have gone so far to the left, along with the NDP, that they're trying to bring it back to the centre. Selling off crown corporations is not part of Conservative tradition or policy. I think they're deceiving themselves and they're trying to be ideologues. Which a Conservative never is. They're not listening to their own pollster, Allan Gregg, who says that the public will never elect a right-wing Conservative Party. The public as a whole don't approach matters ideologically. They're not particularly for or against public enterprise; they just like things that work. A good example is that the public are for Petro-Can but against the post office. Petro-Can works; the post office doesn't."

If ideology and policy are being discussed on the edges of the convention, in its official confines there is a distinct absence of policy discussion. To a large extent, this is a reflection of the personality of Joe Clark. He is obsessed with the practical machinery of politics — organization and structure — at the expense of content. This is very much reflected in the audiovisual "workshop" entitled "Campaigning to Win." So far the "audiovisual" presentations — elaborate, expensive, heavy-handed — have not exactly qualified for any Leni Riefenstahl awards for film propaganda. But "Campaigning to Win" is right out of a company sales convention. It is paint-by-numbers politics for canvassers, the country put under a computer grid, full

13

of demographic analysis, opinion research breakdown of votes into six categories from "hard support" to "hard against". This approach is exactly the same as the one Clark has used to identify his support in the party and to label those opposed to him as "7," a button they now proudly wear.

Clark and his organization resemble the casino owners of Las Vegas in that they are constantly striving to arrange the house odds in their favour. Friday morning, there has been a big squabble over the admission of Quebec delegates to a session of PC youth. Party bureaucrats have not given them the correct starting time, and they have arrived at the meeting to find the doors already closed. The suspicion in Clark's camp, of course, is that these delegates are pro-Mulroney and now they are trying to exclude them from the meeting on a technicality. When Brian Mulroney arrives, he is seized on by the press in that peculiar melee known as a "scrum." To the uninitiated, scrums could be terrifying. They were politics as contact sport. Sometimes as many as a dozen reporters, cameramen and sound technicians charged towards a politician, fire in their eyes. If you got in the way of a cameraman, you could get a knock on the head from his camera that left you spinning. Radio reporters carried their mikes on long sticks, which they thrust towards the pol in questions; a jab from them could smart too. Reporters, such as the CBC's Mike Duffy, were like pulling guards in football: they just flat ran over whatever was in their way. If you weren't a wire service guy or had no immediate deadline on your back, you learned to keep your distance. If something important emerged, you'd find out anyway. As one of the oldest pros on the political beat put it, "Scrums are for amateurs and technicians."

Where Clark is no chin, all jowls, Mulroney is all jaw, all charm. He's really angry about the delegates from Quebec, criticizes the "grossly overpaid party bureaucrats." This is a wonderful chance to castigate the party without attacking Clark openly. Given the premium Tories put on loyalty, no serious leadership candidate can do this. On 6 December 1982, Mulroney, in a supreme bit of farce, had held a press conference at the Ritz-Carlton Hotel in Montreal, protesting his loyalty to Clark. Later it was to emerge that a group of his friends, led by former Newfoundland premier Frank Moores, had been striving for a review of Clark's leadership, funded to the tune of a quarter of a million dollars. The dirty work is left to such lesser lights as John Morrison. Daniel Stoffman of *The Toronto Star* emerges from the scrum around Mulroney and announces: "It's falling apart for Clark."

Early in the afternoon, William Davis arrives at the convention. Taller than expected, carrying his unlit pipe close to his chest like a tiny sceptre, bathed in television light, he makes a regal progress up the escalator to Hall B, where a reception is being held in honour of the provincial premiers. Like his fellow provincial potentate, Peter Lougheed, Davis radiates a sense of self-satisfied power. A leader of the opposition, his manner implies, is not at all of the same status as himself. Yes, he would accept the prime minister's post, if somebody else in the party would go through the nastiness of winning power. But move to Ottawa and eat dirt at the hands of Lord Dracula and the boys? Actually get down in the gutter of a federal election campaign, where, unlike Ontario, he actually stood a chance of losing? That was beneath his dignity. According to my Tory insider, Joe Clark had the following point in his favour: compared to all the others, *he* was the hungriest. He wanted the job most, and was willing to eat any amount of dirt to keep it.

In the afternoon, the mood gets increasingly virulent. There are rumours of scuffles among the women delegates. Late in the afternoon, goaded beyond endurance, the pro-Clark forces are beginning to lose their cool. On the mall, John Fraser (not the cheerful journalist, but the MP for Vancouver South) erupts against one of Morrison's minions, a man called Ross Peart. Fraser is a little bulldog, bleary of eye, a couple of drinks on his breath, and he is furious. "Listen," he says, with considerable heat, "I'm sick and tired of this right-wing bullshit! Every time John Morrison gets up and craps on our party and our leader, I lose votes in Vancouver South. And if you guys think we have all those seats for sure, for certain, forever, you're crazy. I fought for that goddamn seat. I took it away from the people who said that we could never take it. That's what a lot of us have done. And we didn't do it by crapping on our goddamn leader, whoever he was. When you guys are good enough to win a seat with this right-wing bullshit, then you come and give me a lecture!"

Looking on, I had to admire Fraser. His was the first moment of unrehearsed feeling the convention had so far produced. There were real jobs at stake at this convention, cold cash. It was getting to be hard, serious business.

On Friday night, Hall A is jammed with shouting, stomping delegates, for Clark and against. Yesterday Ronald Huntington, chairman of the Tory caucus, revealed to John Gray of *The Globe* that the caucus could be in full revolt if Clark did not do better than 66 percent. The anti-Clark forces have mounted a substantial demonstration: when Clark's supporters chant, "We want Joe, we want Joe," they add, "Out!" With the noise of these demonstrations, the event begins to take on the outlines of professional sport. The convention is now going out live on television across the country; the nation is watching. This convention is a good appetizer for that mass audience that regards politics and sports as interchangeable diversions; the full meal of the Super Bowl is only a few days away.

In readiness for the main event, the Ike Kelneck Band plays the Tory fight song: polka music. Reporters are speculating on who wrote Clark's speech. They agree he has to be personal, ask for the help of the party. Duff Roblin, ex-premier of Manitoba, the Peter Lougheed of 1967, tries to quiet the convention as the anti-Clark forces parade around the hall to a chorus of boos. "You'll get your cheering time later," he says. The Tories allot time for cheering, naturally, but are unhappy when it occurs out of its scheduled sequence. The provincial premiers are introduced like contenders in other weight divisions at a heavyweight fight. When Clark makes his entrance, you feel like the band should be playing the theme from *Rocky*.

Clark clearly has to give the speech of his life. It matters little, in this age of the 30-second TV clip, that political oratory is a declining art. Clark breathes fire against the Liberals, calls for party discipline, but never once speaks personally. Oh, he makes a gesture towards contrition about his mistakes, but never once strikes an intimate note. His personality as leader comprises the real issue of this convention and he refuses to deal with that fact head on. Instead he talks euphemistically about "unity" and "getting our act together." His anger is mechanical, unimpressive. More than ever, Joe Clark seems a hollow man, entirely lacking in soul, as synthetic as his cherished computers. "In the name of our country," he concludes, "let's get on with the job," implying that questioning his leadership is, at heart, just goofing off. Once again, the cheering, for and against, is enormous.

The reaction to the speech is most curious. "I thought it was a good speech. I thought he did well," says tiny perfect David Crombie, met on the floor. The media are impressed. After a straw poll, CTV predicts 78 percent for Clark. Fraser Kelly of CBC thinks it's a good

16

speech. As far as I can see, they're just reacting to the noise of the demonstrations, the nervous hype. CTV gets John Morrison on the air and belabours him for his stupidity. Clark has clearly won it, as far as they're concerned.

Downstairs, on the second floor, it's a different story. The results are brought in to Clark, waiting in the business office of the Convention Centre. Thirty-five minutes later there's no sign of him. Like Blaikie's vultures, journalists begin to gather outside the door. First, Val Sears of *The Toronto Star*, the Silver Fox of Canadian journalism. Then *The Globe*'s John Fraser and myself. Then CP, then Ian Anderson of *Maclean's*. Outside there are Clark staffers in grey suits, with walkie-talkies. A Clark executive assistant, a woman in a blue pinstripe, comes out bearing an expression usually seen around terminal cancer wards. Tim Ralfe, a balding, harassed-looking guy in a blue suede jacket who's very close to Clark, notices that the press has spotted the stricken look on her face and rushes over to her. Sharp words are exchanged and the most forced smile in the history of smiling appears on the poor woman's face. It does not look good for Joe.

"What's going on, Tim?" asks Sears, looking at his watch. "It's costing a million dollars to hold the presses." "Did I mention that I don't really care?" Ralfe replies. Minutes drag by. Don Mazankowski and Erik Nielsen, the men closest to Clark in caucus, are brought in for consultation. It's certain: a disaster is brewing. Sears nods to Art Lyon, the chief convention organizer, and says, "Don't worry, Art, you'll have fun at the leadership convention."

More time goes by. Politics, like war, consists of much waiting. Then Finlay MacDonald, Silver Fox of the Conservatives, emerges from the business office, arm-in-arm with the executive assistant.

"Where's Joe?" asks Sears.

"He's gone," replies MacDonald, silver fox to silver fox. "For serious, Val." Clark has escaped by some back route.

Upstairs in Hall A the delegates are clueless as to what's going on. The Ike Kelneck outfit has brought out its bar band repertoire and everybody is boogying away to "Proud Mary." Beer in paper cups is being sold out in the corridor, and they're getting ready to party all night long. There is no sensation quite so eerie as going into a hall in possession of knowledge of which a crowd of 2,500 is ignorant. It's like waiting for a bomb to go off. After some Academy-Award-style flourishing of ballots, Pat Carney, large, stout, grey, the tears audible in her voice, announces the result. Out of 2,402 votes,

Clark has got 1,607 — 66.9 percent. He appears on the platform with a visibly pale Maureen McTeer. At first it seems as if he is going to brazen it out. After all, he has received a majority. "I asked for a clear mandate," he says. "I received the support of a clear majority of the delegates voting here." Then, all at once, he changes direction. "It is not clear enough to enforce the kind of discipline and to achieve the kind of unity that this party requires." Near me a Young Tory leaps in the air and shouts, "We've got a convention!" Hall A is in shock. The television reporters are scrambling wildly to line up reaction. Their predictions have been hopelessly wrong. The anti-Clark forces are congratulating themselves as Clark calls for a convention and announces himself as a candidate. "He's gone!" they yell. "We got rid of the jerk!"

Then, just like that, the carefully nourished decorum of the Tories falls apart like wet Kleenex. The delegates file out of Hall A in silence, stunned, lobotomized. Many of the women are in tears. Their collective depression has taken a turn for the worse. Otto Jelinek, one of the anti-Clark leaders in the Tory caucus, is giving an interview when an irate Clark supporter in a hockey jacket, somewhat the worse for beer, tries to throw himself on him. The man is narrowly prevented from doing so by his friends. "Asshole," he mutters underneath his breath. Crombie, whose lack of support for Clark is well known, is campaigning already, pressing the flesh on the floor. "Hey," he tells a delegate, "I knew your grandmother."

In the corridor leading to the Holiday Inn, another drunken delegate throws himself on my shoulders, all restraint gone. "We screwed ourselves again, eh?" Beside him, his friend moans, "Joe's a born loser." Spotting Peter Worthington in the corridor, a Clark supporter shouts at him "You happy, Peter? You happy now?" Worthington looks startled by the man's vehemence. In the press room, Fraser Kelly tells Worthington admiringly, "You know the party, Peter." "No," says Worthington, "I know the people."

Back in the hall, John Morrison radiates a positively post-coital sense of satisfaction. "Yes," he says, "we're extremely pleased." For most delegates, however, there'll be no party tonight, but a wake. They had once more pledged loyalty to the leader, but voted their secret resentments. The Tories had again succumbed to their congenital fevers, their chronic syndromes.

The next day, Clark announced that he would step down as party leader. Then he changed his mind. After a few days of further internecine squabbling, the Tory caucus met behind closed doors and emerged three hours later claiming that peace had been restored. Joe Clark retained his position as party leader for the moment but Erik Nielsen became interim opposition leader in parliament. Instead of a wimp, the Tories now had a bully. Ron Huntington was forced to resign his position in caucus, punishment for talking too freely to the press. Lougheed declined to run but indicated he might be persuaded by a draft.

Meanwhile, the Liberals relaxed. The coming Tory victory was no longer a certainty. Some wags claimed that Lord Dracula was working things out so that he could, in the fullness of time, hand things over to Justin, Sacha or Michel. Yet the suspicion was that Clark was not completely through. Possibly his best moment in Winnipeg had been when he called for a leadership convention. If Clark had often reminded one of an actor badly miscast in his role, he had at last found a part he could play with conviction: Sydney Carton, mounting the scaffold to the guillotine, doing the decent thing for his party and his nation. Whatever the case, the coming year of Canadian politics offered intriguing vistas to the future. Now it was all up for grabs. Whatever else our politics would be, they wouldn't be dull.

CHAPTER 2

THE NEW TORIES

For me, Ottawa has always been an enigma. On the one hand, the capital is a one-storey town with leafy, quiet, unpresuming residential streets that remind you of other such streets in Kingston and Stratford. On the other hand, it is the seat of this country's political grandeur, the home of parliament and the embassies of great nations, as well as Canada's most powerful men. The geographical incarnation of the national compromise, Ottawa is one of the few places in the country where you can hear somebody other than a politician start a sentence in English and finish it in French, or vice versa. Yet all too often, Ottawa, as a national capital, lacks majesty.

There is, for instance, the Ottawa Civic Centre. It is a venerable hockey arena that seeks to disguise its age with a modernist façade of glass and steel. Home of the major junior Ottawa 67s, it huddles under the stands of Lansdowne Park, home of the CFL Rough Riders. Across the parking lot stands the tin-roofed Coliseum, a perfect place for a country auction. Down at the other end of the parking lot is the ancient, disused Manufacturers' Exhibition Building, a relic of nineteenth-century artifice that sports gingerbread decoration, carved horses' heads and other period bric-a-brac.

Arriving here on a Thursday morning in June, I think this unimpressive huddle of buildings to be best suited to a rural fair. (One could imagine the dismay of some hotshot all-American from Ohio State or Notre Dame, getting out of the taxi and reporting to the Rough Riders. *This is it?*) Instead, this humble conglomeration of architecture is about to serve as the stage for the largest political convention in the country's history. If, as Dalton Camp once wrote, Winnipeg functions as the New Haven of Canadian politics, Ottawa is its Broadway. The Progressive Conservatives, in the cold of a Winnipeg January, had, almost against their own will, forced their leader, Joe Clark, to throw his position up for grabs. Rather than the self-inflicted disaster for the party that some commentators described, the meeting in Winnipeg had been a pretty good dress rehearsal. As they went through the rigours of a spring leadership

20

campaign, the country's attention remained focused on the Conservatives. They continued to run substantially ahead of the governing Liberals in the polls. The standard refrain of the pundits was that this convention would be choosing the next prime minister of Canada. Now, in the heat of an Ottawa summer, the curtain is going up on the real show. But compared to the importance of the event, its low-rent setting is all out of proportion.

The three major candidates are the ex-leader, Joe Clark, the eventual winner, Brian Mulroney, and the man who, wittingly or not, will make the difference — John Crosbie. At this point, Clark is still the front-runner and, to those observers who look on the Tories with an habitually ironic eye, the favourite. For them, Clark is a loser and the Tories, out of power so long, a party born to lose. Mulroney, on the other hand, is glaringly a winner in life, and it is said that is why some Tories don't like him. He is too pretty, too slick. As a result, he has run a self-consciously "frugal" campaign. Too phosphorescent a manner reminds Tories of the arch enemy, the Liberals, and their habitual winner's gloss. Because Mulroney is so determined to be a winner all the way, he has scorned the loser's traditional place, the backbenches of opposition, with their occupants impotently scolding the government year after year like a shrewish wife nagging her unredeemably alcoholic husband through half a century of marriage. Mulroney would either be leader or nothing at all. Yet, if the Tories stand for anything, it is for dutifully facing up to the tedious in life. There is a school of thought that wants the Canadian people to gulp down Clark, like so much castor oil, punishment and purgative, for having indulged themselves so long with the wicked, heady spirits of Pierre Trudeau. A good, long dose of homely Joe would bring the country to its senses.

John Carnell Crosbie arrives at the Ottawa Civic Centre around 10 o'clock. With some time to spare before the opening proceedings, Crosbie is being piloted by his aides through the blue-and-white striped tent like a large ocean-going liner beset by tugs. Crosbie wears a charcoal suit and severe, steel-rimmed glasses; he is tall, well over six feet — wide-shouldered and heavyset. He has white hair, a florid complexion and a neck that is nearly as wide as his head: a dominating, bullish presence, yet oddly distant. Yes, Crosbie shakes hands with the man fron New Brunswick, the stout ladies with the balloons from his own province and exchanges a friendly word; but then, almost immediately, he leans back, regards them from his great height and crosses his arms across his chest. There are no hugs, no arms-around-the-shoulder, little of the laying on of the flesh that is the stock-in-trade of the ravenous political animal seeking to infuse voters or delegates with the physical evidence of his strength and goodwill.

Not so surprisingly, political aides tend to resemble their employers. Ross Reid, one of Crosbie's top people, also a Newfoundlander, looks more like Crosbie than do the man's own sons. Steve Hastings, another aide, has the Crosbie neck. Audrey King, however, does not resemble Crosbie: she is an attractive woman in her thirties, wearing a red print dress, horn-rimmed glasses and an anxious look. After an arduous team effort, they manage to manoeuvre Crosbie out of the tent and towards his two trailers that stand next to the crumbling Manufacturers' Exhibition Building, beside those of the other candidates.

There, the noise and chaos, which will be the single most distinguishing feature of the days to follow, are beginning to build. The troops of one of the sideshow right-wing candidates, John Gamble, easterners clad in Dallas-like outfits of Stetsons and three-piece suits, mass near their candidate's trailer. Those of another lesser candidate, Michael Wilson, sporting green signs, march off towards the arena, shouting. A radio reporter sticks his mike in Crosbie's face and asks who his favourite singer is.

"Billie Holiday," the candidate replies. "And Sinatra when he was good."

"Are you hearing any winning music this morning?" the reporter says, playing straight man for the famous Crosbie wit.

"Ah, yes," says Crosbie in that beguiling Newfoundland Celtic lilt, "I can hear the violin strings now."

If Ottawa is an enigma, John Crosbie is a mystery. In one sense he is a throwback to another era; to the blood-and-thunder platform orator who stirs great partisan feelings, to the Tammany Hall Irish or red-dirt Southern politician brimming with mother wit and volcanic emotion. At times he could remind you of Broderick Crawford playing Huey Long, or of a restrained, polite Lyndon Johnson. Yet of the major Conservative candidates, he is the best educated, the best read and, what's more, with eight years as a cabinet minister at first the provincial and then the federal level, the most experienced. Despite the fact that he is anything but a TV pretty boy, John Crosbie is one of the more interesting Conservative politicians to come on the Canadian scene for some time. You could never imagine Joe Clark or Robert Stanfield listening to Billie Holiday.

Several weeks before the Tories gathered in Ottawa, I spent some time with Crosbie during his tour of Quebec. At the time, Crosbie's star was spectacularly on the ascent. The major columnists had touted him as the candidate to watch; there had been a *Maclean's* cover. As Crosbie toured Ontario, there was much talk, in a press that embraced cliché with unholy passion, of Crosbie as "a dark horse" in the Conservative leadership stakes race. Yet, as Crosbie campaigned in Quebec, the unfortunate fact that he did not speak French began to slow him up. The night I arrived in Quebec City I saw Crosbie answering questions before a largely French-speaking audience. Crosbie's chief Quebec aide, Gaston Dubé, a portly, mustachioed fellow who bears a striking resemblance to the Parti Québécois' Jacques Parizeau, would field the question in French, then Crosbie would bend down from the podium, Dubé would whisper the translation in his ear, and Crosbie would answer the question in English. This was the arrangement Crosbie was proposing to make permanent should he become leader of his party or, ultimately, prime minister.

The next morning, after Crosbie had met the editor of *Le Soleil* and had his picture taken arduously doping out the front page of the French-language newspaper, he and I had a conversation aboard his silver campaign bus. If the only question the rest of the press corps seemed interested in was the matter of his French, I wanted to know just what Crosbie read and whether his reading affected his political ideas. Seated with him in the back of the bus, I discovered that Crosbie not only reads such political biographers as Robert Caro and Ronald Steel, but is also a fan of the novelists Paul Theroux and Robert Stone. Pretty hip stuff for a Conservative politician.

We went on to talk of his political ideas. Crosbie is a pragmatic conservative, not an ideologue; his objections to excessive state ownership of industry are conceived in practical, not theoretical, terms. He is not a cultural nationalist, but is in favour of a strong CBC. In other words, moderately right-wing. The extreme views of Peter Pocklington he ascribed to "political inexperience"; Crosbie wasn't about to abolish foreign aid or medicare or to privatize Air Canada. All were positions he had arrived at through his practical political experience; there was little connection to his intellectual life.

While we were talking, Crosbie's aide, Ross Reid, approached. He wanted to move the candidate from the back of the bus to the front, to change places with the press so that television and radio could get better sound. "You mean," asked Crosbie plaintively, "there are more interviews?" Indeed there were. CBC was aboard and CTV and CJOH-TV and the Ottawa *Citizen* and Southam News, and they all wanted to talk to John Crosbie, not about literature but about French. As the bus travelled from Quebec City to Longueuil, the questions continued and, subtly, Crosbie's irritation with them grew apace.

When, under a grey sky, Crosbie stepped off his bus and into the lobby of the Holiday Inn, there was a crowd of Montreal reporters, all anglophone, waiting for him. Crosbie went to his room; then he came down to face them. The sole matter they wished to discuss was his lack of French. As Crosbie stood with his back to the hotel elevators, which punctuated his statements with their dinging as they reached the lobby, Ken Ernhofer, a television reporter from CFCF with the small, neat, determined features of a lightweight boxer and a high, urgent voice, pressed the matter home.

"Mr Crosbie," he began, "Mr Mulroney's making a real point about the French business. He's saying that it would be basically preposterous for the party to elect a unilingual leader who simply could not talk to the people of Quebec and get elected there. And you're saying you're going to learn French."

"That expression of view," said Crosbie, "only illustrates the fact that I have become the front-runner in the race. I don't think it's crazy, I don't think it's unheard of, that someone who is not perfectly bilingual should aspire to be national leader. . . . I can talk to the people of Quebec; I understand the background, I like the culture. I don't think it's a conflict at all. It only shows that Mr Mulroney is becoming worried as to my strength in the fray."

"But you say you can talk to the French," Ernhofer persisted. "You can't talk to them in their own language."

Crosbie began to jingle the change in his pocket, a dangerous sign. It's something he does when he gets nervous or angry, and it sounds like a snake's warning rattle.

"I can't talk to the Chinese in their own language," he said. "I can't talk to the German people in their own language. Does that mean there should be no relationships between Canada and China, or Canada and Germany? . . . It is not a great disaster. I am not a criminal; I am just an ordinary Canadian. We have had prime ministers before who have not been completely bilingual. . . . And I don't think the 3.7 million who are bilingual should think themselves some kind of aristocracy in Canada and that only leaders can come from their small group."

The woman from CBC Radio pounced on that one. "Are you saying," she demanded, "the French in Quebec are calling themselves an aristocracy by asking that someone speak French?"

Crosbie's temper slipped another notch. "Did I say that, darlin'?" he said, looming over her intently. "I just said that the 3.7 million people in this country who are bilingual should not think they are an aristocracy and that our leaders can no longer come from anyone but them. I've said nothing about Quebec. Don't you realize there are bilingual people who don't live in Quebec?"

"Do you find it aggravating to be constantly asked about this matter of French?"

"I'm only human," said Crosbie. "Occasionally you wonder, is this the only issue in the country, whether I can speak French or not? Sometimes you get aggravated by it. . . . I think there's lots of other issues. The question is who can lead our party to a majority victory and then go on to lead this country into the land it once was of promise and opportunity. . . . But I'm quite prepared to deal with this all day long if you want me to."

The next day, the press erupted. "Crosbie Says Lack of French Doesn't Make Him a Criminal" read the headline on the front-page story in *The Globe and Mail*. (Christ, I thought, who was the last guy who told us he wasn't a criminal?) Commentators started inveighing against the man who didn't appreciate the difference in Canada between French and Chinese. If, walking into that hotel lobby in Longueuil, Crosbie was the darling of the media, walking out of it he began to be their whipping boy, and going into the convention in Ottawa his momentum started to sag. The question of French did not arise with Mulroney or Clark. Mulroney's French is quite astonishing. Where his English is the Corporation personified, his French is the accent of the street. When Mulroney speaks in French, one instantly thinks of all those dirty tricks played in Quebec, the stuffing of halls with winos and children, the promises of patronage; one thinks of plug-uglies with baseball bats, willing to enforce all the old-style muscle of the Duplessis era. Where Clark's French reeks of the language class, Mulroney's is an authentic, if troubling, French voice. In the years to come, when partisan rancour has died away, historians will be able to weigh more clearly the real and lasting changes Pierre

Elliott Trudeau has brought to Canadian life. Chief among them, perhaps, is the fundamental change regarding language, as those ten minutes in the Holiday Inn proved.

My travels with John Crosbie had been a lesson in politics. In a sense, to be a politician is to answer questions, and the relationship between politician and reporter, totally circumscribed by a structure of question and answer, has become almost inquisitorial. In the collective mind of the press, there was a checklist of qualities that added up to their predetermined notion of a leader. The questions aimed at a leadership candidate were not so much matters of political substance as a kind of probing for psychic weakness. More and more, the price of power was the ability to answer a million questions, then a million more. As Tom Wolfe has observed, the press is the last Victorian gent, perennially anxious to maintain the proper emotion, the seemly sentiment, the fitting moral tone. In English Canada, there was nothing more sacred than Quebec and the French language, even among those who had little knowledge of or interest in either.

For the federal politicians of English Canada, French had become a necessity, not because they were in love with the language of Flaubert, Mallarmé and Voltaire, but because it had become, quite literally, the ceremonial language of power in Canada, in the same way that Latin was once the ceremonial language of the Roman Catholic church. By equating French with Chinese or German, John Crosbie had shown an insensitivity to the realities of the fitting sentiment and the proper moral tone, and the last Victorian gent began to treat him as if he had insulted motherhood, the flag or the Queen.

In Ottawa, as the convention opens, Crosbie is still running third behind Clark and Mulroney. Inside the arena, the low ceiling looms claustrophobically overhead; it is already sweltering. The candidates and their supporters are seated on one side of the rink, curtained off from one another; on the Tory-blue stage sits a Plexiglas, high-tech podium. A connoisseur of omens tells me that Clark is located in the same spot inhabited by Claude Wagner in 1976. With him sit Robert Stanfield and Duff Roblin. Is he about to join them in the party's inglorious past? The floor is crowded with delegates, but more than that, it is a media pit. Delegates in the stands delight in pointing out the celebrities; on the floor, hundreds of cameramen, photographers and reporters swarm: if there are 3,000 delegates, there are 2,000 media people!

As Peter Elzinga, the party president, opens the convention and the various candidates begin to address the policy sessions, you can detect a certain euphoria in the air. In contrast to the gloom of Winnipeg, this gathering gives the impression of irrepressible high spirits. The Tories have been basking in the constant media limelight, warming themselves with the continuing plight of the economy and the resulting unpopularity of Pierre Trudeau. Even the fact that the economy is slowly beginning to turn around offers encouragement. The country is coming out of the wilderness and so are they. In every speech, in every policy session, the message is the same: give Tory enterprise its head and a new Gilded Age is around the corner.

That night, at the various candidates' parties, the air of oncoming good fortune is palpable. Brian Mulroney's bash around the swimming pool of the Holiday Inn has the air of a suburban blowout and it is jammed; a rock band called the Majestics plays, appropriately enough, Roy Orbison's "Pretty Woman." There is rock and roll all over Ottawa; upstairs in the Holiday Inn, a group called the Blushing Brides, shameless imitators of the Rolling Stones, plays for Crosbie; across town the Downchild Blues Band does the same for Pocklington. At last, rock and roll has come to the right wing. You could shake it on the dance floor and still be a good and proper Conservative. Of course, now that Eric Clapton has played for Camels, the Stones for Jōvan, and Rod Stewart for Sony, the former music of revolt is firmly married to the corporation and is about as subversive as Mantovani. Of course, if rock has come to the right wing, sex, at long last, has come to the Conservatives. It used to be said that you went to a Liberal convention to get laid, a Tory convention to get drunk, and to an NDP convention to get 25 pounds of pamphlets. Here at Brian Mulroney's poolside, you get the feeling that, if you are so disposed, you can end up with a bottle-blonde. The crowd is identical to that in the singles bars around the Yonge and Eglinton area of Toronto: highrise swingers in their twenties and thirties, for whom sexual variety is part of the good office-worker's life, along with company paid vacations in the Caribbean, waterskiing and regular promotions. They like rock, good cars, lots of clothes, good restaurants and good sex. If Joe Clark is a young fogy, Mulroney gives the impression of knowing what the good things in life are. Where Clark radiates a sense of tedious labour dutifully fulfilled, Mulroney gives the impression that well-paying government jobs are just around the corner and high good times ahead. "Working for Joe isn't a commitment," a Mulroney supporter says to me, "it's a life sentence."

Later on that evening, I get a glimpse of Mulroney and his wife going through the packed lobby downstairs. The words "perfect couple" must have been invented for these two. While Mila Mulroney, like Maureen McTeer, exemplifies the style of grooming particular to powerful Montreal and Ottawa women, she seems to have come by it more naturally. Where McTeer gives the sense of someone of ordinary tastes and appearance who has blossomed with the attentions and perks of position, Mila creates the impression of always having been the most beautiful girl around. One could already anticipate her face on the covers of the country's women's magazines. The only question was how long it would be before we would know more than we wanted to about her tastes in clothes, food and decor.

Mulroney himself is big, muscular looking. However irrelevant an emotion it may be in reality, there is an atavistic feeling in people that demands that a leader look as if he could give a good account of himself in a fight. Where Joe Clark has the narrowest shoulders I have ever seen, not to mention an impressive pillow paunch that does not speak well of his physical condition, few men would be so brave as to take a poke at Pierre Trudeau, say, or even John Crosbie. Even though he has travelled far in life, Brian Mulroney still has the rawboned body of the Irish working class. More than people know, politics is a matter of sheer physical endurance, and Mulroney exudes the sense that he has not lost pride in his physical strength.

Across town at the Chateau Laurier, some of the other candidates are making merry in its impassable halls. Peter Pocklington has attracted an even younger crowd than Mulroney. Some of them had been the shock troops behind the Winnipeg putsch that deposed Clark. Now they carry the Pocklington banner in Edmonton Oiler's blue and orange, and signs that declare "Let's Make Canada Great." Young right-wingers tend to think of politics as sport and they are as simple-minded as their predecessors of the '60s, though in the opposite ideological direction. Instead of Peace and Love, the slogan is Free Enterprise. Viewing themselves as potential millionaires, they idolize successful entrepreneurs, they hate big government and big unions and big media, and that's why they are with the man who wants to slash income tax, sell the CBC and get rid of Air Canada.

Joe Clark's supporters, on the other hand, tend to be older and more rural and small town than those of the other candidates. Rather than dislike Clark's looks, they identify with his homeliness, his awkwardness. On the plane to Ottawa, I talked with a woman from Clark's own riding of Yellowhead, his former riding president. She teaches social studies and runs a farm. She had no use at all for Brian Mulroney. As far as she was concerned, he was slippery, shifty and shady. For this species of Clark supporter, Mulroney was the archetypal false lover, the travelling salesman who seduces and abandons. For them, nobody that good looking and smooth could be sincere. As for Clark's older supporters, they had always liked their Joe. Not only did he defer to them, not only had he always been a young man with all the virtues of age and none of the vices of youth, but he also gave every sign of needing their advice and, what's more, heeding it. They could not be sure of a similar deference from Mulroney.

At midnight, back at Crosbie headquarters in the Holiday Inn, I have a small contretemps with the Crosbie organization. Earlier in the evening, a senior Crosbie worker volunteered that Crosbie's senior staff had a midnight strategy session every evening. Last night there had been a television crew present and another writer. Maybe I would be interested? Indeed I was. If it was all right, I would be there. Well, I can't let you in, the man said. You'd have to talk to somebody like Ross Reid. And, oh yes, don't use my name.

All I got from Reid was the runaround. He said I would have to talk to Chester Burtt. Where was Burtt? Reid didn't know. After a half-dozen phone calls, I found Burtt. Well, he said, it was a confidential meeting. How about the film crew? I protested. That was different; they were from Newfoundland.

An hour and a half later I talk again to Burtt. Okay, I'm in, just as long as I realize that there's an embargo on everything I hear until after the convention and that I don't tell another reporter I was there. This must really be secret stuff. At ten to midnight I start the ascent to the twenty-third floor, no mean feat since the elevators in the hotel are jammed with delegates and take twenty minutes to arrive. I flip on my portable tape recorder and walk into the Royal Suite, where there are camera lights and a guard at the door. A thin-lipped, grim-faced guy named Howard Dean is talking to one of the Newfoundland TV crew about computer delegate projections. Stale stuff. I sit down and start taking notes on the decor — the beige carpets, the mirrored pillars, the elaborate chandeliers. Dean looks across at me as if I had caught him in the act of child molestation.

"What are you writing?" he demands.

I introduce myself and tell him I'm researching a magazine piece.

"Well," he says, "this conversation cannot be part of it."

"I'm taking notes on the decor," I say.

"Do you want this conversation taped?" demands the guard at the door. I switch off the machine. These guys are paranoid. Something big must be up. Minutes later, the senior Crosbie people — John Laschinger, Robert Wenman, Gaston Dubé, Reid and about half a dozen others — file into the room and sit around the table. They peel down to shirtsleeves; somebody lights a cigar. At last, I think, a smoke-filled back room. What kind of dire deals are they going to discuss? Well, the answer is the blimp. Should the Crosbie blimp come before his speech, or between the speech and the demonstration, and what will the rules committee say? After a few minutes I get up and leave.

It is a political axiom that you can't win a convention with a speech, but you can sure lose it, as Paul Hellyer proved in 1976. Late Friday afternoon, after a barbecue in the parking lot that more than ever gives the convention the air of a country fair, Brian Mulroney is the first to speak. Greyer than his photographs, he strikes me as an unlikely cross between Jay Gatsby and Jean Beliveau. Gatsby, because of the disciplined effort Mulroney must have used to take him on the long journey from Baie Comeau to St James Street, all the effort he has had to put into the construction of that polished, smooth manner, the oleaginous voice. Beliveau, because Mulroney is reminiscent of the hockey players of that star's era, who looked like junior execs on ice, who skated smooth as silk but could take care of themselves in the corners; the type of guy who, far from ending up as a Derek Sanderson style wastrel, finished his career as a corporate officer of the club. Even further from being an ideologue than Crosbie, Mulroney realizes that if the Liberals have been in power all these years by steering a course one degree left of centre, Tories will only gain power by being one degree right of centre. Power, not ideology, is uppermost in his mind as he speaks to the assembled delegates. He tells them that their purpose is to drive the Liberals from office and form a PC government. He talks of a new opportunity, saying the eleventh commandment for the Tories should be "Thou shalt never speak ill of another Conservative." He rules out tests of ideological purity; he talks of better corporate relations with the US and of making Canada "a decent place to do business again." But most important, he tells the delegates that they are losers no more, but are ready for power. "And I tell you we have been in opposition too long," he says, his voice going hoarse and urgent. "Now is the time! Now is the time!"

After Michael Wilson, the Invisible Man, so bland he can't be seen by the naked eye, John Crosbie steps up to the podium. If Mulroney is a better television performer than he is an orator, Crosbie's rhetorical style is calculated to send the hall into an animal frenzy. It is not so much what he says as it is the music, the rolling, impassioned, Celtic periods aimed towards a partisan climax. After the blimp appears, Crosbie doesn't say anything particularly different from what he's been saying on the campaign trail and in the policy sessions, but he works up several more degrees of heat, waving meaty fists above his head as he makes chopped hamburger out of the French language, bringing sardonic smiles to the faces of the press. "Linguistic ability alone will not make anyone a successful prime minister," he says. "Pierre Trudeau is the living proof of that." He talks of his own qualities — his honesty, sincerity, ability; then, ever more fervent, he speaks of the "great electoral victory that now lies on the horizon." He continues: "I come from Britain's oldest colony, Canada's youngest province, a place known round the world for the warmth of its people, the grand, glorious land and the untapped promise of its wealth and bounty. And I say to you that Crosbie plus Newfoundland, Nova Scotia, Prince Edward Island, New Brunswick, Quebec, Ontario . . ." and he goes on to name all ten provinces, the rest drowned out in the largest cheer of the night. It is merely a bit of bombastic flag-waving, but delivered in Crosbie's perfervid style, it brings the house down. "When I have finished my term as your leader," he concludes, "I will want you to be in a position to say this: that John called them as he saw them, that he was a champion of economic realism and responsibility and government. Yes, I want you to say, yes, he confronted our country's massive and increasing economic problems squarely and decisively and, yes, that they are overcome."

The crowd erupts, surely the first Conservatives anywhere to wildly applaud an echo of the anti-Vietnam movement and Martin Luther King: "We shall overcome." Crosbie's speech is considered the best of the night and, sure enough, the press will drag out the clichés. "Crosbie Wows Delegates with Barnburner Speech," the headline in *The Toronto Star* reads the next day.

After Peter Pocklington, backed by Wayne Gretzky in the stands, it's Joe Clark time. There are buttons around saying "The Who Farewell Tour," but nobody is counting Clark out yet. Before the ex-leader speaks, Robert Stanfield and Flora MacDonald are sitting in the corridor opposite the stands, out of the heat — the grandpa and the maiden aunt watching the young folks enjoy themselves.

31

What Clark has to say does not differ all that much from the other candidates. Yet, apart from his own troops, nobody cheers him. Where the Mulroney supporters had applauded Crosbie's best lines and vice versa, when Clark speaks it's like there's a Colgate shield out there in the crowd. If Clark is in fact returned to the leadership, this whole exercise, the millions of dollars spent, the weeks of campaigning, will have added up to an exercise in absurdity, another episode of pointlessness and despair in the history of the Progressive Conservative Party.

The final speaker, except for the bathetic Neil Fraser, is David Crombie. Crombie is a curious case. He was the most successful mayor of Toronto in recent times, yet his career as a national politician has been curiously flat and disappointing. The Canadian equivalent of one of Mrs Thatcher's wets, Crombie had been isolated in Clark's caucus, and all of Clark's Toronto patronage had gone to Ron Atkey. Nor had his leadership campaign been a brilliant one. Organized by the film producer Bill Marshall, it had been a textbook example of communications ineptitude. To this observer, it looked as if Marshall was running Crombie for mayor in the early '70s all over again. First, there was that unconvincing full page in *The Globe*, some $20,000 worth, that read "The Leader." Then there was all the emphasis on Crombie's jogging. "David better stop all that jogging," said John Crosbie, "or he'll have another heart attack." Crombie was small and he was sweet: there was someting about him that reminded one of the American actor Robert Blake, the happy little guy who's all grit and compassion. It was an act that played well in the era of such happy warriors as Hubert Humphrey and the politics of joy, but in the grim '80s it seemed somewhat out of place. If Brian Mulroney had most of young Westmount with him in '76, Crombie seemed to have all of youngish Rosedale with him now, all bright and happy in yellow scarves and umbrellas. ("Did you hear David's speech?" trilled one of the Rosedale ladies after a Crombie policy session. "It was absolutely fa-a-a-bulous!")

If the rest of the candidates, especially Mulroney, have formed a rightist consensus that primarily appeals to the spirit of acquisition, Crombie is here to remind them of their Red Tory heritage, like it or not. Since Crombie's loss is now a foregone conclusion, unlike Crosbie, Clark or Mulroney, he can bare his heart. So, in a speech that contrives to drop every name out of the Canadian and Conservative past, from Susanna Moodie to Georges-Etienne Cartier, John A. Macdonald and Arthur Meighen, he carves out for himself a position as the conscience of his party, urging his fellow Tories that on the way to the Mercedes and the mansion they should perhaps take a detour around grandmother instead of just running her over. "I love Americans," he says, in direct reference to Crosbie's call for closer economic ties with the United States, "but I never wanted to be one. . . . We are Canadians, thank you very much, a proud and daring race of people with hopes and dreams of our own and a sure faith in our destinies as global leaders." All in all, the sermon is well received, no doubt reminding some of the more religious Tories of those they are obliged to listen to every Sunday, when their clergyman recalls them to the claims of the spirit. They were not necessarily going to pay much mind to Crombie's pleas, but it felt good to be reminded of them.

Crombie aside, the major thrust of Tory thought is clear. The speeches all had their share of red-baiting. To Conservatives, the Liberals and NDP are the same thing: goddamn socialists. Just as clear is the notion that the economy is the Tory ticket to power. The hypocrisy on both sides of the fence in this matter reeks in one's nostrils. For the Liberals, the slump was caused by worldwide factors and was currently being cured by their measures, especially "six and five." For the Tories, the Liberals caused the slump — if you believed their picture of ragged masses huddling in the streets, crying out in hunger — and the recovery, such as it was, was the mere result of world forces. In their speeches, all the major candidates demonstrate a touchingly childlike faith in business's willingness to provide full employment and prosperity for all. There was no doubt that the postwar social consensus was evaporating. Just as it was certain that a great deal of money was going to be made in the years to come, it was certain that the gap was going to widen between the haves and the have-nots. There was little question here to which category those present intended to belong.

Saturday morning in the minor-league hockey arena, the resemblance of the proceedings to blood sport persists. There is both an agreeable sense of excitement among the press and a disagreeable sense of confusion. After the papers come out raving about his speech, the media are excited about Crosbie, repeating among themselves his most recent *mots*. When he isn't being clumsy about the sacred issue of the French language, the press love John. After addressing the Ontario caucus at breakfast, Crosbie remarked, "My wife said this morning that tomorrow she was going to wake up with the next leader of the Tory party, and I don't want her in bed with Joe Clark or Brian Mulroney." Now, it seems that his speech last night really has improved his chances.

As the voting starts, John Gamble supporters, already bitter at the inevitable, lurk around the entrance to the Civic Centre like a lynch mob, setting off firecrackers. Each one sounds like a shot. Mulroney's supporters are saying that the media have blown up the impact of Crosbie's speech. At this point, there really is no predicting the outcome, and the media, intent on a result to the exclusion of nearly everything else, continually float "scenarios," masterpieces of mathematical ingenuity as complicated as three-dimensional chess. Listening to them, surrounded by all the signs, wilted by the heat and the noise, the mind starts to boggle, straining under a sense of information overload. Even though scenarios are presented as the result of sober analysis, the product of minds tempered by steel, most often they are the statistical and complex expression of simple prejudice. At this point all I can do is envision the headline should Crosbie win: "Blimp Beats Wimp."

As the voting begins, we are treated once again to Ike Kelneck and his master musicians. Something has changed since Winnipeg. The group has been rechristened the Ike Kelneck Express and it now plays less oompah-pah and more rock and roll. On the floor, two swinging women in their thirties, slightly leathery but still attractive — Mulroney supporters, of course — just keep dancing for the two hours it takes to count the vote. Ah, the old party's changing all right. Though the vote is excruciatingly slow being counted, everything becomes much clearer once it's announced. Gamble and Fraser are quickly eliminated. Pocklington gets 102, Crosbie 116, Wilson 144. Clark comes in with 1,091, Mulroney 874, and Crosbie is well back with 639. Very quickly, Wilson and Pocklington come to Mulroney and the writing is on the wall. Peter Regenstreif, a pollster-for-hire currently working for Pocklington and rumoured to be the link between Pocklington and Mulroney, on being asked why the move was made to Mulroney rather than Crosbie, replies that both men want the economy to be the issue in any future election, and with Crosbie as leader the issue once again would be the French language and Quebec.

In succeeding ballots, Clark loses support, Mulroney gains. Ross Reid and Bill Marshall leave the floor together. Later on it is rumoured that while Crosbie meets Crombie, Joe Clark phones up. "I need your support, David, and I need it now," he says. Crombie, truly a nice man, is hard pressed but he manages to spit it out: "I can't support you, Joe, under any circumstances." Crombie goes to Crosbie, but despite all the nationally televised efforts at persuasion by Brian Peckford, Clark is stubborn and won't go to Crosbie, and the Newfoundlander is eliminated on the third ballot. Crosbie had genuinely expected Clark to cross the floor and deliver the convention to him. He didn't understand that at this point all that remained for Clark was his dignity, and he would rather die than give it up.

I meet a Crosbie supporter on the floor and ask him if there's any chance of Crosbie's supporters going to Clark. Oh, he says, the majority of our people will go with Mulroney.

"Anybody but Clark, eh?"

"It's not anti-Clark; it's not animosity. There's a lot of sympathy for Joe. But we want a new leader."

Now, all confusion is dispelled. More than Tories believe in free enterprise, more than they hate socialism, they believe in value for money. They were not about to spend all that cash, all this time, and wind up with Joe Clark again. At this point, it's all over bar the shouting. When Mulroney's victory is announced, the blood-sport aspect of Canadian political conventions comes to the fore. Unlike American candidates, who watch the results in nearby hotels, Canadian contenders are right there in the arena, while the whole world watches. When the final ballot is announced, Joe Clark looks as if he's been poleaxed, but, to his credit, he regains his composure and gallantly goes through all the right motions. In essence, the Tories had been liberated by what had happened in Winnipeg. They liked the experience so much, they repeated it, only bigger and better, here in Ottawa.

In the days that followed, it was John Crosbie who didn't know how to behave. First, he accused Maureen McTeer of not allowing Clark to throw his support to him. Then, he denounced Clark's "ardent stupidity." This was a puzzling phrase. Perhaps what he really meant was "arrant stupidity." At any rate, a day later, on CBC-TV, he said he couldn't remember ever having said such a thing. Suddenly Crosbie not only began to look like a sore loser, he started to look like that which he had spent so much energy avoiding resembling: a buffoon.

In contrast, Mulroney started to look very good. A man whose major virtue was conciliation — that voice was designed to pour oil on troubled waters — he began to pull together all the disparate strands of the Tories. As Elmer MacKay stepped down to vacate his Central Nova seat, Mulroney seemed more and more like a crown prince and the Conservatives like a government-in-waiting. They were younger than ever before, better organized, better financed. And at last they had a leader who looked good on TV. The Liberals' best chance was to somehow inveigle the Argentinians to invade Sable Island. Otherwise, they would need a miracle, or an unparalleled Tory disaster. While nothing was certain in politics, it was hard to envisage anything but a Tory government. How one felt about the prospect, what their vision of undiluted commercialism in a new Gilded Age would do to the country — that was something else.

CHAPTER 3

THE ENTERTAINER

Almost a year later, in the spring of 1984, Jean Chrétien comes to Toronto — to the financial district — to open his Ontario campaign for the leadership of the Liberal Party. On 28 February, Pierre Elliott Trudeau, a figure of Faustian proportions to the end, had gone for a solitary night walk through the Ottawa streets in a wild blizzard that had kept less intrepid men huddling for warmth at home. It made a striking picture. The head of a great nation, prowling the streets of his capital alone, without bodyguards, undergoing who knows what tumultuous passages of the soul.

The next day Trudeau announced his retirement. John Turner, the Bonnie Prince Charlie of Canadian politics, venturing cautiously out of the exile to which he had condemned himself for nine years, returned to public life on 16 March, and Chrétien followed suit four days later. Soon, there was a second tier of candidates from the federal cabinet in the persons of John Roberts and Donald Johnston. Then there was a bargain basement, consisting of Mark MacGuigan, Eugene Whelan and John Munro. In the summer following his election as Conservative leader, Brian Mulroney had led the Liberals by as many as 30 points, but all fall and winter he was oddly silent in the House of Commons; the country currently believed that he was after all slick and empty, with nothing to say. Now, in the spring, the Liberals are coming back up in the polls. The mood of the nation is that of a spoiled beautiful young girl: perplexed and fickle — unable to make up its mind.

Like Wall Street, the financial centre of Canada is known by the name of its main thoroughfare. In the past decade or so, the country's banks have raised glittering towers around Bay Street that now dominate the city's skyline. Jean Chrétien's local headquarters are not in one of these monuments to the prudence and caution of the Canadian banking system, but in a small, anonymous building on York Street. Crowded together in the small campaign office is an excited group of supporters and members of the local media. Much of Chrétien's support in Toronto comes from the Rev Roland de Corneille, a backbench member from Eglinton-Lawrence and Chrétien's friend from the days when they had both worked for Mitchell Sharp. De Corneille's riding is heavily Jewish and there are a couple of young Orthodox university students here, wearing *yarmulkes*. With de Corneille in his dog collar, they give the room an atmosphere that is at once ethnic, ecclesiastic and ecumenical. There are the usual number of suits, but instead of Tory blue, the Liberals wear brown and grey. There's a fortyish woman in a camel hair coat smoking a cigarette in a holder; the sort who attends Liberal political gatherings in the same way as she does fashionable gallery openings. She fastens the reporter waiting beside her with a flirtatious glance.

"Is your name Sam?"

"No," he replies. "It isn't."

"I thought you looked," she sighs regretfully, "like somebody I know called Sam."

The importance of a political event can be judged by the sort of media who turn up for it. There are a couple of beat reporters from the Toronto papers, a couple of radio people, crews from the local TV news — one with that relatively new component of media life, the muscular female sound technician, proudly toting around her bulky Nagra. But there are no national reporters or network correspondents, let alone major columnists. This is just another night on the hustings.

Chrétien arrives. He is tall, greying, leonine, trim. He wears a nondescript rumpled suit. Afflicted as a child with infantile paralysis, he speaks roughly out of the side of his mouth, murdering the grammar of both French and English with every word he speaks. It is extraordinary the number of politicians who after long years in the trade begin to resemble boxing champions. Years of confrontation with opposition and press leave their mark not only on a man's character but on his face. A veteran middleweight or light-heavy, Chrétien is now trying to prove that he belongs in the same ring as the biggest boys. We see the twisted mouth, the broken-looking nose, the three o'clock shadow; but television and news photographs never convey the extraordinary colour of Chrétien's eyes: a very light grey, suggesting a mildness belied by the rest of his appearance.

He comes into the room, saying hello and shaking hands. Moved from event to event, place to place, by their aides, political candidates sometimes weren't quite sure what they were in a room to do, but they kept shaking hands anyhow.

"We're having what here?" asks Chrétien.

"We'd like you to open this office by putting up the sign," a campaign worker replies.

"And after that we're going to a party next door?"

"That's right."

Chrétien moves back through the packed office into the hallway and tapes a campaign sign to the wall. He's asked by a camera crew to do it again and he uncomplainingly obliges.

"Open for business; we mean it," he says. "We mean it; we're in for a big win." There's a pause. "Are we moving next door?" Chrétien asks. But, before he goes, he can't resist the impulse to address the crowd. Chrétien may look like a club fighter but, in the age of showbiz politics, he has the pace and timing of a stand-up comic. His supporters laugh at his every little joke, eating him up with a spoon. After years of Trudeau looking down his nose at them, years of the wintry Lalonde telling them what to do, years of René Lévesque shrugging hostility and indifference, they are absolutely delighted with a French Canadian cabinet minister who actually appears to like them.

"We have to win in every part of Canada," he says. "I'm running as a Canadian, and there is no better place than Toronto to show your colours." The implication is of course that Trudeau and Lalonde and company were often perceived in English Canada as marauders in a foreign land. Quebeckers first, Canadians second.

"We're having a reception next door with some more people," Chrétien continues. He turns to an organizer and, raising his voice, demands "How many you got there?" Then he confidentially informs the crowd that he never knows how big a crowd to expect. In Halifax on Sunday, he tells them there were 125 cups of coffee and 325 people. "So we look cheap a bit."

After so much chilly Quebec dignity, Chrétien is at pains to expose a sense of his warm humanity. Imagine Pierre Trudeau saying he didn't want to look cheap!

"The problem is that we don't want to peak too soon. We don't want to do a Mulroney-type venture with the Liberal Party. We don't have to be right at the top when we come to the convention. We let somebody else cut the wind for us for many miles and we just do the riding at the right time." And, with his hands, he mimes a racer coming out of the leader's slipstream and pulling out ahead.

"You know," he says, warming to his audience, "Toronto has changed a lot since I come the first time. When I came the first time, Winston's was a cigarette." There are anticipatory giggles and titters at this reference to John Turner's favourite lunchtime watering hole.

"Eventually it became a restaurant." Then he hits them with the punchline: "Now it is a riding without delegates."

Chrétien next holds an impromptu press conference, a quip a minute.

"Where do you stand?"

"I'm certainly not seventh."

"What about the candidates' meeting with the prime minister yesterday?"

"It was a pleasant lunch at 24 Sussex," Chrétien says. "The food was pretty good and I didn't have to pay."

"Do you think of Toronto as being a John Turner stronghold?"

"I will tell you something. I will be stronger in Toronto than he will be in Shawinigan."

There were few guests on Johnny Carson that could do better. If Trudeau had seemed unapproachable and aloof, Chrétien is at great pains to show that he is not only friendly but as wide open as the sky above. "My style of leadership is this," he says. "You can ask me questions about anything — about today, about tomorrow, about yesterday, about the year before. Any questions? I'm not Mulroney; I'll give you an answer."

Chrétien leaves the campaign headquarters to walk a block to the Royal York Hotel, where his reception is being held. It's late in the day, grey and windy, the howling winds created by the bank tower canyons blowing newspapers and grit about the street. Chrétien, surrounded by aides and cameras, walks self-consciously quickly, the better to look energetic and confident. De Corneille is a step behind. "Come on, Rollie," says Chrétien. "Walk with me."

Onlookers in the rush hour traffic are literally open-mouthed at the sight of the Rt Hon Jean Chrétien walking along York Street. For the past twenty years, Liberal cabinet members have been princes of the royal blood in Canada, seldom seen in the flesh, except at times like these when public favour must be courted.

The Royal York Hotel stands opposite Union Station. Like the train station itself, the hotel is a holdover from a vanished era. Although politicians have long since ceased to travel the country in private railroad cars, the old railway hotels like the Royal York in Toronto and The Nova Scotian in Halifax still remain the focus of much national political activity. So many party meetings have been held in these places over the years that they have begun to acquire an historical aura. Inside, the Royal York is gloomy and cavernous, its atmosphere oppressive. Despite attempts to spruce the place up, the heavy maroon carpeting, the enormous looming chandeliers, the well-worn lobby furniture give the hotel a dark, claustrophobic air. The decor is dated without any compensating touch of nostalgia that would evoke the classic. Prolonged periods spent in the Royal York's confines put a damper on even the most effervescent of spirits.

In the lobby, men and women are hurrying in from their offices to hear Jean Chrétien speak. Some of them are delegates, others just the party faithful. Part ideological church, part social club, a political party at the riding level is as close as non-professionals with a lively interest in political life are likely to get to power. Still, that degree of interest in the issues of the day is what distinguishes them from the rest of the population, most of whom would never bother with a political meeting and would thus make their contribution to democracy by virtue of what they saw on TV. Trudeau was not known for his love of these neighbourhood cadres, but Jean Chrétien is eager to demonstrate his intense affection. So, in a crowded ballroom, where the number of cameras has swollen, he reveals just what a down-to-earth sort of guy he really is.

There is, after all, a law of modern politics that states that a leader must be the direct opposite of the man he succeeds. The mass hunger for novelty dictated that after the malevolent Richard Nixon there had to be the sweet Jimmy Carter. After the detail-obsessed Carter came the genially woolly Ronald Reagan, who had only the slightest acquaintance with facts. So Chrétien, besides demonstrating that he is one friendly, open Quebecker, is also at pains to show that he is informal, and plainspun. If Trudeau's discourse was as formal and structured as the gardens at Versailles, Chrétien is at his best when he speaks spontaneously — a few offhand remarks that just happen to grow into a speech through sheer force of high spirits. This evening at the Royal York, he is doing his level best to communicate a relaxed confidence, a sense of the experience he has gained in the major cabinet portfolios of finance, justice, and energy.

"Some people asked me why I took so long to decide," Chrétien begins. "Well, it's very easy. One, is that if I were to declare too soon, it would scare off John Turner. And the last thing the Liberal Party needed was a coronation of Jean Chrétien."

There's deep, appreciative laughter. Chrétien's troubles somehow were always being transformed by his rhetoric into jokes and advantages.

"The other problem I had to cope with was that I never lost an election. So I knew if I was to be in that one, I was to win it. And I reflected a bit because it's a big challenge, a big job. I been sitting

41

next to the prime minister for the past ten years and I know that it is a difficult job."

Since Liberals pride themselves on the unity and harmony of their party, in contrast to the chaotic history of the Conservatives, no candidate who makes a serious attempt at its leadership can directly attack his opponent. Not only is it considered a breach of manners, open attacks are regarded as evidence of bad political judgment. Wounded feelings do not make for the smooth technocratic workings of future Liberal cabinets. Chrétien, if he becomes prime minister, will have great need of John Turner and his supporters.

Still, the campaign is a contest. Chrétien's style is that of a fighter, so he must attack Turner. But only the initiated know when he is doing it. "I stand for Liberalism," he says, "not for opportunism." Turner's name is never mentioned, but all those present know that he is referring to John Turner's sudden return to politics after Pierre Trudeau's retirement. Jean Chrétien is open, but he will not make a frank attack on his chief opponent. That would be bad politics. Tories, after all, do not have a monopoly on hypocrisy. It is an obligatory function of party politics.

Trudeau's assiduous colleague for so long, Chrétien is a forceful apologist for the policies and achievements of his leader's governments. But then, he cannot convincingly be much else. He enumerates the glories of the recent Liberal past: the repatriation of the constitution, the victorious referendum on the independence of Quebec. Then he moves on to the key issues of the present day — unemployment, the economy and the deficit — assuring his audience that the present will be handled with the same dispatch: "As long as we have unemployment in our society and no growth, we have to use the deficit to keep the dignity of our people. I want to bring this party back to the people. I want to make the smallest in this society comfortable with our national institutions. And I think I can do that. I don't think I'm perfect. Daniel Johnson used to say, 'When I look at myself, I despair. When I compare myself, I feel good.' And when I compare myself with Brian Mulroney, I feel very good."

What! A Liberal cabinet minister actually admitting that he was imperfect! They were famous for never once confessing their mistakes. It was the contention of that astute observer, Larry Zolf, that Pierre Trudeau's best strategy, if he had stayed on, would have been to go across the country saying, "Hello, I'm Pierre Trudeau and I'm sorry." There was something of that apology in Chrétien's approach. Finally, having demonstrated his friendliness, his openness, his confidence, his humour, and his humility, Jean Chrétien, echoing his speeches on the referendum, shows that he is not afraid to wave the flag either.

"I'd like to have the opportunity to inspire Canadians," he says. "We're among the most privileged people in the world. Some say I should stop my patriotism speech. I will not. Of course we're having problems. But there is one commitment I will make to you. I will never give up on the problems, and I will never rest until my job is done for this country."

Pierre Trudeau made most Canadians conscious of their lack of brains, riches and looks; he made them acutely aware of their help-lessness to control their own destiny. If homely Jean Chrétien could feel good about himself, feel good about his country, feel good about the past twenty years, he could make you feel good about yourself. In 1968, Trudeau had appealed to Canadians' sense of the higher possibilities of their society. Now, Chrétien is telling them they have come a long way, that what they are now is still very good.

Before the leadership campaign, the public perception of Chrétien was not necessarily favourable. He was no intellectual, and his style was the essence of Ottawa lunchbucket; he was perceived as one of those oppressive and autocratic Liberal ministers of state, the kind you love to hate. Worse, he was, well, sinister. In Dalton Camp's famous phrase, Chrétien "looked like the driver of the getaway car."

Politics, naturally, does not take place in a vacuum. In the course of the leadership campaign, the political background was beginning to change and in consequence so was the perception of Chrétien. Instead of appearing as a backdrop of the Trudeau government, where he seemed little more than a zealous and competent henchman, he was now being seen against a background of John Turner and Brian Mulroney in all their silver-haired, highly groomed splendour. Suddenly all Chrétien's own qualities were transformed.

Instead of being seen as an arrogant top dog, in comparison to the front-running Turner, Chrétien was being portrayed as a gallant never-say-die underdog. His rough edges and rasping voice played well against the oozing chocolate tones of Brian Mulroney. Where he had been viewed previously as a kind of unattractive gangster-type, often caricatured by cartoonists in Chicago-style, double-breasted pin-stripes, he was now being perceived as an attractive *nouvelle vague* gangster type, like Jean-Paul Belmondo in *Breathless*.

The eagerness with which Toronto was drawing Chrétien to its breast disgusted the upper middle class and the media in Quebec.

For them, Chrétien was too eager to play the "pea souper," the Quebec Uncle Tom, in order to win English support, always "*le petit gars de Shawinigan*." Trudeau was one of them, as was Lalonde. François Mitterand was their idea of what a Gallic statesman should be: urbane, cultivated, a phrase from Roland Barthes forever on his lips. The reaction of cultivated Montreal to Chrétien's Toronto reception was precisely that which would occur in Toronto if *Le Devoir* suddenly found that some benighted hayseed Ontario politician reminded it of a great Cockney film star like Michael Caine.

Of course, this image of Jean Chrétien as a populist underdog did have an absurd tinge. In his rough-hewn way, he was an expert professional politician, and the most engaging, proficient campaigner one might hope to see in action. The corporate backdrop provided by Turner and Mulroney was also responsible for the distorted picture of Chrétien's relations to Corporationland. The minister of energy's daughter was married to the son of the president of Power Corporation. His campaign manager, John Rae, was a vice-president of the same company.

"Well," Chrétien winds up, radiating a ton of disarming, sandpaper charm, "I was not supposed to make a speech, so I don't know what the hell I'm doing." Whatever excitement there will be in the campaign to succeed Pierre Trudeau, it will be provided by Jean Chrétien. "Fasten your seat belts," he promises, "because it's going to be one hell of a ride."

An hour or so later, I am waiting in an ante-room to the hotel suite where Chrétien is meeting local riding delegates more intimately. They sit waiting on the beds and standing in the halls, eager to meet the great man. Most of those under thirty who take an active part in Canadian politics seem to be law students; the sort of contacts and experience offered by student politics are essential to the success of future careers. A stoutish young lady informs me that she likes Jean Chrétien because "he's willing to look you in the eyes and listen."

The door swings open and Chrétien's loud voice jumps out. He's talking about the constitution, about how "my practical solution probably saved a revolution in Canada." One of the candidate's aides tries to interrupt: "Excuse me, Mr Minister, there's some other people who want to move in too. I wonder if people who have been here — "

Chrétien keeps on talking. "Think about it, Rudy," he tells a delegate. "I want you to vote for me, Rudy. I like to impress you!"

The aide manfully tries again. "There's coffee and cake in the next room. Please go and help yourself."

"Have we got some more people outside?" Chrétien asks. "Are there any more delegates here?"

I hit on a man who I know is strategically placed in Chrétien's campaign. What sort of thing is going on between Chrétien and the delegates?

"Why don't you go in," he says, "and get a little taste of it?"

Inside, Chrétien, tie loosened, is sprawled regally in an armchair. Night has fallen. Behind the candidate, the window is open and the curtains play in the spring breeze. Out over his shoulder you can see the tangle of the railyards and a green-blue haze of neon. Like most major league politicians, Chrétien takes up most of the space in any room he happens to inhabit. Although there are more than a dozen delegates sitting respectfully, quiet in their Sunday best, Chrétien's domineering personality fills the room to bursting. Crowd-pleaser though he is, up in this private room Jean Chrétien is reminiscent of some feudal lord holding court to petitioners, and soliciting renewed oaths of fealty.

"Have I replied to your questions to your satisfaction?" he enquires of a departing delegate. "You don't want to wear my button yet?" The man is non-committal. Chrétien turns to somebody else and asks, "You're a delegate?"

"No," the man says, "I'm working for you."

The candidate then leaps up to welcome the incoming crowd. "Come and sit down," he says. "I'm having a little press conference here."

I walk into the room and Chrétien sticks out his hand. "Are you a delegate?" he asks. No, I say. I'm on my perennial errand of research, doing a magazine piece. Chrétien's not so sure about that.

"Okay," he says to the room at large. "You ask me questions on anything you want. Ask me anything." Chrétien is like a travelling prizefighter who invites any local to see whether he's brave enough to take a shot at him. Then, suddenly suspicious, he turns to me and demands, "Who ask you here?"

I flourish the magic name. "Oh," he says, "that's okay then."

A phone in the room is ringing. An aide picks it up and begins to speak. Chrétien is distracted by the conversation. "Ask him to call the next room," he snaps. The aide hangs up. By now, there is a fair cross-section of the immigrant communities of Toronto in the room, and they are unhappy. Categorized and patronized under the euphemistic term "ethnics," the Jamaicans, the Italians, the Chinese, the Portuguese of Toronto rightfully feel that they have little real presence in Canada's national life. A black man, solemn as a deacon in a three-piece brown suit, says he's getting nowhere in his local riding association. How does Chrétien feel about "broadening the base of the party?"

Well, Chrétien allows as how "there have been some flaws in the past." He doesn't blame Trudeau, because he wasn't a party man. "He got nominated and elected inside a month. For me, I'm a product of the party." Chrétien tells the man how he has travelled the country for party fundraising more than anyone else. He promises to have more meetings of the party executive than Trudeau. Then, for good measure, he delivers a commercial about his own personal capacities. "I work more than anybody else. So I have more time. And I'm fast. One of my problems is that I'm too fast."

Chrétien goes on to say how he's going to make more contacts with the leaders of the provincial parties, how he's going to re-establish the party in the western provinces. But he is talking on a much loftier level than the Jamaican.

"The people who have been in the party since '68," the man complains, "think they have a divine right to be delegates in Ottawa." He is inarticulate, can't frame his question properly, and goes on repeating his remark about "broadening the base of the party." What he is really saying is: "They won't make me a delegate because I'm black."

The solemn deacon and Jean Chrétien are talking at cross-purposes. If the task before a man in public life is to translate his private personality into the public forum in such a way that its broad contours are acceptable to large numbers, Chrétien has succeeded spectacularly well. It is likely that he is so completely relaxed on the podium because there is now little difference between the public and private man. Chrétien can be all of himself in public and remain confident that nothing embarrassing would emerge from his lips. He has spent so long a time as a public man that he is now a little like an actor who is never offstage.

So Chrétien gives the disappointed delegate a short speech. "The minorities are comfortable with me," he tells him. "Whether it's because I have difficulty expressing myself in English I don't know. But in western Canada, and even in Ontario, there are a lot of NDPers who are uncomfortable with their own party. And if we go with a candidate who looks too much like Brian Mulroney, they might not come with us. If Roy Romanow was not faced with a byelection in Saskatchewan, he might come to be co-chairman of my campaign — between you an' I — "

But the black guy doesn't care about winning over the NDP or Roy Romanow. He's just furious that he isn't going to the Ottawa convention as a delegate.

The next person with a question is called Aldo. He's from the city's Italian community and he too is angry. Aldo is young, intense and hard-driving. As he begins to speak, it is immediately clear that somebody at last is going to take a real shot at the travelling champion:

"I will be open here," he tells Chrétien. "You want my support, I want your support. I'm a candidate in York North. There's a disease in the party. You're right the minorities are comfortable with you, but they're not comfortable with some of the structure of the party. There are people of all backgrounds, mine being of Italian origin, that have been prevented from getting ahead in the party simply because they're Italian or black or Chinese or Portuguese. It's all very friendly at election time, but when it comes time for government appointments, for delegates, it's not coming across. I'll give you an example. There's 600,000 Italians in Toronto. Since 1980 there have been 4,000 government appointments. Four of them have gone to our community." He mentions a prominent Liberal cabinet minister and a meeting he has had with the man's assistant. "He said, 'Well, did you ever think that the Italians aren't sophisticated enough to handle those kind of jobs?' That is the same mentality that says you shouldn't be PM because you're French. You're Canadian, but they don't understand that. I wanted to meet with you, I wanted to make my point, and I'm not going to put you on the spot because you're a busy man. I'm satisfied that I met you, and the next thing I want to do before I make up my mind is I want to meet with John Rae and I want — "

But before he can put Chrétien further on the spot than he already has, Robert Nixon, the former leader of the Ontario Liberal Party, walks into the room, and interrupts Aldo in mid-sentence.

"Got room for another?" he booms, large, bespectacled.

"Hello, Bob Nixon," Chrétien booms back, big man to big man.

"How are you, Jean?" Then he says, all bilingual roguishness, *"Bienvenu à Toronto."*

"Merci."

Aldo, unfazed, just carries on:

"I want to meet with John Rae to work out the details. I have nine

47

votes from York North. Last night we talk with Portuguese and Italian communities, Mississauga South, and we got five there and this is going to happen in many of the ridings in Toronto unless you can sit down and assure us that we are going to get a piece, a small piece of Canada for everybody."

Well, even Chrétien is taken aback at the intensity of this diatribe.

"You will have it," he says. "I can't understand why a Liberal in good standing would say something like that."

Aldo repeats the man's name and the minister for whom he works.

"I don't know," says Chrétien. "He might be a prick." Then he mutters an aside to the giggling listeners. "Of course, I don't know what a 'prick' means." But the candidate squarely faces the issue: "I feel your frustration because I know it exists. There is a kind of elitist connotation to the party that I don't like. We cannot have the Italians or Portuguese vote for us and then they disappear. I'm not like that. If you look at the statistics, you will see that we're in danger of losing the ethnic communities. What is the coalition of the Liberals? It is formed of three groups. The francophones, the moderate anglos, and the ethnics. And in some parts of Canada we've lost it. We used to have the Ukrainian and Polish people in the western part of Canada. We lost them when Diefenbaker became the leader. And we never got them back. So when you lose the ethnics, you might lose them for a long time. Some people compare me to Diefenbaker, but I have one advantage over him. I know how to administer in the party. You don't find any documents under my bed. I don't take any documents home. I can deal with them in twelve hours and that's enough. It's exactly what I'm offering to you, a populist person. You know, I'm not an elitist. I don't use the word 'new' every second phrase like one candidate. But you know, he's still wearing the garters."

"You're not the problem, Mr Minister," Aldo says, "and I want to make clear that the structure behind you isn't the problem."

"It won't be the problem," Chrétien assures him. "I promise you that."

"Can I meet with John Rae some time?"

"Oh, yes."

"We'll make sure you meet with John Rae," says an aide.

Another assistant mentions the aide who had made the anti-Italian slur and suggests some other prominent Liberal ethnic group whom the minister represents. Now they are venturing on shaky ground.

"I don't think we should get into that," another aide quickly interjects.

"I know who said it," Aldo asserts. "I know who believes it. I've been in this party since I was ten years old and I know the personalities in this party."

"But you never have a problem with me," Chrétien concludes.

Despite Jean Chrétien's evident sincerity, there is much truth in Aldo's accusation. Multiculturalism in Canada is a kind of blind for continued domination of political elites. Under Trudeau, it was true enough that Quebeckers and Jews participated in the public life of Canada as never before. But despite the number of Jamaicans in Toronto, or Italians, there was no Mario Cuomo in the Liberal Party, no Jesse Jackson. Instead, the Liberals had a kind of paternalistic connection with these communities, helping them with immigration matters, giving them grants to maintain their distinctive cultures. There was Charles Caccia, there was Anne Cools; neither of them could be called major players in the party or in the cabinet. The main path to political power in the Liberal Party was still the law schools, up through the university student organizations, to graduate work in political science at Harvard or LSE, to apprenticeship as a minister's aide, and from there into electoral politics. You could work riding associations for a lifetime, you could walk up and down knocking on doors forever and still remain in the lower echelons of the party.

It wasn't that Liberals were prejudiced. Far from it; they would have eagerly welcomed some bright new star coming out of any of these immigrant communities, bursting with the proper degrees and the right magnetism. So far no such person had shown up. By and large, multiculturalism meant that Canada's ethnic communities stood at a distance from the mainstream and huddled in on themselves. To date, their bright young men and women had not taken the path out of the neighbourhoods and into the corridors of power. Perhaps nobody was willing to point out where the paths were; maybe the "ethnics" regarded them with indifference. After all, such a path successfully negotiated would take a man far from his roots, and few seemed willing to attempt it.

The previous week in Toronto, three men with just these sort of elite credentials met for lunch to trade inside dope. Naturally, the place they chose to meet was that butt of Jean Chrétien's humour — Winston's Restaurant. Named after Winston Churchill, this eatery, unlike restaurants further uptown, had the courage to stick with the decor with which it set out in life. Where those newer places around

Bloor Street and Yorkville continually changed in order to keep up with the vogues of New York chic, the restaurant on Adelaide Street eternally evoked some long lost period, perhaps the early '60s, when Toronto was making its first halting steps towards becoming a cosmopolitan town. There is a giant portrait of Churchill at his glowering British best in the entrance hall, but the place's atmosphere is a curious attempt at Art Nouveau, though the connection between the bulldog statesman and the *fin de siècle* ethos seems tenuous in the extreme. There are knock-off Tiffany lamps, murals that make a half-hearted effort to imitate Gustav Klimt, and sombre brown curling trellises patterned after those in Maxim's. The whole style recalls the days two decades ago when paisley fabrics and the Beardsley Nineties were the rage with advertising executives, before the hard glitter of glass and chrome conquered all.

Despite this aura of the ersatz, Winston's is well-known as the number one Big Boy Expense Account Lunch restaurant in Toronto. The corporate honchos and big-time lawyers that crowd the place at mid-day know that to be accorded respectful treatment from the place's owner, John Arena, as were the three who are meeting now, is formal recognition of status in the worlds of business and government. Silver head after silver head is bent under the imitation Tiffanys dangling over every table; even the waiters look like corporate vice-presidents. For the first few moments there is nothing in the room resembling a good-looking woman, but soon two strikingly statuesque black girls are seated close by, radiating sex, looking like two big cats on the prowl, clearly on the hunt for a sugardaddy. After all, Winston's gives off a scent of money like a bank vault. But as they look from table to table with glistening, inviting smiles, none of the silver heads pays them the least attention. It would have taken a very brave big boy indeed to tangle with them.

When they were in their twenties, the three men had worked as aides to prominent federal politicians of differing parties. Although they had gone on to various august positions in business and government and are now closing in on forty, they are still steeped in politics. The Liberal is deeply involved in Chrétien's leadership campaign. Like many another Toronto pragmatist, he is walking a tricky line between the federal Liberals and the provincial Tories, an act that requires not a little cunning. All three men have a private appreciation for wit, the more cutting the better, a salty delight in the down and dirty truth of things. Politicians and their advisors could mouth homely platitudes in public all day long but among themselves they were proud of their tough readings of what was after all an unforgiving game. Nonetheless, they are most interested in each other in so far as each one possesses privileged information that he might be willing to share with an old buddy — what a minister had said on such-and-such an occasion behind closed doors; what the premier's present mood was. Not only was this species of information the currency upon which one could dine out in the loftiest social circles; it was a definite strategic aid in keeping one's career afloat in the public and private bureaucracies in which these figures moved. A certain natural respect was accorded those who had access to the ears of the powerful.

The man who advises Chrétien reports that he had strongly counselled his candidate to put more distance between himself and Pierre Trudeau. With an election looming sometime in the year to come, one bedrock certainty was emerging among all the imponderables. The country, after sixteen years, wanted something different. The only question was whether it would settle for a change in style, or whether it desired a sweeping transformation of substance. Yet Canadians weren't known for their revolutionary passions. The astonishing thing was that, in a democratic system, the Liberals still held firmly to the belief that whatever conceivable change was needed, they could supply. If the polls showed that the country required a jackbooted dwarf with a strong belief in the divine right of kings, the party would do its best to produce such a monstrosity, who was in addition a Liberal in good standing. After all, the permanent Tory regime in Queen's Park presented ample proof that a government could indeed go on forever.

Chrétien's advisor tells his lunch partners that he is certain that the humble troops of the Liberal Party are as fed up as the rest of the country, that they have suffered under the autocracy of the Prime Minister's Office and the Privy Council Office, as much as everybody else. The Liberal Party, in power so much of the past seventy years, is broad and deep. There are a multitude of currents, shoals and eddies of alliance and opposition, some of which have been washing to and fro for decades. Chrétien's advisor is a good specimen of those people in the party who still hold grudges from the 1968 leadership campaign, who still, despite his two decades of dominance, regard Trudeau as an interloper. It wasn't only John Turner who felt that now, at long last, it was *his* turn. Even in the Liberal Party, Chrétien's friend says, there is resentment at the notion that only those who attended Oxford or the Sorbonne were entitled to the leadership.

51

Much of that feeling was naturally going to coalesce around Jean Chrétien. At the same time, there was a lot of respect for "*le petit gars*" here in the environs of Bay Street. He had been, after all, one of the major players in Canadian politics over the past 20 years.

Glancing over at the empty table where John Turner invariably ate his lunch of steak and tomato salad, Chrétien's advisor laughs and says, "He's so rusty, they're calling him the Tin Man." The art of politics was after all like any other art: it required constant practice. So far, Chrétien was like an athlete on the top of midseason form, effortlessly dancing through the opposition. By contrast, Turner's reflexes were slow. He had made a bad mistake on the language rights of the French minority in Manitoba. Chrétien's man voices the suspicion that Turner is not up to the bruising game of electoral politics, that he isn't back for the long haul in any event; he had still not made up his mind when Trudeau resigned. Turner is running a hastily improvised, scrambling campaign. Despite his loyalty to Chrétien, the aide prides himself on his political detachment. Canadians are looking for politicians to define a new social consensus, he opines. The Liberals are waiting to see which of the major candidates are most capable of holding on to power. In that sense, they were failing to see that he who was most ideological would be most pragmatic.

The conversation now turns to the Tories. There had been a rumour abroad that Brian Mulroney was doing his best to attract star candidates from the Toronto region, that there was a Mulroney bandwagon on which prominent provincial cabinet ministers, Roy McMurtry for one, and media celebrities like Adrienne Clarkson were eager to jump. Now, with the Liberals coming back up in the polls, maybe these people were having doubts. Well, says the Tory, William Davis was not too encouraging about his cabinet ministers jumping to the federal camp. The candidates in Toronto were not going to be that glitzy.

Several weeks after his meetings with the Jamaicans and Italians of Toronto, Jean Chrétien is wooing quite another type of delegate, in rural Nova Scotia. If other politicians finely calibrate their pitch according to what part of the country they are visiting, Chrétien is always himself. On a late May morning, he arrives at the Halifax airport. He has not stopped once, barnstorming across the country, and now looks like a man running entirely on his nerves and his iron will. There are those observers who believe that Chrétien's handlers should have taken him off the delegate trail and rested him up for the convention. But he takes pride in claiming that he is the hardest-working man in show biz, that nobody is going to put out more effort, that if there is one delegate to be won over, he, Jean Chrétien, would travel a long way to meet him.

The Halifax airport is a small 1950s box of yellow brick. Big-bellied fishermen, awaiting their own flight, are talking, in the near-Irish brogue of Atlantic Canada, about ships "doun ounder the say." They are decked out in black denim jackets and fancy-stitch cowboy boots; the entire working class, from autoworkers to loggers, are C & W numbers these days. Along with the usual camera crews, Chrétien's advance party stand chatting and drinking airport coffee as their leader gets off the plane. Unlike Tories, Liberals not infrequently have a faintly academic air. One of the advance men is wearing professorial tweeds, cords and wire rim spectacles. Yet he stands in the Bad Hombre Gunslinger stance popularized by his party leader. His feet are spread wide and planted firm, as if he is expecting imminent physical assault, the thumb of his clenched fist hooked into his belt, as if ready to snake towards some imaginary Colt on his hip. Here is one Tweed Jacket ready to come out of the library and shoot it out with the real world.

A poll in the morning's *Globe and Mail* says that Turner now leads Chrétien by just four points. Although conventional wisdom has it that Gerald Regan is going to deliver the Atlantic region's votes en bloc to Turner, a story in the *Halifax Chronicle-Herald* quotes Chrétien's Atlantic coordinator as saying that his man is out in front. There was a custom in politics, as in professional sport, that no matter what the circumstances, you always said you were going to win. It was showing the flag, it was loyalty, it was the done thing.

After a brief scrum, Chrétien takes off in a rented car, leaving the press scrambling. Some of them feel that he has deliberately given them the slip. The Chrétien camp is claiming that it is the delegates that want the press excluded but, judging by the session at the Royal York, some pretty frank exchanges are taking place that neither candidate nor delegates are eager to see in print.

Canadian Press, *Le Soleil* and Radio-Canada rent a car and do their best to follow Chrétien into small-town Nova Scotia. They travel through a landscape as green as the British Isles, past red brick textile mills, industrial relics of Charles Dickens's century, past K.C. Irving refineries standing out prominently on the hills, dominating the countryside like Druid temples. Soon they are lost. When they turn off the sideroad to find a map, the guy at the gas station says yes, he has a map, but no he can't sell it; it's his only one.

"Don't you miss Trudeau already?" CP says to *Le Soleil*. Trudeau would have made this trip, if absolutely necessary, in regal style, tightly organized, motorcycle escort at full speed, the press bus contentedly trailing along behind.

In Kentville, Chrétien is just winding up his meeting when the press roll up. The town has a clapboard, New England feel. The candidate, in his blue-grey Ottawa lunchbucket suit, stands orating in a backyard of a house with a white picket fence, while the local Liberals, dowdy and plain, keep an awed, respectful distance. The house is on the outskirts of town; beyond is the perennial Canadian bush. For a second, before the cameras and microphones swarm all over, one has the sensation of a timeless scene; one that might have taken place in the last century: the Big Man from Ottawa come to tell the villagers his story.

When his meeting with the delegates is over, Chretien presents an award to an ancient couple who have performed decades of local service. The minister of energy pumps the old geezer's hand and says "A good Grit, eh?" A teenage girl in a purple pant suit fumbles with an Instamatic and says nervously, "I'm not a professional at this."

"You better be," says Grandpa.

The media is now swarming into the quiet, well-tended backyard, which is awash in spring flowers. The first question to Chrétien makes reference to the fact that most of the federal cabinet has gone over to John Turner.

"A lot of ministers have concluded too early who will be the next prime minister, but I have faith in the delegates that they will come to their own judgment. If I had listened to the press, I would have stayed home and I would not be campaigning this morning."

A reporter from the *Kentville Advertiser*, wearing a windbreaker with a shirt and tie — that characteristic small-town combination of informality and respectability — asks Chrétien if he will increase the federal subsidies for farmers in the Maritimes. Kentville, after all, is farm country. "I'm not going to make promises about spending money," the candidate replies sternly. "Mulroney will tell you that he will increase the subsidy, but I'm not like that. I don't buy votes." Then, perhaps with second thoughts, Chrétien softens. He praises farmers in general, and says maybe he'll be able to fix interest rates for them, something along the lines of government-supported interest rates for housing.

Jim Munson of CTV is covering Chrétien on this swing. Munson is tiny, barely five feet, but is one of the few journalists who is a politician's equal in his ability to dominate any room he happens to be in. Chrétien treats Munson gingerly, just as he does Jason Moscowitz from the CBC. Newspapers and magazines could do their damndest, but no major candidate wanted a Munson or a Moscowitz to be out of sorts with them. A disaffected network reporter could make you look very bad indeed night after night on the national news. And that was where the battles of present-day politics were won and lost. *The New York Times, The Washington Post* could rail away at Ronald Reagan forever and he would still be smiling. But woe betide an aide if he lost Sam Donaldson's luggage.

Munson asks Chrétien about a poll that shows that John Turner can now beat Brian Mulroney and also indicates that Chrétien could trounce him too. He wonders if that little bit of information is going to change Chrétien's strategy in the last weeks of the campaign. "I always knew that I could beat Brian Mulroney," Chrétien boasts. Then he loads his voice with deep irony. "I mean, I knew the guy." The Kentville audience laughs appreciatively. The utter contempt in which the weak, divided, none-too-smart Tories are held has been a deep and abiding tenet of Liberal faith for decades. For Liberals, Diefenbaker, Stanfield and Joe Clark were all figures of elderly futility. There was no reason to suppose that Mulroney, slick though he might be, would be any different. Stanfield fumbled the football, Clark fumbled his chance at government. It seemed like a law of nature that Brian Mulroney would soon trip over his shoelaces. Besides, the Tory leader was being buried by the media; all its attention was fixed on the Liberal leadership and the question of whether Turner would let his lead slip to Jean Chrétien.

"So in this campaign, where I've caught up very rapidly with my friend John Turner, it's a sign that to catch up on Brian Mulroney will be very easy. I'm already ahead of him. So I won't change my strategy. It's working very well so far."

"You said you won B.C. Do you think you're winning Atlantic Canada?"

"I'm informed by my coordinator here that it's a neck-to-neck situation. There's a lot of uncommitted. That's why I'm here this morning."

"Is it important," Munson inquires, "that Allan MacEachen gives his word which way he might go as far as influencing delegates in Nova Scotia?"

"I don't want to comment on that. Mr MacEachen will make his view known when he is ready."

Allan MacEachen was the most important cabinet minister in the Maritimes and still a force in the party. Clearly, Chrétien cherished a strong hope that among all the other ministers, MacEachen would eventually join his cause.

The girl in the purple pant suit with the Instamatic is now perched on a picnic table. She is one of the Kentville delegates and is passionately in favour of Jean Chrétien. She has a pale, pinched face and a kind of ecstatic aura, more associated with religion than politics. A reporter asks her why she is so set on Chrétien. Well, she says, she has no use for John Turner. Why? "First of all," she declares fervently, "he deserted the party, left it in limbo. Secondly, there's too much polish. There's something so *real* about Chrétien, so honest."

After the meeting, Chrétien piles into his rented car with his local coordinator, Wilf Moores, his press secretary, Brian Smith, and a driver from the local party organization. He's making his way across country to Liverpool. Moores is in his forties, prematurely grey, with a country squire's red complexion, and a general air of provincial gentility. Smith has smooth manners, and a dulcet, radio announcer's voice. He is given to calling Chrétien "boss."

"That's a beautiful town," Chrétien says.

"See that guy. Look!" Moores exclaims. "Somebody recognized you back there."

"Yeah?" Chrétien is not particularly impressed.

"Actually he probably said, 'There goes Brian Smith.' That's what he said."

Chrétien is more interested in delegates than in banter. "I said to a reporter here, we have two or three delegates and he said we have gained some."

"Yeah."

"You know, everybody prefer not to have the press."

"You think so?"

"I think some of the questions asked of me would not have been asked. The questions that she asked me, the girl, about Turner, I was happy that she asked. But she would have not asked that if the press had been there."

56

"And I've got a good idea where she is," says Moores, "and she's not with us."

"She with Turner?"

"She announced Turner at her delegate selection," says the driver. He is bursting with the front-porch gossip of Kentville politics.

"I don't know if she was trying to embarrass us or what," says Moores.

"She was trying," Chrétien replies. "She was. She was trying to say that there is nothing sinister about resigning; it was exactly that. It's what I say, that he resigned because he wanted to go back to his family and make more money. It was completely honourable and I was tempted to do the same thing many times."

"Actually, that wasn't the point that she wanted to hear."

"I wasn't too offensive," Chrétien insists. "I'm telling you what Turner told me at the time. He might have had other reason to resign. But if they're going to pretend that he have other reason, they should make them public."

"It was almost like she was trying to build a defence for Turner in front of those people because Turner wasn't there to answer for himself."

"No, I enjoyed it. She provided me with a good occasion. And the other thing I like, the issue's alive."

"People are thinking about it."

"She was a Turner and she was extremely defensive. The bottom line means that it's hurting."

"Yeah," say Moores and Smith in unison.

The talk then turns to the rough ride the press is giving Turner. "They set him up," says Moores. "He was the white knight at the start. Now they say 'wow,' this isn't the guy we thought we had. Now we have to somehow save our ass here. We can't seem to shape him up and we don't like it."

"Richard Gwyn wrote a column where he said I've won the campaign but I'll lose the convention. Have you read that? What is that? It's based on nothing?"

"But we have an example right here in Kentville," says Moores. "Right here we lined up two or three of the uncommitted. We're winning the majority of the uncommitted in every riding."

"We've got to do better than split the uncommitted," cuts in Smith. "We've got to split 60-40."

"This is my own score among the uncommitted," says Chrétien.

"We're ahead in Newfoundland. We're neck and neck here. We're ahead in PEI. I haven't heard about New Brunswick. I'm ahead in Quebec among the uncommitted, I'm ahead in Alberta and I'm ahead in BC. That proves that I'm ahead in the majority of the provinces."

"And Quebec offsets Ontario."

"And when I say I'm neck and neck, the growth is on my side."

"That's right. The momentum is there."

"The press look at it as if the winner is going to be there on the first ballot. And I'm telling you that it's not impossible that I will be first on the first ballot."

It's a long way to the south shore of Nova Scotia, and Smith thinks Chrétien ought to get something in his stomach: "We've got some lunch for you in the trunk because you didn't get anything to eat."

"I'm not that hungry," Chrétien says in a low voice.

Smith insists. "You better have a bite anyway because you won't be eating until later on tonight."

Chrétien waves him off. His mind is on one thing. "Anyways, guys," he says with enormous satisfaction. "We're winning it. Beating Mulroney is going to be small potatoes. It's going to be tougher to beat Turner than to beat Mulroney. Anybody that beats Turner, they will say this guy is unbeatable. If I defeat the champion, I become bigger than the champion. It's like I say at the beginning. I have nothing to lose. If I win, they say he's done the impossible. If I lose, they say 'Poor Jean, he deserved it, but he was born on the wrong side of the river.' "

Moores laughs out loud. "Lots of people on this side of the river with ya!" he reassures his man.

Chrétien talks unceasingly throughout the trip. In order to campaign convincingly, full out, the first person you have to persuade of your eventual victory is yourself. The man seems to be undertaking some strange course in autohypnosis. Talking about Turner, he announces, "I just take a little piece of him every time." Chrétien makes a picking, pinching gesture. "I hurt him," he says, "but I don't kill him." Let Eugene Whelan make the kamikaze attacks.

The candidate's mind then turns to the Quebec cabinet ministers who have gone to Turner. Some of them were close friends and their defection has hurt. "You know what it is? They're saving their own asses. They don't love the man. They love power." Unavoidably, the appetite for political power gets in the way of friendship, and old ties are betrayed.

As the car moves through Nova Scotia, the conversation returns to the meeting in Kentville. In every town there is some bullyboy who thinks he can mix it up with the champ. In Kentville, it was a local lawyer who for years had been inflicting his political opinions on the town. The driver evinces great satisfaction at the comeuppance the man apparently received at the hands of Jean Chrétien. "It's strange," says Moores, "He's a fan of the minister's — he's got the button on — but he's asking questions that are contrary to the party's main programs. It's like I've finally got a chance to talk with ya and I'm going to vent within me all the things that I dislike. It was an awful shouting match."

"He was opposed to everything," Chrétien agrees.

Moores does a quick sketch of a small-town redneck: "He was opposed to universality, he was opposed to the baby bonus, he was opposed to unemployment insurance."

"He got carried away," says Chrétien. "I asked him if he was doing worse than he was twenty years ago . . . I mean, come on."

Moores and Chrétien discuss just how much money a lawyer could make in a small Nova Scotian town. For all the long distance he had come, Chrétien was still the product of Shawinigan. A big man had a fine healthy body, a big house, a big car, and big dough. A smaller guy would do well to have respect.

As they get closer to Liverpool, Moores briefs Chrétien on the couple they are going to meet there. Their son is the local delegate. He is undecided.

When they arrive, the house is on the water, looking out on a pulp mill, which is sending up a plume of pollution. It's a ranch-style house with a colour-coordinated beige interior. The local gentry assembled to meet Chrétien are more refined than their Kentville counterparts; they have wine glasses in their hands, not Instamatics. These are the cultivated small-town people, the sort who read *The Globe and Mail* every day, and make frequent trips to Toronto, Montreal and New York. If there was one subscription to *The New Yorker* in Liverpool, it would surely come to this house.

"Isn't this a nice place to campaign?" Chrétien booms out to one of the assembled matrons. She's apologetic, a trifle embarrassed. "Yes it is," she acknowledges, "even if there is a smelly pulp mill along the way."

"Oh, a paper mill is part of my life," Chrétien assures her. "I was born across the street from a paper mill."

That night a thick fog rolls off the Atlantic and envelops Halifax. The city has improved over the past few years. The fashion for renovation has come east and has brought a great deal of the city's colonial architecture into sharper focus. Halifax now has a somewhat more civilized air, there is a slight tinge of the picturesque; an Anglo Quebec City. The night fog softens the dour grey contours of the city and transforms it. Traffic signals, their lights smeared by the rain and mist, shine in dreamlike shades of plum, peach and lime. The head-lights of the cars stab out into the dark so tangibly, the beams look like they comprise a solid mass.

Over in Dartmouth, Chrétien is fundraising in a roller rink called Wheelies. The crowd is sparser than his organizers would like. There is plenty of ginger ale and cake.

"I never complain about being tired," Chrétien begins his address, "but I am a little tired tonight."

"Good boy, Jean," somebody in the crowd shouts. "You've worked hard."

Chrétien's complexion is indeed grey. He looks exhausted. But once again, he rises to the occasion and, off the cuff, creates a remarkable atmosphere of intimacy and candour. Far less important than the issues are the emotions a politican sparks in his audience. Chrétien is all heart. He tells the East Dartmouth Riding Association that he has come across the country from Vancouver to talk to them. "When I make a commitment, I keep it." He talks about his own candidacy in first-person terms, insisting that he isn't in the race for his own vanity. "We already have enough clippings in the name of Chrétien." The message is: You can trust Chrétien; he is not arro-gant. Then, a battler to the end, he takes on Mulroney with brawling humour: "I don't understand why we should be a Tory party when the Tories are adopting our own policies. On Medicare, Mulroney has come with us; on Manitoba rights he has come with us. So why should we look to *his* position? Brian Mulroney is a man of experience in the international field. Oh yes, he went to Cleveland, Ohio many times to receive his orders to close the mine in Schefferville, and when he have no more job, he kicked out Joe Clark to take his place because he was unemployed — it's understandable."

The partisan audience roars with laughter. Humour has a narcotic effect in politics. North Americans trust men with humour. They naively believe that a man with a sense of humour has essentially gentle intentions towards them. Trudeau was all business. Chrétien's is the only Liberal wit to match John Crosbie's. Now, with the au-

60

dience under his spell, he continues, once more emphasizing his experience, his well-earned trust, the years as minister of finance, the Charter of Rights, making the deals in the west after the National Energy Program.

"Now," he roars, "the task of beating Brian Mulroney — it's *nothing* compared to that. It's always the same, the Tories win the election one year too soon. Look at the polls! We're moving up! We're moving up! I will have won the country and I will have remained a Liberal."

This was the point where Chrétien should have ended his speech, but he enjoyed talking so much, he invariably went on ten minutes too long. There was little doubt: Jean Chrétien was lovable, the country had increased affection for him. But he was not listening to his advisors, he was not moving away from Trudeau on the issues. If the Liberal Party was coming up in the polls, there was little doubt that a good part of the credit was due to his exertions. The sole remaining question was whether this change in style, this new popularity, could propel Jean Chrétien past John Turner, as he was predicting, and over the top.

CHAPTER 4

THE ICEMAN COMETH

Just as much as it is a function of rank or position, privilege is a quality of the mind. The elites of business, government, bureaucracy and the media, which in effect ran Canada, believed not only that it was their meritocratic duty to guide the modest fortunes of the nation, but that, like any eighteenth-century aristocracy, it was their destiny. It was partly a matter of birth, partly of talent and ambition, but those who ran the country had a strong sense of entitlement, a passionately held conviction that it was theirs to rule. Imagine, then, the inner bitterness of those who believe they have been unjustly deprived of this rightful destiny. What floods of resentment can equal those of the princely exile, deprived of his birthright?

Consider the case of John Napier Turner. Although not born rich, he had nonetheless spent his childhood within the orbit of power. His mother, an unusual woman for her time, had been a government economist during World War II. There was the family cottage at Kirk's Ferry, next to that of Lester Pearson, the Ottawa glimpses of that arch-ghoul Mackenzie King out walking the dog. Canada was a democracy, but John Turner had grown up in a milieu where people talked about running the country as a matter of course. Just as a child of musicians has an early ear for music, and the children of farmers have a nose for crops, power and its conundrums formed Turner's infant environment. Later, his mother married a rich industrialist. He had been a golden boy at UBC, Oxford and the Sorbonne, the heralded consort of Princess Margaret, a young man whom the Liberal powerful had marked out early as a "winner." Liberals, whose grip on power consisted almost entirely of the politics of compassion for the weak, loved nature's favourites like few others. The crown prince of the 1950s' fraternity boy, John Turner had been the promising young MP in Lester Pearson's Ottawa.

Then that most notorious decade, the 1960s, intervened, epitomised by Pierre Trudeau, who wasn't Dobie Gillis, but Marlon Brando. Turner, who was famous for his anxiety to do the right thing, who was the quintessential example of a man who leads his life according to the expectations of others, was upstaged by a usurper who had resolutely devoted a lifetime to pleasing himself. Nevertheless, hemmed in by inhibitions as he was, Turner was a man of enormous, princely pride. Finally, he had found playing a supporting role to Pierre Trudeau's leading man intolerable and in 1975 had left the cabinet for the golden towers of Bay Street, where his expertise and connections in governments at home and abroad were worth considerably more than a minister's salary.

Although Turner obeyed the code of silence that distinguishes politicians as well as Sicilians, it was generally understood that he disapproved of the leftward, statist drift of the Trudeau administration. The exile on Bay Street, like most men, had been formed by the verities of his childhood. King walking the dog. Jimmy Gardiner running the West. Ernest Lapointe running a quiescent Quebec. Government as the consensus of regional elites. Across the nation, big man talked to big man and matters were settled by them, not by a technocratic apparatus of committees run by the acolytes of a solitary philosopher king.

But it is the rare exile who is returned to usurped privilege with such consummate ease as that afforded John Turner in the spring of 1984. Pierre Trudeau was a dogmatist who had scant tolerance for independent minds. His ministers were either disciples or they were nothing. Consequently, except for Chrétien, there was no strong personality in sight who might have proved a natural successor. Apart from Eric Kierans, John Turner was the only figure of substance who had been unwilling to sacrifice his pride for whatever crumb of power Trudeau might condescend to apportion. He had waited in silence; now the kingdom was his, apparently there just for the asking. Only, in *his* mind it was as if the years of the interregnum had never happened, should never have happened. As Christina McCall-Newman had pointed out, Turner was a perfectly preserved relic of the days of St Laurent and King. The press were beginning to call Turner "The Iceman," and indeed he seemed like a specimen of a vanished world come back to life. He may have been the white-haired boy of the Golden Towers, but out on the streets he was a stranger in a strange land. Watching his campaign for the leadership was breathtakingly close to science fiction.

This is an impression well confirmed when, late in May 1984, Turner comes to Toronto to address a party held for his youth workers in a disco at the top of the CN Tower. Unlike the casual Chrétien campaign, Turner is already enveloped in a prime ministerial cloak of security. Reporters covering the event are taken deep into the concrete bowels of the tower, asked to show identification, asked to sign a ledger, and made to wear a numbered lapel button. Then they are individually escorted by a young security woman in a velvet aerospace jumpsuit up an ear-popping high speed elevator to the tower's top. The security guards around political events are invariably youthful and badly paid. On their employers' orders, they treat the press like dangerous criminals, after which they inevitably ask them how to get a job in the media.

The disco is called Sparkles. Gazing out of ceiling-to-floor windows, one sees, as from a 707, Toronto Harbour and the Islands. At the turn of the century, the Eiffel Tower gave poets an opportunity to sing the wonders of the coming Modern Age. The CN Tower offers a glimpse of the nature of the coming era of travel in outer space. Your life would be entirely spent in that particularly excruciating physical state enforced by air travel. You would always be cramped in too small a space, you would always breathe air that was reconditioned, your ears would always be at odds with cabin pressure, and terra firma would always be too far away. Even if nobody was dancing just yet, socializing on top of the CN Tower was like going to a cocktail party in the aisles of a passenger jet.

If Jean Chrétien was a big draw for the Jamaicans and Italians of Toronto, John Turner attracts a young crowd that can only be called first-plateau chic. A spectacular girl in a backless dress and gloves, with long red hair coming down over one eye like Veronica Lake, sits perched on a stool, a drink in front of her, staring moodily out at Lake Ontario. Supervising the music, there is a disco DJ in a New Wave crewcut, a tiny braided pigtail dangling back onto his collar. He wears a black Hamlet suit of extreme cut, the trousers as tight as leotards. His fingers work continually at his nose and nostrils, the telltale signs of a dude who has snuffled down many a line of coke. The socially idealistic hippies have all disappeared; now there is Punk, its style of consciousness nihilistic, bitter, its fashions intentionally harsh and extreme. The punk DJ is at Sparkles this evening just to do his job; only the law students are here out of enthusiasm for John Turner. Their hair is razor cut, they wear swingers' moustaches. For a showbiz gathering, the crowd is dowdy; but for politics, it's high fashion.

I ask one of these young lawyers why he's supporting Turner. You could ask questions all night and not hear an original word. Much more likely to get yesterday's newscast. The lawyer feels, predictably enough, that Turner is going to bring western Canada back into the Liberal fold, that Turner, in some way I cannot see, is going to make the party "vibrant again" and this will appeal to youth. I asked the lawyer why he preferred Turner to Chrétien. "Chrétien's always joking, eh?" he replies. "He's not serious." For young Liberals, there is such a thing as too much humour. Politics, after all, are serious.

When John Turner arrives at Sparkles, however, the mood is not so much vibrant as deeply respectful; the same emotional ambience one might expect from a visit by Prince Philip. An august personage has descended on multitudes presold by a reputation. This reputation of John Turner's is a mysterious thing. Almost a decade out of public life, he cannot have made much of an impression on the twenty-year-olds in the crowd. His accomplishments as a corporate lawyer are not terribly well known. Perhaps it is enough that he reputedly brings home a large salary. Respect for money has never been greater.

Well, Turner certainly looks prime ministerial, what with the beautiful silver hair, the laser-blue eyes, the lordly carriage. And there is something truly ceremonial about his progress through the Ontario youth. Turner would certainly make a fine prime minister, if all the job meant was making a good appearance on those occasions when foreign dignitaries came calling. Unlike Chrétien, who pounces on delegates loud and ebullient, his appetite for power nearly palpable, Turner looks less like a man who is courting his party's favour than one who has long since won it. And if he reminds one of Prince Philip, then his wife Geills is not at all like Queen Elizabeth, but more like the Duchess of Windsor. There is something in her thin lips of that brittle feverishness of ambition that recalls the elegant Mrs Simpson.

Turner negotiates his way through the crowd with all the slow pomp of a royal barge coming down the Thames. Tall and bulky, he rests both his hands on the shoulders of a smaller man, earnestly entreating him to make up his mind. The Hep Cat of UBC 1948 grapples a young black guy, far more stylish than Chrétien's deacon, in all the thumb-twisting intricacies of a soul shake. Eyes and teeth agleam, Turner greets the preppies in their TCS ties, and the aging balding workers, in a game where "youth" seems to refer to anyone under the age of forty.

Turner is introduced to his audience by a young university Liberal, a Japanese kid, articulate and self-consciously enthusiastic, who speaks of the problems facing young graduates looking for work. Where my university generation of the late 1960s saw a mere job as the most

65

prosaic destiny you could explore after graduation, the current one regards a good berth as a rare and priceless commodity. Unlike the Italian who was finding a frustrating dead end in the riding associations, the Japanese kid is handsome and well-spoken — clearly a Liberal "comer." His introduction over, Turner bestows a bear hug of endorsement upon the young Liberal. Then, stepping up to the microphone, he says, "Welcome to Sparkles. The campaign has reached a new high."

Turner conceives of campaign politics as good healthy exercise, along the lines of touch football or tennis. So he thanks the young Liberals for their enthusiasm. "I told Geills," he says. "If this isn't fun, we're not going to do it. You've made it fun and I couldn't enjoy it more."

Turner had a great journalistic reputation for smoothness. Yet he had stumbled badly over language rights in Manitoba; he had earned a quick rebuke from Pierre Trudeau when, on a bus near Trenton, Ontario, he revealed to Val Sears that he had left the government over a dispute with the prime minister to do with wage and price negotiations. On television he glared with such concentration that he appeared slightly demented. The television audience had no idea of the pressure of politics, the mood of hysteria that scrums engender. They didn't see the charging cameramen knocking down anybody or anything in their path; they didn't experience the reporters' desperate intensity. They just saw what the results were in John Turner's face. Now, watching him in public for the first time, it becomes apparent that for all the deep tones, the rich voice issuing out of the powerful chest, he is far less relaxed in the spotlight than Jean Chrétien, far less able to communicate the attractive portions of his personality. His delivery is clipped, as staccato as a jackhammer. Worse, his thought is convoluted, choked; you have to work hard to extract the sense: "I remember what one of my heroes once said and I had the honour of knowing him and giving him a bit of support — that ended in tragedy — Bobby Kennedy — Geills and I both knew him well."

Here Turner pauses to accomplish that familiar phlegm-removal manoeuvre that had prompted CBC sound technicians to dub him "Throat Cancer." Over a headset, the operation must have sounded like some kind of industrial process concerning the unblockage of municipal drains.

"Ahhhhhauhurgghhh," says Turner. "Bobby Kennedy said to the young people of the United States, and I'd like to say it to you. You have more stake in this country than I have. You're going to live longer in it, and pay attention to the future because you're going to spend the rest of your life there."

How's that again?

There is something quaint about this evocation of the lost era of Camelot. Turner had always been likened to the Kennedys in his golden boy days. But then, the press had compared every handsome young politician of the early '60s to the Kennedys. The Kennedy name, the preppy sense of "fun," used to be a sure way of reaching young people. But, biography after recent biography seemed intent on discrediting the whole Kennedy clan as a pack of rogues and lechers. The focus on Jack Kennedy's fondness for skirt, and plenty of it, was characteristic of the public obsession with purity of character, in what was after all the worldliest of professions. In any event, the name of Bobby Kennedy no longer represented a magical talisman for youth, but was now more in the order of a historical personage, as much a figure of the distant past as Franklin Roosevelt. The sense of social idealism awakened, however expediently, by the Kennedys has long vanished for these job-hungry kids of the 1980s. They see themselves not as potential civil rights workers bringing the benefits of their compassion to the disadvantaged, but rather as the objects of their elders' compassion. Turner's unthinking appropriation of the disappearing mantle of the Kennedys is just another symptom of his distance from the present moment, another indication that he has returned to Canadian politics as a lordly visitor from another time warp.

The next afternoon, a Saturday, Turner attends a Liberal policy debate in the glooms of the Royal York Hotel. This is the last of these debates for the leadership contenders, a travelling roadshow that has previously visited Vancouver, Halifax and Montreal. The Canadian Ballroom, a large oblong rectangle, is dressed up with a chic grey backdrop, featuring a stylized red maple leaf that radiates lines out from its points like some primitive Aztec power symbol. Grey, of course, is this year's modish interior design colour. Every bar, restaurant and hotel with aspirations to style features some variation of grey. Tory political decor never strays beyond the primeval patriotism of red, white and blue. As far as they're concerned, the absence of Tory blue from the national flag is just another instance of Grit treachery. The NDP is militantly anti-style — nothing so frivolous as art direction for them; they're always represented by varying combinations of muddy oranges and sincere browns. But the Liberals, those champions of first-plateau chic, can be relied upon to replace their traditional red-and-white with red-and-designer-grey.

Liberals also pride themselves on their media smarts. So these policy sessions are designed to focus attention on the leadership race in a kind of thundering crescendo, like playoffs in hockey or football. As such, they serve as mini-conventions, gatherings of the faithful.

The room is jammed, the walls festooned with the candidates' posters. Turner's supporters wear the same bright yellow scarves that David Crombie's legions wore last June in Ottawa. Is this the emblem Rosedale and Forest Hill have identified as their distinctive political insignia?

A good part of the federal cabinet is present. And there too is Bryce Mackasey, keeping the lowest of profiles behind the banks of television cameras, but unable to stay away. Mackasey, having undergone one trial for alleged influence peddling, now stands as the Liberal pork barrel personified, although he had been acquitted.

The bargain basement candidates are all present: John Munro, who has also been touched by rumours of scandal, Eugene Whelan, and Mark MacGuigan. Whelan has his own bucolic style, but Munro and MacGuigan are of a piece. They wear dark, severe, well-pressed suits, shoes shined to a high gloss; they are blessed with plentiful heads of hair. They both exude a comfortably fed, sleek sense of well being. They have a high colour and radiate an agreeable sense of just how good it is to be a minister of state. Judging by the looks of these three men, power must be a rare tonic for the metabolism. In effect, the world always extended a red carpet for you. Your actions had real consequences in the lives of millions, your every utterance was taken as a matter of the utmost respect. You could indulge your bad humour, your irritations, with little consequence.

Now, it is all changing. Although there is a lingering admiration for Trudeau, his henchmen inspire a rare contempt. They were too desperately positioned on the greasy pole of life, squirming and writhing to retain their patron's favour above, while gazing down on the populace below. It is not a posture to compel admiration.

Whelan, Munro and MacGuigan have no chance whatsoever of winning the leadership of their party. Their motives in running are usually attributed to some combination of vanity and delusion, but after all, they are practical men. With their leader about to go, Trudeau's cabinet members, if they wished to maintain that eminently agreeable station in life to which they had grown accustomed, had a choice that only appeared simple. In truth, it came loaded with a weight of dread. First, they could support whomever they determined to be the best bet for leader. This had to be done quickly and with evident sincerity; bandwagon-jumpers could not expect much in the way of welcome. Accordingly, cabinet members like André Ouellet, David Smith, Francis Fox and Robert Kaplan had all plumped for Turner. It was the conventional wisdom. Still, the message of Turner's candidacy was that the sixteen years of Trudeau's leadership had been a mistake, which he, Turner, was going to correct. Willing followers of Trudeau, like Munro and MacGuigan, were not sure of the reception they might receive from John Turner, even if they did tender their support. It would be an inconceivable humiliation to support Turner for the leadership and then be dropped from cabinet anyway. So the three men were not really contesting the leadership. They were anxiously attempting to drum up sufficient delegate support in the party to enable them to barter for a cabinet post in the new leader's government. Unfortunately, they had little to say beyond the usual Liberal pieties; nor did they have the crowd-pleasing personality of a Jean Chrétien. Their candidacies were sounding an ever-increasing note of desperation.

Conducting the proceedings is Paul E. Martin. The son of Liberal paterfamilias Paul Martin, and a Montreal shipping tycoon, Martin has all the platform smoothness that Turner is lacking. He has a distinct resemblance to the movies' Bill Murray and an easy humour. Martin was the kind of new face the Liberals sorely needed. They were always trying to recruit him into active electoral politics, but he had so far evaded the call. After his father — one of the few surviving links to the King and St Laurent governments — is pointed out to the crowd, sitting in the front row, Martin introduces the first speaker, Iona Campagnolo, the party's president.

Her appearance on the platform is greeted with such a volume of spontaneous enthusiasm that even Campagnolo seems alarmed by it, unwilling apparently to accept the intensity of her own popularity. It is possible that the outburst that greets her is having the uncomfortable effect of making her second guess her decision not to run. After all, she had a more legitimate chance of victory than the bargain basement candidates.

Glimpsed for the first time, Campagnolo is possessed of an extraordinary glow of appeal. There is something of the countess about her. Her height, her perfect features, her silver hair, her predilection for long skirts that trail the floor, make one think of European royalty.

After all, the current phase of Canadian politics suggests that there is no single more powerful group than women, and no issues, even unemployment and the economy, that are more important than those that concern them. Party politics are usually a good half-decade behind the larger society in reflecting cultural trends. The rebellious fervour of American youth started out in the early '60s, but did not fully translate itself into political terms until the candidacies of Eugene McCarthy in 1968 and George McGovern in 1972. While the Women's Movement seemed to reach its peak in the mid-1970s, it is only now that women are beginning to be recognized as a formal, legitimate force.

Campagnolo tells the crowd to cool it with the signs and the noise because "Here at these forums we're at work." Pay attention now boys and girls, or nanny will spank. She speaks with the force of a Canadian Margaret Thatcher. From Judy LaMarsh to Flora Mac-Donald, there have been important women politicians in Canadian public life, but watching Campagnolo and the Liberals, one has the definite impression that the historical moment is exactly right, and that a woman with a more Thatcher-like sense of ambition would have had a very good chance of becoming the country's first woman prime minister.

The Countess Campagnolo goes on to talk about how some Canadians are trying to hide from the changing nature of society by listening to that nasty Brian Mulroney's promises about "a restored yesterday." The reference is directed more at Reagan than Mulroney, but the Liberals love to tilt against the opposition by running against the American president, a person still profoundly mistrusted in Canada. Setting aside Reagan's right-wing politics, many Canadians still had Victorian notions about the acting profession and what they considered the exaggerated importance of Hollywood in American life. The most esteemed Canadian actors were not likely to get far in politics, even in the unlikely event that the notion appealed to them. The idea of Donald Sutherland or Christopher Plummer running for high office was unthinkable for a people who were willing to laugh at Chrétien and Crosbie, but were reluctant to have them as prime minister.

Campagnolo goes on to say that, in their policy sessions, the Liberals have "pointed the way to a new political generation." It is of course the party's desire to renew itself without the inconvenience of a period out of power, sans perks. But the last thing they want to do is suffer the painful self-examination necessary for a true transformation. Real change in the Liberal Party necessarily would have to include the admission that they had erred in one or two particulars over the last couple of decades. The fact that they have held office for the best part of the century has encouraged a godlike sense of infallibility among them. If Pierre Trudeau had been Napoleon, you could easily have imagined him defending the retreat from Moscow as an essentially good thing for France. While it was regrettable that so many thousands of troops had frozen and starved to death, there was nothing wrong with invading Russia in the winter. Anybody who suggested otherwise was probably both a fool and a coward.

The Countess Campagnolo repeats the usual pieties about the Liberals remaining a "commonsense, middle-of-the-road party, believing in a strong private sector, a strong public sector, and the greatest social safety net in the world." Still governessy, she reminds the party that they have urgent work to do, that they must remain a united, disciplined team. But, if on the surface she looks like European royalty, Campagnolo now reveals herself to be, deep down, a good old rootin' tootin' Canadian cheerleader: "Liberals are *smiling* all across the country," she croons in yearning tones. "The sun is *shining* and it's summer once again. The polls are up and, under a new, confident leader, we will *beat* the Tories in the next election."

Despite such Pollyanna-ish optimism, the Liberals are a party in trouble. The creed of Liberalism, largely unexamined since the 1962 Kingston Conference, held during the hiatus of the Diefenbaker years, is under serious attack from conservative ideologues in the United States and Britain. The real question before the Liberal Party was how far they were willing to abandon the watery socialism of the Trudeau years and for what. If Liberals prided themselves on being more reflective sorts than the proudly know-nothing Tories, the debate that follows reveals the current paucity of the party's thought. The Liberals seem to be counting on the country's distrust of the Tories to mask the fact that, after nearly two decades in power, they have little to *say* to Canadians.

In his pinched, nasal voice, MacGuigan, a professor of jurisprudence, quotes that great founding prophet of liberalism, John Stuart Mill. And even though he earns mild applause for his strong statement against American intervention in Central America, he says nothing that is likely to stick in the mind.

Whelan, in his fluorescent green cowboy hat, is forced to spend the better part of his time at the podium countering a racist remark he recently let drop about Africans. The minister of agriculture, with his hayseed demeanour, looks like the shrewdest, most prosperous farmer on the face of God's earth, one who takes the purest delight in getting the best of city fellers who ain't half as damn' smart as they think they are. Whelan demands, "Why is there gold flake on the winders of the bank when people don't have cornflakes on the table?" The Royal Bank Tower, in which John Turner had offices at McMillan, Binch is, in a remarkably frank celebration of Mammon, covered in gold plate. Whelan's jibe is, of course, another coded slam at the silver-haired front-runner. But Turner just grins affably. It's Marquess of Queensberry rules here, and a gentleman sportsman is happy to let a rube take his best shot. After all, the grin shows how pathetically little damage has been done.

Donald Johnston and John Roberts are the second-tier candidates. They have no real chance to win either, but are nonetheless accorded a certain respect as they jockey for the number three spot. If things are close at the convention, it is possible that their support might make a difference. There is no love lost, the story goes, between Turner and Roberts. Like the bargain basement candidates, Roberts is trying to do a salvage job on his political career. Roberts and Johnston have been vying for the title of campaign intellectual, the source of new ideas about liberalism. During that short season when Gary Hart had been in vogue, Roberts had made an attempt to label himself as a "neo-liberal." But, given a close reading, there was nothing terribly new about his liberalism.

Johnston, on the other hand, was like Turner trying to move to the right, but in a more thoughtful way. He had notions about re-forming the social welfare system by combining unemployment in-surance and other benefits into one guaranteed annual income. Just at the moment, Canadians were nervous about the possible dismant-ling of social welfare programs, and Johnston's notion had the timely virtue of wanting to save money and be compassionate all at the same time. Such thoughts had earned him the respect of various com-mentators and he had begun to move ahead of Roberts. Then, in Vancouver, a few weeks before, Johnston had broken into public tears when talking about his daughter and her horror of the nuclear holocaust. It was a moment reminiscent of the time that Edmund Muskie had wept before the voters of New Hampshire after a scur-rilous newspaper attack on his wife; that little outburst had torpedoed the man from Maine. While Canadians weren't as obsessed as Amer-icans with swaggering toughness in their leaders, neither did they want a man with his hands on the controls who was given to weeping in public.

Donald Johnston looks enough like Joe Clark to pass for his more intelligent brother. However, in the age of the television close-up, his lack of strong, distinctive features is no advantage. Yet he has the benefit of being a comparatively fresh presence. This afternoon in Toronto, he proceeds to attack the party's powerbrokers and vested interests. Making a kind of snout-grabbing gesture with his hand, Johnston promises to "yank their noses out of the trough." The remark might have appealed to a country and a party losing patience with blatant patronage, but to those of the Liberal establishment, a thousand of whom had votes out of approximately 3,500 at the convention, and who evinced an iron-willed determination to stay guzzling at the trough up to their very eyebrows, Johnston's threat seems less than endearing.

Turner is next. He has a deeper voice than the others, a richer tan, but somehow the mind just drifts when he speaks. In part this is because he presents his thoughts in the jargon of management science, incessantly talking not of choices but of "options," and making constant use of barbarous neologisms like "priorization." Not only does the pseudo-scientific language make Turner sound like a cross between an efficiency expert and the Bionic Man, it makes him dull. Politicians are not poets but, little as they like it, they do have to use the English language. There is no colour in Turner's discourse, no trenchancy. While Chrétien at his best brings all of himself to a platform, with Turner you are left wondering who the man is behind the manager. The language of management science sounded fine in the backrooms of business and government; it sounds like Martian in the backyards of ordinary folk. Worse, there is no avoiding the comparison with the man he aspires to follow. The unavoidable impression, now that Turner is out in plain view, is a thump of a letdown. Trudeau, as a political performer, shared with other star performers, such as Brando and De Niro, a certain dangerous unpredictability. Whenever Trudeau was around, you were never sure where he might lash out, what he might say or do. While you might conceivably not like a word of what he said, you could never take your eyes off him. Without a similar imperative demand on the attention, Turner is drearily predictable. Listening to him, you can always sense the inner machinery lugubriously working towards what he perceives as the current consensus. One has the feeling that John Turner has never held an unpopular opinion about anything in his life.

So, here in the ancient caverns of the Royal York, the Iceman dutifully emphasizes the importance of free enterprise, while pledging not to disturb social welfare. Even now he is mouthing the received wisdom of Winston's Restaurant about the party's past attitude towards business, and the received wisdom of the Liberal Party itself about social welfare. Business first, welfare second. Turner, unlike Trudeau, is a deeply unoriginal man. It was, after all, the conceit of any gent who thought enough of himself to aspire to the leadership of a people that he could translate his own private vision of their future into public reality and persuade millions of them to help him achieve this end. While Trudeau spoke directly to the nation from some fiercely guarded inner portion of himself, Turner always made you think he was delivering a message from a committee.

There's a big demonstration for Chrétien, who speaks after Munro. But he makes a costly tactical error. Instead of speaking spontaneously, as he had done in Dartmouth, he's stiff, formal and humourless. It's as if Chrétien feels he has to be dead serious in the serious company of his fellow ministers. By sacrificing the natural colour of his personality, he's playing to his weaknesses, not his strengths; none of the attractiveness of his personality shines through. Chrétien would have been better advised to tell ten minutes of jokes, without once mentioning an issue, than strive to be as portentously solemn as John Turner. In this formal setting, itself deprived of humour, Chrétien seems once again the standard Liberal cabinet minister. So, while he calls for equality of opportunity, for compassion, tolerance, and a new open style of government, he is not making the overwhelming impression he needs to.

Seen on the same platform as Turner, Chrétien's disadvantages become more apparent. The Liberal elite, who pride themselves on their cosmopolitan manners and who regularly congratulate themselves on how well they can negotiate the drawing rooms of Washington, London and Paris, cannot help but think of what an embarrassment Chrétien would be abroad. Although he had endeared himself to Canadians over the years, the prizefighter face and Godfather manner were at first guaranteed to frighten small children. To Americans, who had funny ideas about Canada anyhow, Chrétien would seem like a stereotype of the backwoods pea-soup lumberjack. His first trip to the United States as prime minister leaps to mind. The American papers would play it as "Lucky Jean the Voyageur Goes to Washington." And the goddamn Brits! They thought the country still hadn't made it out of the logging and beaver pelts stage. Bad enough, without handing them Chrétien, so they could look down their fine Whitehall noses at him.

Style aside, the difference between Turner and Chrétien is one of emphasis. For Chrétien, maintaining the Liberal social welfare net came first; then everything would be done to help the economy. For Turner, the economy came first: that safeguarded, he would do everything possible to keep the social reforms. Chrétien was offering a more open style than Trudeau, but essentially the same approach to government. Yet it was a mistake to put a damper on his personality. The champ who invited any brave bucko to ask him a question was here playing things too scared and cautious.

If John Turner is the Prince of Boardrooms, John Roberts is the Duke of Dinner Tables. With his double chin and cupid's mouth, he shares the glossy ruddiness of the bargain basement candidates. Roberts's voice isn't a Mickey Mouse squeak like MacGuigan's, but compared to Turner's sumptuous tones it is light and mild. You could see how Roberts might be impressive at an elegant dinner party; he would dominate the table with his aura of power, his inside dope, his charm. The voice was perfect for the chamber music of the dining room. Big halls required more throat muscle, demanded symphonies.

But Roberts comes out swinging and, unlike the others, scores a few hits. He attacks Ronald Reagan's ambassador, who has pronounced Turner, Chrétien and Mulroney to be acceptable as prime minister to his country. He attacks the media, always a sure bet, for having counted him out. He attacks John Crosbie; he attacks Brian Mulroney, "who has not asked one question since he came into the House of Commons about jobs," and who has "refused to define what a Conservative alternative for this country would be." In Roberts's opinion, without the social net, the recession of the early 1980s would have resembled that of the Depression years — all soup kitchens, jumping freight cars, and Woody Guthrie songs.

Roberts makes an all-out plea that the Liberals not move to the right. He says that he believes in an active role for government, that Canadians "shouldn't let the strong fight it out for status and success in our society." It is odd to hear the impassioned language of social justice in such a plump and rosy representative of established privilege. Reform held a powerful grip on men's minds when it provided a dream for the future, but it was not convincing out of the mouth of the overripe past. Roberts, presumably eager to demonstrate that his attachment to social justice is no dreamy idealism, finishes, urging that "it is because we have remained liberal that we have won election after election." Somehow, the higher-minded nuances of social reform were lost when they were presented as self-interest. Preferably, reformers should be lean; they should not look so well-fed as John Roberts.

After an intermission, the floor is open for questions. One very pointed enquiry concerns the adversarial nature of trade unions. The labour movement in North America had never been more unpopular; the only time the public ever heard about them was when there was a strike. Still, the question puts the candidates in a fairly awkward position. They can bash the unions and appear for all the world like any Tory hog jowl, or support them and look anti-business (at a time when business had never been more popular, this would be a dangerous thing to do). After all, when Whelan and one or two of the other minor candidates had tried to whip up some populist fervour by attacking the traditional target of the banks, Paul E. Martin had become very nervous. "Whenever these guys start talking about the banks," he had said, "I want to get out of camera range."

Jean Chrétien, the man you can ask anything, ducks the question. Turner comes up with the "right" answer. Although predictable, Turner does have the ability to create occasional small surprises. So, asked how business and labour are going to live together in the near future, Turner, with his instinct for consensus, answers that Liberals "have to create a constituency of working men and women in this country. And I would think the first priority is to renew the dialogue that has lapsed over the years. After all, we can show common cause with labour. They know we have challenged in our own markets, we have challenged abroad. They also know that productivity is a shared responsibility. Not just labour, but management, better get to be more efficient in this country." It wasn't particularly eloquent, it was couched in the damnable jargon of management science, but, for the candidate from Winston's, it was manifestly decent.

Even though John Roberts maintained that "what we need is not a chief executive officer but a leader," it is clear that Turner has made the strongest impression. In his concluding remarks, he is all fiscal responsibility, emphasizing the importance of reducing the deficit, but not, of course, in Draconian fashion. He says he's going to create a climate for expansion. Then, not having said a partisan word all day about any of his opponents or the opposition, he proclaims that he is going to take the high road. It was true that people were tired of Trudeau's unending appetite for conflict, but Turner is giving the impression that he would just as soon not mix it up with anybody, that it was in fact beneath his august dignity to enter into unseemly brawls. So far he hasn't had to. The only man with a genuine talent for ridicule, Jean Chrétien, has suppressed his natural high spirits, true to the code of unity. The risk of venturing a shot was that it might not land. And to swing and miss, leaving your opponent untouched, was the mark of a loser. At the core of Turner's appeal lay the idea that he was all winner. Nothing was going to make him start mixing it up.

In the last week of the campaign, John Turner goes to Peterborough, the most average place in Canada. Prone to odd bouts of book-banning, the small Ontario town is so characteristically representative of the heart of the heart of the country that it has become one big social laboratory for market research — the ultimate test-tube city. If anything from pet foods to Petro-Can wows the folks in Peterborough, the chances are that the rest of the country will love it too.

On the bus out from Toronto, Turner heads for the very back, takes off his seersucker jacket, puts on a pair of black hornrims and buries himself in papers. With the red tie, the white seersucker, and the blue shirt, he looks like a walking tricolour. Politicians always travelled at the front or the very back of a bus or plane, *never* in the middle. It was like the corner office in a building — a power position. After the furor in the newspapers about Turner's unguarded remarks about the prime minister, he is keeping his distance from the press.

"Come on, John," says a reporter, not loud enough for Turner to hear, "what do you think of the PM? You can tell *me*." The story is that Turner and Trudeau almost certainly detest each other, but it didn't look good for the party to have them indulge in open squabbles.

With Turner today is David Smith, the minister of small business, and one of the leading pro-Turner Liberals in Toronto. In shirtsleeves and bright red suspenders, Smith is the plump incarnation of Liberal smugness. As the bus travels along Highway 401, he's talking to Craig Oliver, the CTV correspondent, about Jim Coutts's chances in the coming Turner government. The inevitability of such a government seems a natural fact of life to Smith; so does his own high place in it. There had been early rumblings about Coutts making a leadership run for himself, but he had been talked out of it. "Well," says Smith, with the air of a man who knows he's going to be consulted on all cabinet appointments, "if Jim had gotten on board early and meant it, it might have helped, but I don't know what good he thinks he's doing himself by chasing after the Spadina vote." In any event, it doesn't seem likely that those Liberals closely associated with

Trudeau, Coutts and Keith Davey especially, are going to have much to do in a Turner administration. He has already gone on record as saying there would be no "rainmakers" in his government.

Arriving in Peterborough, Turner moves through the crowd at the Red Oak Inn before making his speech. Watching him, you don't have the feeling that he's really connecting with anyone. He grabs the men with his patented two-handed shake, massaging their elbows, and fixing them with the laser beam eyes. With the ladies, he grasps their little paw with both hands and caresses the back of it. But little real warmth comes across. When Chrétien finally did shut up long enough to listen, you felt the words sinking in. With Turner, one felt they were going into a data bank slugged "Demographic Opinion." Even in the sauna-like atmosphere of swarming supporters in the hotel's poolroom, the Iceman does not melt very much.

On his way through the crowd, Turner is stopped and challenged by a tall man in a small-town check suit. The contender's face clouds over; he gives a clipped answer and quickly moves on. Turner doesn't like unpleasant disagreements. A CBC radio reporter buttonholes the man and asks him what the conversation with Turner was all about.

"I asked him why he hasn't spoken his mind more as a private citizen," he says. "Basically with John Turner you're trying to re-member what he did in politics ten years ago. With Jean Chrétien I can look at his recent performance; I don't have to look back ten years. With Chrétien you've got lots of actions. You only have mem-ory with Turner."

"Did Mr Turner win you over with his answer?"

"He seemed to express the view that it would not have shown any loyalty to the Liberal Party to have criticized its policies. He said when he was asked, 'I'm a private citizen now.' There's something incompatible for me in saying 'I'm a private citizen' and then saying you're part of the party."

"In a word, what's your impression of John Turner?"

"I feel he's going to have a lot of problems." If this small confron-tation was any measure, John Turner had an overly optimistic view of his own persuasive powers.

The front-runner gives his speech in his usual barking tones of assertion. He doesn't stroke an audience like Mulroney, or rough it up like Chrétien; his words just seem to hang there in the centre of the room, in a void, without striking home. Today's main topic is youth unemployment — a program to give youth experience in short-term jobs, particularly reforestation and "upgrading the municipal infrastructure." Once again Turner underlines his lofty, non-partisan nature, high above the petty fray. "I have not come back to fight Liberals or Tories, but to take the high road. And I have resisted the temptation to reply to some of the shots that have been taken against me."

Turner gets enthusiastic applause from the Peterborough audience. In the heart of the heart of the country, nothing is more admired than restraint, especially of unruly emotions.

Leaving the Red Oak Inn, the media surround Turner on the steps. The candidate looks around and says, "Where's Dennis?" refusing to utter one word until his press secretary, Dennis Baxter, arrives with a tape recorder. Politicians' press advisors now lurk in every scrum, taping everything in case their man is misquoted. There's a long impatient pause while somebody goes in search of Baxter. The press and Turner stand facing one another, the media making nervous quips, Turner, lips tight together, grimly silent. Finally, when Baxter doesn't appear, a soundman offers to pass on a copy of his tape to the Turner camp. Assuaged, Turner gives the go-ahead to questions. Craig Oliver asks him whether he expects to go into the convention ahead, "neck and neck," or "behind."

If Pierre Trudeau could easily be goaded by the press into speaking his mind, Turner is clearly a man bent on saying nothing that might inflame further controversy.

"Well," he says, "we have our tracking systems, you have your tracking systems. I'd want to let you make an objective judgment about that."

"I don't have any tracking systems," says Oliver.

"You work for a cheap network," offers Richard Gwyn, standing nearby. Gwyn is a short, sturdy Brit about fifty, with greying hair worn in an odd, combed-forward style that gives him the aspect of a Roman centurion in a film starring Charlton Heston. He is probably the most respected political columnist in the country.

"What do you mean by 'municipal infrastructure,'?" Turner is asked by the reporter from the *Toronto Sun*, a puzzled look on his face.

"Well," says the candidate, "you look at our parklands . . . "

"You talking about repairing roads?" the journalist demands.

"Not necessarily," hedges Turner.

Whether "municipal infrastructure" meant jobs cleaning up parks

or working on roads, beneath the jargon it sounded like small potatoes. Another reporter asks Turner whether he feels that the party's
concerns are different from his own.

"I know exactly what's on their minds," claims Turner. "I'm right
in synch."

Heading back to Toronto, the bus stops at the York Mills subway
station so that some reporters can head out to the airport. Turner
gets off the bus too. Those journalists who choose to stay aboard
are treated to the odd sight of John Turner, the betting favourite to
be the next prime minister of the land, accompanied by only a couple
of aides, walking up the slope of Hogg's Hollow, looking in vain for
a taxi and entirely ignored by the passersby.

CHAPTER 5

APRES MOI . . .

Since the war, with the exception of Marshall McLuhan, he had been the country's only great man, but nobody could ever make up their mind whether he was a force for good or bad. He had been the most unexpected, exceptional entity ever to arrive on our national scene, but he had dwindled into a routine, partisan politician. His early career was linked inextricably to an unprecedented era of hope, but in the end he had come to symbolize, justly or not, everything that was wrong with the times. He was physically small, yet in the funhouse mirror of television he seemed overwhelmingly formidable. He was a theoretical intellectual, who had become a master of bare knuckles politics. He was a cold logician, who could arouse the most torrid extremes of emotion. He was a dedicated apostle of freedom, who had ended as an autocrat. He was a rich man's son, who was the most socialist prime minister the country had ever had. He was a hothouse exotic in a land that prized the mundane. He was a lone virtuoso, who practised a mass art. He was a famous lover of beautiful women, whom rumour forever cast as homosexual. And now, in the early summer of 1984, he was leaving office. It was far from certain that he really wanted to go.

On 14 June, the eve of the convention that will replace him, Pierre Trudeau stands in a crowd on the second floor of the Westin Hotel in Ottawa. He is flanked by security people, attended by a diminishing huddle of media, waiting to be presented with a parting gift by the National Women's Commission, minutes before he goes into a dinner that they are giving in his honour. At sixty-four, Trudeau looks ten years younger than his age, not a man ready for retirement but still in the prime of life. Yet his hair is now steel-grey, not shoved forward, Julius Caesar-style as in the 1960s, but spikily brushed back from his high forehead. No longer fashionable, the sideburns of the 1970s have disappeared. Even though Trudeau is in immeasurably better physical shape than most men of his years, there is at last a kind of paunchy thickening around the middle. Age has made his features less sensual; even more ascetic. He no longer looks like a hybrid bit of casting against type — the social philosopher as practical politician; now his face coincides exactly with the role, that of the immensely distinguished elder statesman.

The magnetism, though, is still there. Trudeau has run the country for close to two decades by the sheer force of his personality. But, unlike other politicians, he does not boom out the loudest parts of his character in order to dominate. He is still enigmatic, deadly quiet. In its last phases, the Trudeau legend had begun to carry some of the tragic resonance of Hemingway; the veteran warrior, trying to wrest victory from pathos one last time. Still, despite the troubles of the past years, he is retiring unbowed. And any room he enters is still electric with anticipation.

Yet what had been original and spontaneous in Trudeau's public personality to begin with has become as formal and hieratic as a minuet. Waiting for the presentation, the prime minister assumes his shy-and-timid stance, the introvert complement to the extrovert gun-slinger pose. In his shy-and-timid, or Bambi pose, the tiger-souled Trudeau clasps his hands in front of him, fixes a virginal glance on the ground, and gives the sweetest, most bashful smile ever seen on the most diffident four-year-old in the daycare centre. If Trudeau has long been the nation's father, he has besides the self-absorption of its most spoiled child.

Up on the platform, a group of singers is belting out, in rococo four-part harmony, a song written especially for the occasion; it expresses a grateful nation's thanks. The singers are polished and poised. The gift of the National Women's Commission is wittily symbolic — gardening tools and gloves. However, you couldn't really see Pierre Trudeau on his knees in the grounds of his Art Deco manse on the side of the mountain in Montreal, planting a prize rose bush; it wasn't really in character. Nevertheless, the crowd oohs and aahs at the sight of the gardening gear as if it has been plated in gold.

The president of the women's organization gets up on the platform to make the presentation. Naturally Ms Talmey seizes on the gardening metaphor in paying tribute to Trudeau's achievements as the provider of big jobs for aspiring women: "Here," she says, "the Master Gardener has not created flowers, he has created soil. Mr Trudeau, you have given us the climate, the roots and the nourishment to flourish."

There was something about Trudeau that inspired admiring metaphor. He had variously been The Philosopher King, The Northern Magus, The Lone Gunslinger. Now he's The Master Gardener. Taken together, they read like the attributes of a constitutional monarch. All that was missing was "Defender of the Faith."

So, in tribute to The Master Gardener, Ms Talmey goes on to enumerate a "harvest" of achievements on behalf of women: the Royal Commission on the Status of Women, a minister for that same department, a Council on the same subject, numerous judgeships for women, the first woman justice on the Supreme Court of Canada, the first woman Speaker of the House of Commons, the first woman Governor General, and the appointments of countless women to boards and commissions. "We miss you, we love you," she concludes, "and we just want to say goodbye."

After the cheers, the Master Gardener himself gets up on the platform and addresses the crowd in his smallest, most uninflected voice. He informs them that he well understands the symbolism of the garden tools: "I always did call a spade a spade," he says. "It did lead me into a certain number of confrontations. Now, I'm going to become a homebody. I'm looking forward to the next period of my life. I will now be able to join all those who help our government from the outside."

It is said quietly, the irony is gentle, but the statement hints at bitter depths. Canadians famously had tired of confrontation. If Trudeau conceived of public life as an occasion for uninhibited debate, with little quarter asked or given, there were now large portions of the population who saw the back alley rumbles between east and west, the provinces and the feds, business and government, not as the free contest of legitimate difference, but as embarrassing public squabbles, far better decided in private by the proper authorities. To the genteel mind, ugly confrontations, verbal brawls, were the intolerable essence of the sordid; an eruption of irrational violence, evidence of a lack of control. In the years of affluence when Trudeau came to power, the years of sit-ins, marches and demos, public conflict gave politics a piquant edge. Now, after ten years of economic disappointment, it spoke too loudly of real anarchy. Besides, the country had given every sign of tiring of the man who had triumphed in so many bouts over the years. The impression was that Trudeau had won all these fights not on the people's behalf, but at their expense.

As for "all those who help our government from the outside," Trudeau's message was simple. It's easy to carp at my leadership. Let's see how well you'll get on without me.

The man's resentment was understandable. While there were still many, like the women's group, who adored Trudeau, how great were the legions that despised him. Think of the abuse he had suffered over the years and which, goaded beyond endurance, he had amply returned. In a certain portion of the national consciousness, perhaps not the highest, Trudeau would be best remembered for his extended middle finger, and "fuck you" recalled as his most memorable message to the nation.

Because Trudeau had aroused extraordinary expectations, because he had dominated the country's public life for so long, the feelings he aroused exceeded rational politics and began to encroach on the domain of the religious. Max Weber had spoken of the routinization of charisma, but what had happened to Pierre Trudeau over the years superseded all such categories. The political bond had taken ascendance over those of family, culture and religion. For Canadians, Trudeau had become more than just a mortal; he had become the Modern Age incarnate, or perhaps just Fate. There was inflation? Blame it on Trudeau. Crop failure? Blame it on Trudeau. Adolescents were illiterate? Blame that on Trudeau, too. There were no jobs? Trudeau again. After all, governments were omnipotent and could spin the planet on their fingertips like so many satanic jugglers. It was a folk-belief that had nothing to do with issues or economics or the salient qualities of a leader's personality, or even with reason itself. If the economy was bad, it was only Trudeau's perversity that had wished it on everyone; and, somehow, if there was less government and fewer politicians, there would be less bad news on everybody's television sets.

"You were kind enough to point out," continues the Modern Age incarnate, "some of the appointments I made over the years to women. I must say that it happened without me being aware of it. People show me these lists with these names on it, and I say 'Did I?' I took the best person at the time. I'm not sure it will be to your advantage to quote statistics on that because I just learned that women are now the majority in this country, and I always fight for minorities."

In front of this small, impromptu gathering of women, Trudeau is tender, thoughtful and intimate. He still has an undiminished ability to reach an audience. The conversational tone, the pensive air make it seem as if he is talking to a couple of individuals, not a room. And what's more, that he understands them better than they do themselves. In part, it was a trick, this knack of creating a sense of high-toned intimacy, of noble purpose. In part, it was a matter of somehow abolishing the space between himself and an audience, no longer a separate "you" and "I", but the materialization of a credible "we." So, this evening at the Westin, Trudeau finishes by speaking of "the many fights we still have to fight together, the fight for peace in the world." It is the classic rhetoric of high-minded reform, the rallying of the troops for another Long March on history. You are no longer struggling on your own, but are now enlisted in a noble crusade. It is potent music, but sadly it now has a nostalgic ring. In the Age of Reagan, moral commitment and idealism seem self-defeating, the notion of "the great cause" foolishly naive. There is a genuine feeling of loss in the room; Trudeau's time is passing. Perhaps he has stayed too long, maybe it would have been best for him to go in 1980. But power was addictive, as murderously difficult as heroin to kick. Even now, you sensed that he was leaving office with enormous regret, that he would have liked to stay, but couldn't see any conceivable way of doing so.

The proof of his reluctance has been his total lack of concern with helping his party find a successor. An egotist to the end, Trudeau was not likely to look with paternal benevolence on anyone who followed him. "If you are politically ambitious," Trudeau was said to have remarked to Senator Peter Stollery, who had complained that Trudeau had left the party rudderless, "you'd be best off to join the Tories."

Out in front of the Westin, a small band is whooping it up for John Roberts. If there is a certain sadness at Trudeau's leaving, there is no sense of irrevocable change, and the atmosphere in Ottawa is determinedly cheerful. Trudeau's era is at an end, but the Liberal era will go on forever. During the past year, even when the Tories were far ahead in the opinion polls, the Liberal strategy was plain: drop Trudeau, and find a new leader and cabinet more in touch with the right-wing times. It was one of the Liberals' perennial articles of faith that Tories were incompetent, always had been incompetent, and always would be. It was Trudeau's force of personality and intellect over the past couple of decades that was responsible for this confidence, but the party seemed to believe that his magic would remain with them even when he had gone.

Unlike the Tories, who hired musicians as if they were so many waiters, the Liberals loved to demonstrate amateur enthusiasm. Walking around thumping a drum or blowing a cornet was beneath the dignity of even a Young Conservative, but Roberts's little band evoked a kind of antique collegiate high spirits, Varsity vs. Queens 1926. Worse, the little ditty that spells out R-O-B-E-R-T-S was as damnably catchy as the worst of radio jingles; it stuck in your head for a long time.

Just across a canal from the National Arts Centre, the Westin is the capital's newest hotel, airy and modern in comparison to the seedy genteel Chateau Laurier. It was beginning to draw a good number of political events away from the older hotel around the corner. The Westin is decorated in oyster greys and creamy beiges. The carpeting is lush under one's feet. Like Halifax, Ottawa is sprouting the occasional sign of civilization. From the restaurant on the Westin's second floor, you can look out through floor-to-ceiling glass windows on that square mile near Parliament Hill, and given the right company and a glass of wine, feel that Ottawa isn't entirely despicable as a city.

As the guests swarm into the Westin for the dinner, it seems like every ambitious careerist of a lawyer or academic is there. As well as being the party of social reform, for decades the Liberals have been the party of power. Those Canadians most pragmatically attracted to power seem naturally to find their way to the Liberals, not waste themselves on the quixotic fumblings of either of the other two parties. Looking at the faces coming into this dinner, though, it strikes one forcibly that the careerists are beginning to outnumber the reformers by a considerable amount. Outside the banquet room, Turner meets Chrétien, and there are smiles and handshakes. The flashbulbs go crazy. There is no evidence of hard feelings, certainly not in public. (Earlier, waiting in the departure lounge at the Lester B. Pearson International Airport in Toronto — its new name evidence of the near-totalitarian Liberal compulsion to leave the party's prints everywhere — a delegate from southwestern Ontario had said to his friend, "I want 'er neat and clean, real decisive." Everything would be civil, orderly and upbeat. Power would change hands with no undue mess, the party would emerge from the convention still united and yet possessed of the country's confidence.)

That formidable battleship, Bella Abzug, is the evening's keynote speaker, but Trudeau leaves before she addresses the dinner and Turner does so too. Why? asks a reporter. "Because," says Turner, radiating self-importance, "there are a thousand people waiting for me in Confederation Park." *One thousand . . . waiting . . . for me!* Outside the Westin, Turner and his wife climb into a white Buick convertible and drive the few blocks to the park. Leaning back on the maroon upholstery, Turner finally has an air of glamour. If Trudeau was Brando, then Turner was some kind of wooden Cary Grant, come out of a decade-long obscurity for a movie-of-the-week. He's followed to the park by a double-decker London bus jammed with his young supporters chanting "Come on guys, we're number one!"

In Confederation Park, an indifferent jazz-rock group is playing. There is a tent striped in Turner's colours, red and yellow, where the Canadian equivalent of bread and circuses — beer and the Blue Jays on television — is being served up to all comers. Turner makes his speech, but few of the beer drinkers in his marquee come out to hear it. After all, the Jays have a 7-3 lead in the ninth; there's still a good chance they can catch the Tigers for the pennant.

Down the street, opposite the Four Seasons Hotel, Canada's favourite Arkansas cracker, Rompin Ronnie Hawkins, veteran of a quarter of a century on the southern Ontario bar circuit, is singing for Jean Chrétien. Hawkins, close to fifty, in black T-shirt, Texas hat and red neckerchief, is singing "Forty Days." The song is to Hawkins as "Over the Rainbow" was to Judy Garland. Now grey-haired, grey-bearded, with a great gutbelly hanging over his belt, Hawkins is living proof that respectability can come to anybody who waits long enough. Watching him and the band pump out nostalgic fifties' rock for the legions of the ruling party, one cannot help but think of the days when Hawkins played the roughest club on the Yonge Street strip, the Coq d'Or, a spa that catered to a whole Beggar's Opera cast of rounders, hoods and mafiosi. In those days, dressed all in black from boots to hat, Hawkins looked more like Orson Welles at his most Mephistophelean than he did like Elvis Presley, and he sang songs from the Deep South with the loudest, most primitive beat, complete with lyrics full of sex as murder, voodoo and menace.

Tonight he sings the more innocuous songs of Chuck Berry and Little Richard, the sentimental songs of the yuppies. If Canadians ever went to war again, they would be dying not to Roll Out the Barrel but to Roll Over Beethoven.

"We're singin' for the next prime minister of Canada," Hawkins states with nightclub sincerity. "We're singin' for John Chrétien." In Hawkins's drawl, "John" Chrétien sounds not so much like a candidate for prime minister of Canada as like Lyndon Johnson, looking for re-election in Texas. Self-defined winners, the Liberals believe in the best of everything, and Hawkins, now launching into a jumping rock-abilly version of "Orange Blossom Special," has always had the best bar band in the country.

Near the tent, listening to the music and chatting with a couple of reporters, is Chrétien's daughter, France Chrétien Demarais, and her husband André. If Chrétien were to be chosen leader, one of the nicest things about it would be the presence of his daughter. If Iona Campagnolo and Mila Mulroney were some of the queenly figures in the nation's life, France Chrétien Demarais had to be its first princess. In her twenties, she has a full, pouting mouth like Natassja Kinski's and is dressed not in first-plateau chic, but in true elegance. Peter Stollery is also in the crowd, wearing a Chrétien button, and so is the candidate's old mentor, Mitchell Sharp. The Pearson cabinet minister is still spare, lean and distinguished. The juxtapositions of public life are sometimes startling: I suddenly have a crazy vision of Mitch Sharp getting down in the old Coq d'Or.

Over in the bar at the Skyline Hotel, a bunch of journalists are gathered around a table. They are trying to talk themselves into being interested in the convention, attempting to convince themselves that Chrétien still has a good chance, telling of rumours they heard about soft support for Turner in the Quebec delegation, floating various eventualities whereby Chrétien could take it. If politicians had to do a job of self-hypnosis, just to keep themselves getting on and off airplanes and delivering speeches, convincing themselves that they were eventually going to prevail in spite of the odds, then journalists had to make themselves believe that they were on to the world's most fascinating story if they were going to write it at all. Inevitably, their best tales and one-liners were the ones they could never use in print. Tonight they are swapping Turner stories, precious few of which will ever see the light of day. For the press, Turner has become a kind of good-looking Joe Clark; that is to say, the chief butt of bar-room humour. Roy McGregor, a novelist and one of the best magazine writers in the country, tells a story about Turner, on a trip out west, eating Chinese meatballs with chopsticks. The front-runner suddenly becomes aware that he is being watched by reporters; realizing that, if he drops one, it will be Robert Stanfield and the football all over again, with infinite, desperate concentration, he steers the meatballs into his mouth.

"God," says Dan Smith, *The Toronto Star*'s western correspondent, "his mouth has a life of its own. It's like it belongs to another person."

Turner has little idea of how much the media have changed in the years he has been away from Ottawa. Not only have their numbers swollen, not only is it harder to get buddy-buddy, but also, after

Vietnam and Watergate, they are all more sceptical of politicians in general. Nor has their attitude been improved by their undisguised contempt of Pierre Trudeau. (One of Trudeau's top advisors tells of how he kept trying to improve the prime minister's dealings with the press. He would suggest having Richard Gwyn and Allan Fotheringham in for lunch, say twice a year; that ought to help relations. No dice. He tried to persuade Trudeau to read David Halberstam's book, *The Powers That Be*, a definitive account of how Roosevelt and Kennedy got the press working on their side. Trudeau didn't open it.) Besides, many of the media are no longer the under-educated, baggy-pants, provincials of Turner's salad days. One of television's better-known personalities likes to recount how he once came to interview the Iceman at home. The filming over, Turner and Geills relaxed with a pitcherful of Martinis while the interviewer was offered the same beer as the goddamn prole soundman. Turner didn't realize that television interviewers were globe-trotting sorts, fond of holding forth about the best place to eat in Jakarta, the best tailor in Jermyn Street, and the best way to rent a house in Sardinia for the summer. You didn't offer a television star a bottle of Molson's Ex while you sucked back Martinis without insulting his hardwon sense of status, and consequently lessening yourself forty percent in his estimation for life.

The Family of Man, to which the Tories had paid vain lip service back in Winnipeg during their leadership review, begins to show up in earnest the next morning when the Liberal leadership candidates address The Native People's Caucus at the Westin Hotel. The native politicians — Indians, Métis, non-status peoples — are striking-looking dudes with a presence that combines the C & W swagger of the Canadian hinterlands and a distinctly militant style. Big, rangy men from the reserves, some of the Indian delegates wear white Panama hats, shirts unbuttoned to the sternum, and fancy vests that would pass inspection on Harlem's hippest street corner. But, instead of Afros, the Indians sport long, black, braided pigtails that reach down to the small of their backs; there are many turquoise and silver bracelets on their wrists. Sometimes, laid in among the silverwork, you can spot a digital watch. This dandyism also has a homely touch, something of the time-honoured bush-country macho of the logging camps and mines; there is often a big comb, stuck fifties' greaser-style, without an iota of retro irony, in the back pocket of their jeans.

It is a style of militance dating back to the great days of the American Indian Movement and *Bury My Heart at Wounded Knee*, when celebrities like Jane Fonda patronized Indian causes. But like Black Power, Indian militance has been running out of steam for years, and is having to make do with the synthetic fuel of lip-service.

As the meeting begins, an Indian delegate steps up to a microphone placed for questions in the audience and states with no irony at all that "the delegates would like to see the expression on the candidates' faces as they make their commitments." It comes as little surprise to the media pundits, but the native people's delegates are right in tune with the tribal sensibility of television. Unlike newspapermen, who harp on politicians' consistency in an obsessively linear way, they know a man's expression is more viscerally important than his words.

The Indian delegates and the Great White Chiefs now perform the tired ritual of militance. Talking as if he is already elected, Turner tells the native leadership what his government is going to do for them. He congratulates them on their "forceful representation," talks about the "ongoing process that will bring us together and bring Indians into the mainstream of Canadian society" — the usual Turner nerve gas. When other men paused in their speech, it could make you believe that they were endeavouring to scale some great contemplative height of truth. When Turner halted for a second, it just sounded as if he was stumbling around, lost for words.

Characteristically, just as Turner presents himself as part of a corporate entity — in this case "my government" — Chrétien sets forth another chapter in his intimate autobiography. He informs the Native People's Caucus that the best years of his life — 1968-74 — were spent as minister of Indian affairs and northern development. "People kept telling me," he says, "that I was creating my own problems when I gave the Indian Association money to express themselves. Oh, you gave me hell a lot of times. . . ."

Chrétien is interrupted by large, self-congratulating applause. It was the Indian part of the ritual of militance that you came and blitzkrieged the white man with rhetoric. The Liberal part was that you gave them a grant to do it. "You've come a long way," Chrétien continues, punching up one of his most kneejerk catchphrases, "but you've got a long way to go. Be proud of your heritage, your culture. We made enough mistakes for you that you should make some mistake for yourself. Keep fighting! Be proud!"

Everybody seems satisfied with the enactment of the ritual, but as a minority movement, they are far from commanding the momentum that is propelling middle-class women into positions of power. Despite the bellicose rhetoric, the Native Peoples, like the "ethnics," are passive clients of the Liberals, on the sidelines of Canada's political and social life. At the end of the meeting, all the cameras, mikes and notebooks head for Chrétien and Turner as if the other candidates are invisible. Mark MacGuigan sinks his face into his hands. All morning, Whelan, in his egregious cowboy hat, has looked as if he is just going through the motions. As MacGuigan comes off the platform, a professorial-looking supporter peers through his wire-rim specs and says, "Way to go, Mark." MacGuigan doesn't look encouraged. There is a rumour afloat that he has tried to make a deal with Turner and has been unceremoniously repelled. From now on, for the third-string candidates, life is becoming an exercise in humiliation, embarrassing to watch.

Behind the scenes there is much busy manoeuvring. The two major candidates are trying to determine what the five lesser lights are prepared to do after the first ballot. Naturally, these negotiations require a certain amount of delicacy. A candidate like Jean Chrétien would have to make such overtures himself. He couldn't send any mere flunkies to parley since at this point the feelings of the bargain-basement chaps are raw and bruised as they watch whatever political respectability they ever possessed go shuddering down the chute.

For the Liberals, technocrats though they may be, delegate-tracking is not nearly as scientific as it was at the Tory convention. Where Brian Mulroney had Paul Weed of the Big Blue Machine and a bank of computers tracing the shifts of delegate support, the Liberal candidates, amidst the gathering chaos of the convention, are still endeavouring to judge how well they are doing by less technological means. Although one or two of the candidates have computers, their input is almost entirely based on non-objective assessments — the casual conversations of friends working for opposing sides, mutually assuring each other that, if their own candidate fails, they will come over to their buddy's camp. As a result, there is a great deal of wishful thinking and self-deception among the delegates about who is willing to move where. For the candidates' close advisors, the trick is to stay detached.

For instance, Jean Chrétien's Ontario campaign chairman, Patrick Lavelle, had sat down on Friday morning with his counterparts from the other provinces and come up with a total of 1,250 votes, a surprise and a disappointment. Lavelle, prematurely white-haired, is astute, in his early forties, and speaks in a loud bark. With these numbers, his candidate will be in poor shape on the first ballot if Turner has 1,600 votes. Chrétien feels that the other candidates are better disposed towards him than they are to Turner because he knows them better, from the years they have spent together in cabinet. But now, they could come over to Chrétien and still bring little in the way of hard votes. By Lavelle's count, the also-rans have a maximum of 500 votes between them, and that number is fast plummeting. There is Don Johnston, for instance, whom the media has been heralding as the man of ideas, a fresh candidate gathering tremendous support. By Lavelle's estimation, Johnston has 40 votes in BC, 29 in Ontario and 30 in Quebec. Johnston's main notion is to pull the noses of the Liberal establishment out of the patronage trough. As far as Lavelle is concerned, that is just more wishful thinking. The line is too heavy, too long and far too wide.

Since the Liberals' main objective is to assure themselves of a continuity of power, Chrétien, although he is taking "little pieces" of Turner here and there, is being careful not to provoke open antagonism. As the leadership race began, Lavelle had gone to see Turner at Chrétien's request, and had told him that Chrétien would run a "civil, decent campaign." Turner replied, "I've got a long memory."

Inside Chrétien's campaign there is naturally a good deal of jockeying for turf and position. After all, if their man should happen to win, his key advisors would be catapulted from relative obscurity to some of the most powerful positions in the land. In this fight, the most important commodity was access to the candidate. At the moment, except for John Rae, everyone is severely restricted from reaching Chrétien. The loser in this contest, according to Lavelle, is Eddie Goldenberg, another aide, who was being too aggressive about his own views.

Chrétien had been counting on Lavelle bringing over Allan MacEachen, with whom he had long been close. After taking a bad beating as minister of finance in the worst years of the slump of the late 1970s, MacEachen's power was now on the wane. But back in the early 1970s, when the Liberals governed only with the support of the NDP, MacEachen, an exceptionally wily House Leader, had saved the government's bacon on more than one occasion, some of them still not on public record. MacEachen told Lavelle that he would not declare for any candidate. This neutrality he considered a personal favour to Lavelle. It was a measure of MacEachen's down-east shrewdness that he could proffer non-support and hold it out to Chrétien as a favour. MacEachen, as they say, was keeping his options open. Still, he was the only major figure in the cabinet who was not himself a candidate or committed to Turner. If Lavelle could pry MacEachen loose, it would be counted a major victory, since MacEachen still carried much prestige within the party. So Chrétien kept pressing Lavelle to bring him over. But MacEachen believed firmly in the alternating "principle," which said that French Canadians and Anglos took turns leading the Liberals. That too had been part of the Liberal formula that had kept them in power for the best part of the century. After Trudeau's sixteen years, the Quebec wing of the party had come up with the lion's share of appointments; the Anglos and the ethnics were hungry.

Lavelle had spent many fruitless hours trying to persuade MacEachen to declare for Chrétien. Home, at midnight, Chrétien would be on the phone asking "What about MacEachen?" Lavelle would return to his task the next day, for another two hours, with the identical result. Still, Chrétien pressed him to see MacEachen one more time. In the absence of other favourable developments, the coming of MacEachen had taken on an overwhelming importance in Jean Chrétien's mind.

Finally, Lavelle had told Chrétien: MacEachen isn't coming.

Later on, Eddie Goldenberg had said to Lavelle, "I don't know what you said to the minister today, but you really upset him."

"If you're telling me," returned Lavelle, "that I told him MacEachen isn't coming, should I have told him different? Should I have said he was coming?"

"Maybe it was the way you said it."

"I said, 'He isn't coming.'"

When Lavelle told John Rae about MacEachen's rebuff, Rae groaned and said, "That's the convention."

According to Lavelle, Rae had wanted Chrétien to lie low two weeks before the convention; play it safe, shut up like a clam, front-runner-style. For Lavelle, this advice was proof positive that Rae didn't understand the guy he was working for. As far as Lavelle could see, Chrétien only looked like a populist when he was compared to Mulroney and Turner. To those who would have him transform his personality into a corporate stone wall, Chrétien would only say, "Hell, I'm not going to change. You can't change me now." Nor, in Lavelle's opinion, was Chrétien eager to become the prince of patronage; he had little appetite for his fellow Liberals' habit of dangling

93

perks, such as Air Canada passes, in front of people who had not necessarily thought of themselves in government jobs before. Nor did he enjoy the way these people were made to sweat while the appointment was being decided and were soon transformed into panting idiots, ringing up ten times a day and demanding to know about their new job. Chrétien found the whole thing distasteful.

As Friday wears on, the Liberal troops drag themselves from forum to forum in the dank bowels of the Ottawa Civic Centre. Liberals are truly different from Tories. Their pride is that they are completely fashionable and up-to-date. There is a black girl in a jump suit and braided corn-row hair; husband and wife teams attending the convention *en famille*, struggling around the junior hockey rink with a child in its carriage, part of the liberated school of family life that inflicted children on all conceivable social occasions, and were surprised and insulted when others didn't always share the awed enthusiasm they had for their offspring.

In one of these forums, John Turner is asked by yet another dreary partisan of decorum and order whether the House of Commons should be made to behave itself better. Canada's parliament is indeed one of the most freely rambunctious in the world. In response, you would expect some uptight, let's-make-the-boys-behave-themselves nod to propriety from John Turner. Amazingly, he informs the man that he believes the House of Commons should remain "the popular forum of our national life," that the parliamentary rules of debate should be left as they are, so that discussion can be "stirring and adversarial and bring out all points of view." Turner adds that the Canadian parliament of the nineteenth century presented considerably more of a free-for-all to public view than its modern descendant and that "what Sir John A. was dealing out in the early days of our country makes the average MP today look like a milquetoast."

Turner's defence of open democratic debate isn't all that wildly daring, but, in the present climate, you have to be grateful for whatever support for the free expression of opinion you can muster. After all, Trudeau's own dislike of the press had determined him and his government to try to manage all expression. Although in the early days Trudeau had shown a strong concern for civil liberties, his governments had done little for the untrammelled freedom of expression. The Kent Commission, formed ostensibly to investigate concentration of ownership in the Canadian newspaper industry, had given rise to a sinister bill, which would have made newspaper editors

94

responsible to a government-appointed committee, rather than to the proprietors of their publications. The bill never became law, but it was a fair measure of the Liberal government's disposition. Then there was Bill C-21, which had been intended to give cabinet full control over the heretofore-autonomous Canada Council, turning that venerable institution into just another Liberal patronage pork barrel and Agitprop centre. During the Trudeau years, the traditional Liberal concern for the freedom of the individual had given way to a control junkie's lust to dominate everything that lived or breathed north of the 49th parallel.

A few minutes before, I had encountered the man who was the embodiment of this illiberal attitude — Trudeau's minister of communications, Francis Fox. It is one of the great pleasures of political conventions that you can catch cabinet ministers out in the open, away from aides and all the usual paraphernalia of prudent retreat. Fox is tall, bespectacled and stooped. Habitually black-suited, severe — an exemplary picture of bureaucratic anonymity — Fox, striving to demonstrate his ardent devotion to John Turner, is here decked out in a bright red-and-yellow outfit that makes him look remarkably like a circus clown.

I ask Francis Fox a few questions about what seems to me to be an increased zeal for censorship and book-banning, especially in Ontario. Does he think our society is going to have to drag itself through another debate about freedom of expression, like the one that occurred in Britain at the time of the paperback publication of *Lady Chatterley's Lover* in 1960; that we are going to lose a battle against censorship that had so recently seemed to be gained for all time? Fox chooses to discuss the issue in terms of broadcasting, but he is anything but sympathetic.

"Well," he said, "some of the broadcasters have indeed been irresponsible in their programming. They bring it down on their own heads. The state doesn't want to be in this kind of thing, and then you have excess on the part of the broadcasters and I think you have to intervene, quite rightfully so. The public airwaves don't belong to broadcasters; it's a privilege to have access to them. They don't have the right to turn them into smut programming."

"Doesn't the zeal for censorship in this country disturb you occasionally?"

"Not really," says Francis Fox, guardian of public morality. "Just as governments come into the marketplace at times to prevent out-

95

rageous market power there, they have to intervene in what has really been a poor exercise of responsibility of some broadcasters in this country. Listen, I gotta run."

Somehow, Fox did not strike you as a man who became passionately concerned with the value of free expression in an open society. It was a lack too often found among "liberal" ministers.

In the Civic Centre itself, the dress rehearsal for the coming evening's tribute to Trudeau is underway. Maureen Forrester is running through the national anthem. There is no Ike Kelneck Band, no Kapuskasing Polka; just an orchestra up from Toronto. These musicians were the giggers, the proficient journeymen who amassed small fortunes out of jingles, television and the big theatre orchestras. If some thought the press cynical, they should have seen the faces on the boys in the band as they rehearsed "O Canada." Trudeau's farewell may have been a big deal for the Liberal Party; for Russ Little's musicians, it was just another job.

As another performer runs through his routine, a flying squad of young, surly, minimum-wage security guards, much more numerous than those employed last year by the Tories and ten times as officious, come to evict everyone who doesn't have a floor pass. For the Liberals, not only must a journalist possess general accreditation to the convention; a special plastic laminated card, coded "O," is required before one can step onto the convention floor. Each news organization, seemingly in descending order of prestige, is allotted a certain number of floor passes. At the very bottom of the list are those writers working on books. There is a story going around the convention that the Liberals were appalled at *Contenders*, Martin, Gregg and Perlin's account of the inner workings of the Tory convention, which probed a little too deeply for their tastes into the wheeling and dealing that took place down on the convention floor. So, lacking the proper floor pass, I am unceremoniously asked to clear out by a fat young woman.

That night, not in the best of moods, I watch the tribute to Trudeau from the rafters of the Civic Centre. The show does not make for a happier state of mind. It is quite simply awful, more like a low-rent show-biz "roast" than a farewell homage to a prime minister: the Holmby Hills Rat Pack salutes Frank Sinatra's fifty years in showbiz. But, sad to say, the tribute to Trudeau is the perfect expression of the decadence of Liberalism.

The other two parties, for varying reasons of ideology and temperament, avoided this extreme degree of intrusion of borscht-belt showbiz into their politics. For them, it was bad enough that television had forced feckless theatricals into the sepulchral business of politics. The Liberals, notorious pragmatists, were willing to use anything that might hold the public's famously wandering attention. This time around, you had to wonder at their taste. The whole production gave off the aura of SCTV's parodic lounge lizard, Bobby Bittman.

The stage is a crimson red with a shiny black tile surface, a garish neon maple leaf hovering in the background. Huge speakers of the sort used for Van Halen arena rock are aimed at the audience, but the performers — Rich Little, Paul Anka and René Simard — are all regulars in Las Vegas. Clearly they have been chosen because they are Canadians who have substantial American reputations. The Liberals like to emphasize that they are players on an international stage.

Up in the cheap seats are a bunch of young Turner supporters, all in their early twenties. Fans of more current entertainers like Talking Heads and Michael Jackson, they jeer sarcastically every time one of the cornball Vegas acts is introduced. Rich Little brings on his usual sheaf of imitations: out comes dithering Pearson, quavering Dief, glowering Nixon. Then, in Trudeau's musically genteel voice, Little informs the audience that after he resigns, the prime minister is going to take a job as a washroom attendant in the House of Commons. There is dead silence: the Liberal audience is stunned at Little's apparent lack of taste. But he makes everything all right again by saying, "It's the only place in parliament where the Conservatives know what they're doing." The audience breaks into the huge applause of evident partisan relief.

After René and Natalie Simard do their Canadian Osmond routine, film director Norman Jewison tells the audience how much Trudeau is respected in bigtime New York (even though at the moment all these provincial, petty bastards up here seem to be howling for his blood). Then, it's Ottawa's own Paul Anka. The singer comes out on stage and, not having troubled to learn his lyrics, reads them from a scrap of paper held out in front of him. Pure class. Anka belts out a doggerel version of a song he wrote for Godfather Sinatra, that self-complacent hymn of Hollywood self-justification, "My Way."

Consider the profundity of:

> *I feel ten feet high*
> *Because I*
> *Don't have to supply*

97

The usual translation.
They've sung his praise
A thousand ways,
And he survives in such a way
That Peerless Pierre,
Extraordinaire
He did it his way.

And finally, for the last word in mindless showbiz vanity:

You must agree
That Canada gave you him
And gave you me. . . .

Vegas North, baby.

If Anka, Little and the Simards bring back memories of 1959, black-
and-white television variety, there had previously been a well-pro-
duced film, considerably less repellent, which was a trip down the
nostalgic lane of the 1960s. While members of the Civic Centre
audience wave the orange posters fixed with the image of the younger
Trudeau from the leadership campaign of 1968, the speakers thunder
out a soundtrack of Jimi Hendrix, and Steppenwolf. Interspersed with
the more dramatic moments from Trudeau's long career — from the
early near-hysteria to the War Measures Act and the fight against
Quebec separatism — are the newsreel stereotypes of the key events
of the American 1960s, the civil rights marches, Vietnam, the Kennedy assassinations. The production gave an eery sense that a Canadian era was indeed passing and that its leading spirit was leaving
the public stage. Because of the historical weakness of the Progressive Conservatives, the attack on liberal values that had taken place
in recent times in both the United States and Britain had yet to find
its full political expression in Canada. Canadians could look with their
customary smugness at the Reaganite government south of the border and say that it could never happen here. Now, with Trudeau
stepping down, there was a palpable nervousness among the gathered
Liberals about what lay in store. Pierre Trudeau had led the country
for the better part of the adult lives of anyone in the audience under
forty. Watching the film, remembering the magnetic leader of 1968
and comparing him with the bloodied but unbowed veteran of 1984,
evoked in Canadians of this generation not a few elegiac sentiments
about mortality and the melancholy flight of youth. The wild freedom

and generosity of the past decades had been squeezed almost out of existence by leaner times; the new age was a deadly sober affair. Trudeau's initial exuberance and nonchalant style, the dates with movie stars, had all been part of the gaiety of the era. As the years passed, the man had become more austere and forbidding. Now, his leaving was a bruising reminder that the fun was over for real.

When Trudeau finally comes out on stage, the crowd starts up the old battle cry, "True-dough, True-dough, True-dough," the chant under which Liberals have conquered so many times. After the obligatory standing ovation, Trudeau plants his feet in the gunslinger stance, one last time, and says farewell to the Liberal Party. Characteristically, he does not indulge in Crosbie- or Chrétien-style ham emotion. Rather, we are treated to a cool, scholarly lecture on the recent history of the Liberal Party, "the fifteen or sixteen years we have spent together."

Trudeau declines to talk at all about the future, and does not divulge whether he has a preference about his successor. Instead, he takes a ride on (what else?) that ancient warhorse, Canadian Identity. Four centuries after its discovery by Europeans, Canada was still a new land, forever making the adolescent attempt at self-definition. So Trudeau talks about how his era was a time of "turmoil and revolt, and a search for identity and the slow learning of maturity of our country." As to the adult future: that has nothing to do with Trudeau, but with "you delegates." It was instructive to hear how the warmth of his "we" system collapsed, when it suited Trudeau, into the chilly wastes of "you" and "I." "We" had spent fifteen or sixteen years together; in the future, "you" were on your own.

Nonetheless, the prime minister goes on to expound the Liberal philosophy, arguing that it is not so much a program or a series of policies as an approach to politics. "A country," he says, "is not something that is built, like the pharoahs built the pyramids and left standing there to defy eternity. A country is something that is built every day out of certain basic values." One would have liked to hear more from Trudeau in this vein — politics as existential choice — but, as he himself goes on to say, the mentors of Canadian Liberalism are not Nietzsche, Heidegger and Sartre, but Locke, Jefferson, Montesquieu, Acton and Mill.

"Liberals see the difficulties," Trudeau continues; "they look for rational solutions. They make sure that reason appeals over prejudice. They tear down the barriers of what separates a country from what it can become. They remove the obstacles to freedom and liberty, so that each human being can fulfill himself and herself according to their potential. They do not seek to equalize everybody. They do assure that equality of opportunity is there for all. They confound the powerful, they confound the secure, they challenge conventions; they're asking questions all the time. They're looking for answers to problems that prevent a country from fulfilling its destiny."

Here Trudeau changes gears. The philosopher of values becomes Canadian historian. He traces the achievements of Canadian Liberalism from Laurier to King, from St Laurent to Pearson, taking good care to honour the spirit of *l'alternance*, speaking in French for Laurier and St Laurent, in English for King and Pearson. "Mackenzie King saw," he says, "that true Liberalism is not giving freedom to everybody and freedom to the strong to oppress the weak, and he ushered in that great series of Liberal reforms from old-age pensions to family allowances to unemployment insurance. . . . Lester Pearson, with all his love and knowledge, who gave us the Canada Assistance Plan, who taught the world the way of peacekeeping. *These* were leaders."

Although he has said he won't defend the record of his governments, Trudeau starts to describe Canada as it was before he came into office. "Fifteen years ago," he recalls, "a woman had never sat in the Speaker's chair in the House of Commons; a woman had never occupied the post of Lieutenant Governor, let alone Governor General. A woman had never sat on the Supreme Court; a woman had never sat as the chief justice of a superior court in Canada. And nobody had voted until they were twenty-one. And there was no Jew in the Canadian cabinet and there never had been, and there was no French Canadian who had ever been minister of justice or minister of trade. [Trudeau seemed to have forgotten that both Ernest Lapointe and Louis St Laurent were French Canadians who had served as ministers of justice.] There was no Negro Canadian sitting in the Senate, or Greek or Italian. There was no provision stating that aboriginal rights were entrenched and did exist. People abroad look at Canada and see a country with compassion, with an idea of sharing. . . . Liberalism is not only a party of purpose, it is a party of the people. . . . Whenever the going was tough and we were opposed by the multinationals or the provincial premiers or by the superpowers, I realized that if our cause was right, all we had to do to win was to talk over the heads of the premiers, over the heads of the multinationals: over the heads of the superpowers, to the *people*."

Throughout the speech, the prime minister has been subtly, gradually intensifying the emotion. Now he talks of the repatriation of the constitution, of the charter of rights. He tells of asking his caucus in 1980 how they should proceed if they couldn't get it past the provincial premiers. Would they have a referendum for repatriation or just linguistic rights. "They said 'Hell, no!'" Trudeau shouts. "'Let's go first-class. Let's get the whole bag. *On va en Cadillac, mon dieu!*'" It was safe to say there was still much fight in the man who once styled himself Pierre Esprit Trudeau. "Remember this," he concludes, "because I'm stepping down as your leader, and in two days you'll be choosing a new leader, and you'll find me there with you following him. And we will dream some more. Our hopes are high, our faith in the people is great, our courage is strong, and our dreams and the truth will never die."

Well, there it was — the last outing of our national philosopher. But tonight at the Civic Centre, although there's a standing ovation and a few moist eyes, no great outpouring of emotion is felt. There is a certain complacence about all the reforms Trudeau has outlined, a feeling that they had not been hardwon victories in the face of much resistance, but a taken-for-granted way of life; a feeling that the party had now dealt sufficiently with reform, it could go on to more fiscally minded things.

If there are those who think they have just watched the exit from public life of a great man, there are others who strongly disagree. Peter Worthington, who has had many a skirmish with Trudeau, including an arrest under the Official Secrets Act in 1978, is standing outside the arena. He says that in his opinion "Trudeau's done more damage to this country than any man in my lifetime. I think he divided the country, ruined this party." One could have remarked that *The Toronto Sun* would have had very little to froth about throughout the entire course of its existence without Pierre Trudeau to serve as cosmic villain.

Of course, Trudeau's essay in mini-history put the best rhetorical face on the contribution that the Liberal Party had made to Canada. It was a vision of a benign dynasty of Liberal prime ministers from Laurier to himself, bestowing the paternal blessings of modern enlightenment on a perennially adolescent and backward people. There were other analyses of the historic role of the Liberals that painted not quite so disinterested a picture. It was the great virtue of the socialist inheritors of Karl Marx that although their remedies for the cure of capitalist society have proven mistaken beyond measure, their diagnoses of the political economy of nations had the matter-of-fact ring of cold cash. There was a dissenting history of the Liberal formula for power, promulgated by political scientists like James Laxer, that was hard to dispute. It went as follows:

The Liberal system, the formula that had kept the party in power for almost seven of the nine decades from 1896 to 1984, served to act as a fulcrum amidst the country's contending political and economic elements. The Liberals contrived to referee the many vying forces of a country with a harsh climate, enormous and far-flung territories, and no abundance of fertile land. At home, they created a balance between French and English, capital and labour, the status quo and the agencies of change. Abroad, they positioned Canada the correct distance between the countries that were most important to it — Britain and the United States. Not too near, not too far.

Originally, John A. Macdonald had designed a confederation that cut a deal between the elitist Tories of Upper Canada and the ultramontane Catholic Church in Quebec, that relied on open access to British markets and capital, and that ran smoothly on the grease of railway patronage. After his death, this system collapsed. As Wilfrid Laurier began to put the Liberal formula to work, Quebec bargained off its interest in the preservation of French-language rights across Canada in favour of greater provincial autonomy. More important, Laurier had effected an essential realignment of Canada's relationship with Britain and the United States. Wary of Tory British connections after the hanging of Louis Riel, Laurier had encouraged closer economic ties with Washington. Although he was careful to speak the language of British liberalism, Laurier opened the door to American liberal democratic values. For economic nationalists, like Laxer, and Empire diehards, such as George Grant, this realignment was the great Adamic sin of Canadian Liberalism. But, given the fact that Britain was on the wane and that the twentieth century, like it or not, pre-eminently belonged to the Americans, Laurier's practical choice could hardly have been otherwise.

Laxer argues that the Liberal system recognized that Canada's political stability depended on coordinating the economy on behalf of the banks and the railways, while providing hope to the disadvantaged and the underprivileged. After giving the Rockefellers a hand in crushing the Wobblies in the mines of Colorado, Mackenzie King, between bouts of anti-semitism and table-tapping, reconciled Canadian labour to the corporate economy, through paternalistic company unions. It wasn't modern labour practice, but compared to union-busting Tories like Arthur Meighen, the Liberal system was thoroughly enlightened.

Laxer points out that as American liberal attitudes crossed the border, so too did the American Dream. If the eighteenth-century Republic depended on the sturdy Augustan rationalism of Hobbes, Locke and Jefferson, the late nineteenth gave way to this half-secular, half-religious creed of mythic potency, which owed as much to P.T. Barnum as it did to Emerson and Whitman. Its appeal yet undimmed in 1984, the dream combined a pragmatic belief in hard work and an idealistic faith in equality of opportunity. Where old Europe envisaged Time as a tragic descent from a Christian Fall, new America saw History as a never-ending ascent. Nature, by definition, was beneficent; present inequalities and limitations were merely God's test of every man's ambition. The hard-working Elect would prosper, the slothful Damned would rightfully perish. Private business was the dynamo of the dream, not only for itself but for all society. American workers would never jell together in a Marxist scheme of class solidarity because each immigrant generation saw its children moving up and out into management or the professions.

Even though there were Tory interregnums, they did not disturb the unbroken success of the Liberal system. In order to be elected at all, they had, like John Diefenbaker, to convince the nation that they were really liberal populists. The Tories, with their lingering hierarchical ties to the British class structure, still believed that society belonged to those of superior quality and Anglo-Saxon descent, whose families had been socially prominent. The Tories under Meighen, Bennett, Drew, Stanfield, Clark et al could never convince the disadvantaged that they really approved of their dream. Diefenbaker, whose roots were German, and Brian Mulroney, coming from the Irish working-class, both fought uphill struggles against this lingering sentiment.

After World War II, with Attlee in office in Britain and the New Deal going full steam under Truman, Mackenzie King brought in the welfare state, not out of the goodness of his heart, but to combat the growing popular support of the CCF, who offered wage-earners more money and power. With the German and Japanese economies in tatters, the United States became dominant in the post-war world. Canada prospered as the Americans invested in resources and established local factories, seeking Canadian markets for their manufactured goods. Socialists wished to believe that the monopolist corporations transformed the American Dream into illusion. It wasn't true. Along with much else, the Corporation had taken over the American Dream. Americans began to believe in social mobility not in terms of creating their own flourishing businesses, but in scaling the corporate ladder. Once again, in their more subdued way, Canadians followed suit.

Pierre Trudeau came to power in 1968 at the end of "a long economic upsurge," which had transformed the country into a different place from the provincial boondock of Diefenbaker and Pearson. As Laxer says, Trudeau's cosmopolitan style was the perfect adornment for the nation's substance. In previous generations, those like Trudeau who had been educated abroad — those best and brightest sons — would have left Canada behind and made their lives and careers like the more proletarian Roy Thomson in Britain, or like John Kenneth Galbraith in the United States. It was a premise of Trudeau's era that Canadians would stay home and help transform their modest birthplace into a first-rate nation. Assuming a belligerent independence equal to the Americans', Canada would come to economic maturity as a fully developed, self-reliant industrial nation.

In many ways Pierre Trudeau was the latter-day incarnation of Wilfrid Laurier. Both used the rhetoric of classic British liberalism to fight off the Catholic conservatives of rural Quebec, with their hatred of the modern world. Although Trudeau was the embodiment of the modern spirit, believing in business, labour and science, he was no populist. He had scant faith in the little man, except as the grateful recipient of the cool wisdom of a refined technocratic elite. Keeping the United States at ever further arms length over issues like Vietnam, Cuba and nuclear arms, Trudeau gave Canada a more independent place in the world.

If he had entered public life in the 1960s as the spirit of liberation, by 1975 Trudeau had been transformed into the spectre of regulation. Gone was the nonchalant hero; now, for Laxer, he was "gloomy, stern, aloof." In the new economic climate of the mid-1970s, Washington was investing more in Western Europe, South-East Asia and at home. Canadian imports were far outstripping exports. Things were bad. In 1975, in a televised new year's speech, Trudeau announced the end of the dream of individual ambition. Under the influence of the limits-to-growth doctrine of the Club of Rome, he pictured the desire for self-betterment as a menace to the nation's collective well-being.

Suddenly, Trudeau's style was no longer seen as cosmopolitan adornment, but as self-indulgent extravagance. The hard-nosed realpolitik of Jim Coutts and Keith Davey, the collectivist message of the 1975 New Year's address, so like Jimmy Carter's 1979 "malaise of America" lament, bespoke an oppressive, hopeless future. Suddenly, the Liberal system no longer represented the rising hopes of the underprivileged, but the preservation of what had become their entrenched interests. Moreover, the candidacy of Trudeau's probable successor, John Turner, spoke not of lofty dreams of the future but just more realpolitik. The pessimistic vision of 1975 may well have approximated the sad truth of things — that the perennially ascending line of history had at last stopped, that the fluid mobility of Canadian society had finally congealed. It was nonetheless a state of affairs that few were willing to accept. Perceived as the steward of the dead present, having lost its vision of hope, the Liberal system was deep in malfunction.

What's more, many of Trudeau's cherished values, expressed in his farewell convention speech, no matter how appealing, seemed as out of step with the times as the music of Steppenwolf. Now, a philosopher could ignore the *zeitgeist* with impunity and hold on to his beliefs in magnificent and defiant isolation; a philosopher-politician who did so was one headed away from office and into the exile of opposition. In the Age of the Squeeze, the powerful were not to be confounded but to be cravenly appeased; the consequences of challenging convention seemed overwhelming. In recent years a counter-agenda had arisen, which seemed like an almost mechanical reversal of the policies of the Trudeau years. This program set forth a policy of less government intervention, a dependence on the private sector to spur economic recovery, encouragement of foreign investment, less sturdy self-reliance and more ties with the United States, and a halt to nationalist policies over American magazines, television and film.

John Turner was being seen in the press and by his Liberal opponents as a right-winger. It was a false description; he was only a man with a practical nose for opportunity. The most significant act of his political life had been his dissenting resignation from Trudeau's government in 1976; the future of Canadian politics lay in taking Trudeau's policies and setting them precisely on their head.

The farewell speech over, the delegates and the media are left to debate its quality. Even if Trudeau's policies evoked more of the past than the future, his powers of fascination have not dimmed; he can still engage the nation by sheer force of character. On the pavement, outside the Civic Centre, yet another rock band is playing. Mac-

105

Guigan's besuited professorial supporter is performing some weird abandoned dance among the ass-shaking multitudes, all restraint gone. Larry Zolf, finished with his CBC duties for the night and heading off to dinner, hears the thump of the rock and roll, sticks out his tongue, squeezes his eyes ecstatically shut, and starts heaving bearishly from foot to foot in a hilarious parody of the revellers. Today the philosopher king has decamped; tonight they will dance. But tomorrow the Liberal dynasty will surely continue.

Friday morning is spent in the acquisition of a floor pass. In a Dostoevskian cubby-hole outside the chilly basement room that houses the press, a guy in a scraggly blond beard is making a limited number of passes available to selected journalists. Once again I explain the nature of my mission — the magazine articles are turning into a book — but there seems to be something about hard covers that spooks the Liberals. The guy in the beard says, "I wouldn't use the book as a selling point if I was you." While we're talking, another writer attempts to engage his attention. The scraggly beard pauses, turns, and says, as if from a great distance, "Don't you see I'm having a conversation?"

But since he's an admirer of my *Globe* column, he manages to come up with a pass from his private store as it were. "Go over to the accreditation centre and get it laminated," he says, "but don't tell a soul."

In the accreditation centre, the man in charge of press relations, another beard, only this time one of those awful Solzhenitsyn jobs with a shaved upper lip, snatches the pass right out of my hand as I proffer it for lamination. "Was it a guy with a blond beard standing at the door who gave it to you?" he demands. I'm forced to admit that it was and have to do some fast talking to get the pass back. Forewarned, I say nothing about books. Just writing a few columns for Canada's national newspaper.

In the early afternoon, large cranes shift scenery in the Civic Centre, dismantling last night's Vegas supper club stage and building a new one. Later on, outside, the candidates throw food into their supporters: burgers for Turner, a fish fry for Johnston. Although such spreads are the routine stuff of political conventions, they do have a certain echo of the bad old days when political support was bought and paid for. This outlay of food, drink and entertainment, even if it did nowadays occasionally carry a nominal price-tag, was a kind of symbolic indication of the good things that would eventually flow from a candidate's government. A couple of days ago, Jean Chrétien had put on a lunch of corned beef sandwiches and beer for Ottawa's cabbies. *Le petit gars de Shawinigan* was their kind of guy anyhow, but the lunch had done him much good.

At 5.30 p.m. the delegates are thronging at the doors of the arena, crazy to get in and secure turf for their candidate. Barry Callaghan, covering the convention for *Toronto Life*, reports on the latest excess of the security thugs. At the doors of the Civic Centre, it seems, a paraplegic in a wheelchair has proved to lack the proper credentials. The security goons grab hold of the chair, turn it around and send the paraplegic whizzing right back out the door.

As the delegates rush in, there's some shoving between the Turner and Chrétien troops. "Get over to that seat," bellows one floor manager to his followers. Then, just as a sweet little incident is about to develop, the two camps recall the need for party unity and start making nice with one another.

Then the evening of speech-making begins. Once again in tandem with Paul E. Martin, the Contessa Campagnolo, resplendent in white jacket, red scarf and black skirt, acts as MC. She informs the convention that they must choose the best candidate because he will become prime minister. Forever alternating between scolding schoolmarm and upbeat cheerleader, Ms Campagnolo doesn't improve on her initial impression; the more you heard, the less you liked. Trudeau arrives and takes his seat in his shirtsleeves, Roman emperor style, in a box high up but directly across from the stage. With a woman stationed behind the candidates, signalling in sign-language for "the hearing impaired," the speeches begin.

Except for the increase in noise, nothing much has changed since the policy sessions. Whelan, glistening with sweat, comes into the arena accompanied by a full marching band. But he's just going through the motions, repeating his line about the dastardly banks and the gold and the "winders." Munro is evidence of the fact that political defeat is physically debilitating. His eyes are red-rimmed and popping from their sockets; he sweats heavily, mopping himself ferociously. The unprepossessing MacGuigan counsels a "tough stand against an illiberal future."

John Roberts, who has had a disappointing campaign, partially redeems himself with a strong speech. "My Liberalism does not imagine Canada to be a limited liability company," he says. "We do not hire and fire our citizens. We do not simply calculate the costs and benefits, and our bottom line is not balance sheets, but people. My Liberalism fights to retain the heritage of social security that Liberal governments have fought to maintain in Canada. These programs aren't frills, they're essential to the stability of our society. A liberal society cannot be polarized into two solitudes of rich and poor or unemployed. It cannot save the rich against the retribution that social justice will surely bring. I do not believe that we should quietly tiptoe to the right. I do not believe that you, the grass roots of our party, want us to be some smudged photocopy of a know-nothing party. We know we must win elections, but the one thing we must not lose is a Liberal Party that is a driving force for opportunity and social justice. It is because that passion for opportunity and social justice has been at the heart of our party that we have won election after election. . . . "

It was, one had to admit, a cry from the heart, a statement of genuine principle, made by a man with little to lose. Roberts ends with a quotation from Browning, and warns the delegates that "there will be several ballots tomorrow."

Disco Don Johnston comes on to loud synthesizer music playing Van Halen's "Jump" as if the candidate was descending from a space capsule. Does this mean he stands for high tech? Johnston subtly tries to link Turner with Mulroney. The leadership, he says, "is not something to be given away on the basis of charm or friendliness. It's not a vote for the best-looking candidate either." He points out that the Tories are down from 62 percent to 40 percent in the polls. "[They] are now finding out that beauty is only chin deep. . . . The Tories went for a quick fix; face and tonsils and smoke and mirrors. That will not get them elected. Image is not enough for the Canadian people."

It is the perennial bitterness of the homely towards the beautiful. But, in truth, the point does little for Johnston's prospects because it sounds like another plaintive cry from the Vancouver weeper. Worse, it shows a fundamental misreading of "image" politics. The television electorate of the 1980s do not scan their Japanese TV sets looking for great beauty, although it doesn't hurt to be easy on the eyes. What they are looking for is the projection of confidence and competence; not so much the face, as what a politician's expression reflects of his inner disposition. The television electorate has little memory for issues, or past records, but they are hypersensitive to the emotion that leaps from their screens. A trained actor like Ronald Reagan could manufacture a feeling of confidence as easily as any other emotion; it was just part of the thespian's job. A politician could have the looks of Quasimodo and still throw out an air of fatherly, calm confidence.

Turner arrives to drums and electronic music, flying medieval pennants representing the ten provinces. He receives a deafening applause. The favourite runs in a jock's charge to the stage and starts licking his lips like crazy, his tongue darting around like a lizard's. The first thing Turner says is how much he likes Trudeau: "Last night the party paid tribute to the PM and tonight I want to pay tribute to him personally." The task before Turner tonight is to affirm Trudeau as "the most remarkable Canadian of our generation," but then subtly to move away from his policies. He calls for new prosperity, new confidence. "Whatever we do," he assures the delegates, "however we do it, it will never be at the expense of the unemployed, sick, old aged or disabled." Turner goes on to make the usual nods at youth, women and peace, and pledges to "go out and sell for Canada, sell our products." He makes more nods in the direction of the West and party unity, but — in a direct slight of "the most remarkable Canadian of our generation" — promises to make the Liberals "a national party once more." Then, never once naming Mulroney, he makes a rare attempt at partisan rhetoric: "I don't think Canadians will buy a let's-pretend Liberal. I think Canadians will choose a real Liberal every time. I want to assure you that we won't let the Conservatives sweet talk Canadians by painting over the old-style Tory principles of privilege and progress for a few. They don't fool me, they don't fool you, and they won't fool the Canadian people. Mr Chairman, there is a sense of urgency in the land. This is not a time for business as usual; it is a time for action and initiative. My friends, to implement my agenda I need your support tomorrow and I ask you to give me your vote. With your help, we will build a truly national party, we will mobilize a new coalition of Liberals, we will mobilize a new confederation. Together, *ensemble*, we will win the next general election. . . ."

It is a solid speech, the tone confident, but it does not smack of new beginnings; the note of urgency is anything but convincing. One does have a sense, after all, of business as usual.

Next is Jean Chrétien. The order of the speakers is so fortuitous for the needs of prime television time that some of the press are suggesting that it has been fixed. The two major candidates one after another in the heart of prime time. Chrétien comes out to the theme from "Chariots of Fire," this year's upbeat anthem, replacing the fanfare from "2001" for pols and prizefighters alike. Chrétien's signs — a plain red maple leaf on a white background — are not art-designed like Turner's, and there is no elaborate exhibition of pennants or other paraphernalia as he is announced. The no-frills candidate, the plain man, Chrétien just bustles, all business, up to the microphone. Naturally, he strikes a combative note from the start. "Millions of Canadians are watching tonight. One Canadian who is watching us is Brian Mulroney." Then to huge partisan cheers, Chrétien rhymes, "Brian, Brian, do not adjust your set. What you see is what you're going to get."

Chrétien's speech itself had become an issue with his campaign staff, after a first draft had been shown to his advisors. Those who dissented from its contents were cut off from seeing further drafts. "It shall forever be the pride of my life," he says now, "that I was able to serve beside Pierre Trudeau." Chrétien persists in presenting himself as the candidate of the *status quo ante*. It was a move of touching loyalty to what had been some of the country's best years: it was a romantic act, but it was in support of a lost cause. "I will not move," he says, "I will not move this party to the right. . . . I know that some of you are struggling about whether you should vote with your heart. Of course you should vote with your heart. If your mothers and fathers did not vote with their hearts, this country would not exist today." All the candidates had made strong pitches to the delegates' sense of compassion. Increasingly, for the Liberals, compassion seemed a mere cloak for their will to power.

The reaction, after the speeches are over, seems to prove the adage that oration does not really move anybody from their set positions. A Liberal member of the Ontario legislature, Vince Kerrio, says it's clear that Turner now has the best chance to defeat the Tories: "I think Mr Turner is telling us that there's a way to be financially responsible. Chrétien and those boys are talking about not moving to the right. There can't be much room for them to move left."

I bump into Jim Coutts, the man who has been running in Spadina riding in Toronto for the last four years. For many years Coutts had done many of Pierre Trudeau's more unpleasant chores and had never been able to shake the reputation that had come along with that job in the Prime Minister's Office. Asked for his impressions of the speeches of the two major candidates, he demonstrates the lack of plainspokenness, the compulsion to equivocate, that had so contributed to his failure to endear himself to the voters during the by-election in Spadina in 1981.

"I think both of the leading candidates did very well," Coutts says fearlessly. "One was saying I know how to manage the country. One was saying I know how to lead the country and I care about the country."

"Any clear winner?"

"No, I think both of them did very well."

Outside one of the exits I encounter Peter Stollery, dressed in a blue Chinese quilt jacket. He is perhaps the first member of the Senate of Canada to attend a Liberal convention in a motorcycle helmet. If Coutts is depressingly pragmatic and non-committal, Stollery is endearingly outspoken in his support of Chrétien.

"People generally hear what they want to hear in a speech," he says, "but I know that what I just heard was one of the greatest goddamn speeches ever."

"Turner didn't say anything," a bystander interjects. "All he did was yawn."

"He didn't say anything," Stollery agrees. "All he did was cover bases and say how much he liked Trudeau, and everybody knows he's lying. I mean, I've always voted with my heart. What's this about anyway? I mean, if people don't vote their hearts tomorrow, they can stick it up their ass."

On Saturday, there is a demonstration on behalf of the unemployed outside the gates of the Civic Centre. There are many beards, T-shirts and guitars, signs proclaiming "People, not profits," placards excoriating the American interference in Nicaragua.

"We're the union of unemployed," they sing. "All of us are really annoyed."

Annoyed? Not fighting mad, blind with rage, or ready to kill, but "annoyed." Nonetheless, it's hard to find a member of the great unemployed among the protesters. They're all poverty bureaucrats.

"Are you unemployed?" I ask one of the protesters.

"Me personally? No, I'm not."

"Where do you work?"

"The post office."

Out on the floor, both passes dangling in my shirt, I run into Patrick Lavelle. Although the talk around the convention is that MacEachen

111

has definitely gone to Turner, Lavelle still sounds brave; nonetheless, he has spotted the writing on the wall.

"We're still in there kicking and kicking hard. Turner's going to have between 1,500 and 1,600 on the first ballot, and we're going to be between 1,300 and 1,400. But my prognostications with the leaders of the other camps is that we're going to have problems there. They're not good."

"There's hostility?"

"Yeah, there's hostility."

"With Whelan there's no problem; he's coming. But he brings nothing. But if I look at Munro, Roberts. . . ."

Just then Lavelle spots a film crew picking up our conversation a few yards away, a mike pointing in his direction.

"How are *you* today?" he says to them. "Nice to see you." But Lavelle moves out of microphone range. "It's going to be tough," he confides. "Extremely rugged."

A Johnston man is saying to a Roberts girl, "I'm going to Turner." "I want to know the reasons," she replies.

A Turner supporter is going around telling other delegates that they "still have time to join the winning team." Richard Gwyn's column in *The Toronto Star* quotes a cabinet minister as saying "This is no time to be romantic." And sure enough, there is the complaisant Allan J. MacEachen sitting with Turner in his box. The Liberals were being realists, not a particularly attractive sight; especially considering that it was their supposed idealism that had appealed to Canadians over the years. The high-mindedness of the Trudeau years was sadly over, but his cohorts were failing to find anything with which to replace it. Nor did the convention give the impression of a party in genuine renewal. All the candidates were retreads. Iona Campagnolo had declined various entreaties to stand. Lloyd Axworthy, against his own best judgment, had not run but was backing Turner. There was not a fresh face in sight. The Liberals were a party in need of severe reform, but there was no will to accomplish it.

As the delegates vote, the band plays the mindlessly upbeat theme from *Flashdance* and The Beach Boys' "Help Me, Rhonda." Three girls supporting Chrétien are having their picture snapped by a photographer. Seated on the convention floor, they have assumed the classic poses of bathing beauties. They are long-legged, sexy, but still small-town wholesome, lacking the professional model's sheen of some of the women supporting John Turner.

Waiting for the first vote to be counted, Johnston and his supporters heave soft Nerf balls onto the floor. Iona Campagnolo, her mothering instincts combining with her public relations skills, has a bushel of BC apples distributed.

Chrétien is cheerleading his delegates with both arms aloft when the results of the first ballot are brought to him. By the gravity of the expressions around him you can see it is bad. His wife grabs hold of his arm and forces a smile. When the vote is announced publicly, Chrétien has received only 1,067, much lower than expected. Turner's at 1,596, Johnston third with a paltry 278.

Whelan right away comes over to Chrétien. He attempts to place his emerald cowboy hat on the energy minister's head. Chrétien waves the stetson aloft, but he's damned if he's going to put the thing on. Some Munro supporters also trickle over to Chrétien and their candidate then comes too. With five minutes to go before the next vote, it looks as if John Roberts is moving over to Chrétien. Making theatrical gestures, Chrétien beckons Roberts and soon he is on his way. It is a gallant walk.

Down on the floor, in front of Chrétien's section, there is a frightening mob scene. One gets a disturbing hint of how a crowd in a moment can turn into a beast. Between the pushing cameras and the shoving delegates, there is an incredible crush, with the cameras colliding, onlookers being knocked off the chairs on which they have perched to improve their view, everybody pressed solidly together on the edge of panic.

"I've had about enough of you, boy," one young delegate says to another who is jammed right up against his body. "I can't fucking move," the other complains, through clenched teeth.

"The message to Chrétien's supporters," a Turner organizer is pronouncing blandly, "is that for the good of the party we have to pull together." If patriotism is the last refuge of a scoundrel, then party unity is the last refuge of a Liberal politician.

Then MacGuigan, earning himself little respect from the Chrétien camp, slides over to Turner. "Maybe he thinks Turner will help him with his campaign debts," quips a cynic.

While the second ballot is underway, I talk with a western delegate who feels that Turner will bring more members into the House of Commons from the West, and that will bring more pressure on him to make rulings in favour of the West when a conflict arises between Quebec and western Canada. As a minister, he says, Chrétien was at the mercy of the bureaucracy. "He's really just a simple guy . . . ."

The fact that the result is still in doubt means that Chrétien won't have been humiliated. Still, his supporters are refusing to give up in the face of all odds. One of Chrétien's workers from Ontario is claiming that it's still up for grabs, that Turner only got half of MacGuigan's 135 votes. Out on the floor, TV is doing an interview with Léonce Mercier, Chrétien's Quebec organizer. Mercier, in his windbreaker and pinky ring, looks like the essence of backwoods Quebec, the richest man in a very small town. Around Mercier and the interviewer, the beefy technicians have linked arms, shutting everybody else out. This was physical proof of television's pre-eminence. The TV crews believed they had first call on any turf and were generally willing to back it up with brawn. "Fucking electronic idiots," says one newspaper correspondent held at bay by the television musclemen.

It's all over on the second ballot. Chrétien, with the support of Whelan, Munro and Roberts, only improves his vote to 1,365. Johnston stays in but falls back to 192 votes. Turner gets 1,866 and wins handily. Lots of folks, apparently, were eager to be on the winning team. Up on stage for the acceptance speeches, Chrétien talks about "John Turner, my friend since 1963" and acknowledges "there is only one winner and I am not the one."

Turner makes the nod to Trudeau, to Iona, to the people who helped organize the convention, and generally expresses his leaden sense of duty. "In every generation," he says, "Canadians have had to rework the miracle of their political existence. . . . Canada is a supreme act of faith. . . . I come to this task with conviction, passion for progress, dedication to human dignity, and a belief in the underlying goodwill of Canadians. These are the qualities of the Liberal faith — your faith and my faith. You have given me the task of translating the values of that faith into action during the years ahead, and it is a stewardship that I accept. It has been a remarkable, eventful day. The drama of democracy never fails to excite us. Thank you from the bottom of my heart for that confidence that you have given me."

The Liberal Party had done its duty and now John Turner was going to do his. As a personality, Turner was the essence of the quotidian, and his candidacy carried a heavy sense of obligation. He was the boring job that you couldn't leave when no others were in sight; he was the bad marriage that keeps going out of fear of what family and friends might say if it fails. The Liberals had chosen him not out of any sense of excitement, but from dull duty. They left the Civic Centre, however, with the sure sense that their dynasty was in good hands. Pierre Trudeau had stepped down and had, it seemed, taken most of the party's intellect and strength of character with him.

Leaving the convention, I come across that Canadian institution, Pierre Berton, who has just been interviewed on television. Off camera, Berton has a more rugged, formidable presence than his avuncular TV image. I ask him whether he thinks the sense of romance has vanished from the Liberal Party now that Trudeau has gone. "Well," Berton says, "you didn't see much of it in that last speech. If there's any romance around now, it's with Brian Mulroney."

During the weeks that followed, the pragmatic wisdom of that Liberal establishment that had swung the convention to John Turner seemed well rewarded. Allan MacEachen was named government leader in the Senate. Of Turner's opponents, Don Johnston was awarded the justice ministry, while John Roberts held onto his old employment portfolio. But Munro, Whelan, and MacGuigan (despite his attempt at ingratiation at the convention) were promptly dropped. There were reports that Jean Chrétien, mentally and physically exhausted, like John Crosbie the year before, had taken his defeat extremely hard. It was understandable. The investment of such vast amounts of ego, energy and emotion in a losing cause had to play havoc with even the most well-knit personality. Chrétien was said to have pushed Turner to the wall in their post-convention meetings for what he considered adequate consolation. Not satisfied with his appointment as minister of external affairs and deputy prime minister, he demanded to control the patronage for the province of Quebec. The cruel dangling of government appointments, it seemed, was not as distasteful to Chrétien as he had previously claimed.

Still, as far as anyone could see, the orderly Liberal transfer of power had been a success. Although there was little fresh blood in Turner's cabinet, and none of the new faces he had promised during the leadership campaign, polls commissioned by the Liberals in the weeks after the convention showed him to be leading Mulroney by between 6 and 10 points nationally and by much more in Quebec. It seemed natural for Turner's advisors to argue for an early election. The campaign and the convention showed the party in its most open and appealing guise. To attempt to govern without a mandate, the argument ran, would emphasize the worst non-democratic aspects of John Turner's Liberals. It was best to take advantage of their current popularity. There was, of course, another, less flattering, explanation for the Liberals' high standing. The leadership battle had claimed all the country's attention for months. In the media age, the voters were most in favour of what most occupied their consciousness. Because Jean Chrétien had succeeded in making the campaign a contest, the convention had contained sufficient drama to hold the public's generally wayward attention. He who had the country's attention had its vote. It had little to do with issues, it had little to do with intellectual nuance; it was a brute mechanical yes or no, and that was all.

Pierre Trudeau, to the end, followed a private agenda. Leaving office with scarcely concealed reluctance, he apparently had decided that if he was less able to savage his enemies, he could yet reward his friends. Bryce Mackasey was appointed ambassador to Portugal at upwards of $75,000 a year; Eugene Whelan was made ambassador and permanent representative to the United Nations Food and Agriculture Organization in Rome at a similar salary. Mark MacGuigan was given a judgeship of the Federal Court of Canada at $89,100 a year (plus an allowance for robes and wigs) until age seventy. Munro was appointed to the Canadian Transport Commission at an annual salary of more than $63,000 for a ten-year term, and on and on and on.

Patronage had been the fuel that had run the Liberal system for close to a century. It was the reward for loyalty, the real motivation for all that unity; no political party could hope to function unless its troops had hopes of tangible recompense and security at the end of the day. In making allowance for the future of his loyal warriors, Trudeau was merely holding up his end of the perennial bargain. This at long last was the reward for never once speaking one's true mind, never doubting or challenging the leader, always toeing the party line. The press and the public, though, saw it differently. They watched a bunch of played-out pols assuring themselves of a soft berth for life, while plain folks struggled. Turner could not have liked the appointments, but there were reports that Trudeau himself, in a private meeting, had convinced Turner, on doubtful constitutional grounds, that a parliamentary crisis would result if he refused to make them. Never a match for Trudeau one-on-one, Turner chose not to make a fuss. The new prime minister flew to London and asked the queen to postpone her scheduled visit to Canada in the fall. Back in Ottawa on 9 July, the new prime minister called a summer election. Canadians would go to the polls on 4 September.

CHAPTER 6

THE LIFE OF BRIAN

Gate C, at the Ottawa International Airport, serves as the point of departure for the election campaigns of all three leaders. Set away from the main passenger traffic of an airport that seems permanently under construction, Gate C is a dingy, anonymous waiting room, built around two dull brown columns, a baggage carousel, and a few scattered seats. Here, one afternoon in the first week of August 1984, the American Dream, in the person of Brian Mulroney, is making ready to descend on eastern Canada, a tour that will take him at breathtaking pace through Moncton, Bathurst, Newcastle and Saint John in New Brunswick; Halifax and Sydney in Nova Scotia; Chicoutimi, Jonquière, Roberval, Quebec City, Baie Comeau and Sept-Isles in Quebec.

Out on the tarmac stands an Air Canada 727, wearing its familiar red-and-white trim. In the late, or corporate phase of the Dream, nothing is left to chance; the Mulroney campaign is organized right down to its toenails. On the nose of the 727, in the stylized script that adorns most of the posters and other print effusions of Mulroney's campaign, is inscribed "Brian Mulroney" and "Manicouagan One," the latter referring to the hometown riding on the north shore of the St Lawrence where Mulroney has chosen to run. Inside the gate, handing out plastic ID. tags for the media's luggage, assisted by a couple of elaborately groomed woman press aides, is Ross Reid. Last seen toiling on behalf of John Crosbie, Reid is now in charge of the practical arrangements for the press travelling with the Mulroney campaign. He has been roaming around Africa in the interval between campaigns and is now decked out in a deep tan and a blonde beard. Riding herd on the swarming droves attracted to Mulroney, Reid has developed a manner that varies between that of the most popular young housemaster in prep school and some latterday reprise of P.G. Wodehouse's Jeeves, sparing no effort to keep the pampered little Bertie Woosters of the press fat and happy.

Before boarding, the correspondents are either immersed in *New Yorker*s and King Penguins or are recounting the details of last night's fun. "A heavy day of sex," says the Ottawa *Citizen*, "and I'm ready to go." Disapproving of such coarse male camaraderie, the tiny female press contingent huddles together for protection against a couple of dozen males away from home. When it's time to climb on the 727, Reid, playing the wagonmaster role to the hilt, waves everyone aboard, singing out "Ho!" as if he were Rowdy Yates in person and the journey of Manicouagan One some species of cattle drive.

Mulroney, his wife, and his campaign manager Norman Atkins are out of sight in the first-class compartment. The rest of the plane is taken up by the large Mulroney support staff, including press secretaries Bill Fox and Michel Gratton, senior advisor Charles McMillan, pollster Allan Gregg, Mila Mulroney's personal secretary Bonnie Brownlee, as well as numerous aides. In addition, there is a production staff that sets up Mulroney's public address system and his blue PC portable platform backdrop, so that every time a speech is televised, the figure and background look consistent. Already, one of the production crew, crop-haired in a short-sleeved blue polo shirt, on which "PC Production Team" is inscribed in both official languages, has whipped out a guitar, strapped on a harmonica in a Woody Guthrie-style holder and is churning out an off-key version of "Ghostriders in the Sky."

The media pack lowers in the back of the plane. They have plastered up signs jealously reserving their seats. On the overhead baggage compartments, the photographers have taped an ever-increasing number of comic shots of the Tory leader, his aides, and members of the press, taken along the way. The correspondents are uniformly equipped with Radio Shack TRS 80 lap-size portable word processors that can be plugged into a phone when they touch ground, sending their stories instantly to their newspaper's computers. No sooner have the lads staggered aboard than the stewardesses are serving drinks. As Manicouagan One takes off for Moncton, the theme from *Flashdance* booms out from speakers at the front and rear, counselling all within hearing to "take your passion and make it happen." The song is a celebration of just that American Dream, taken from a film written appropriately enough by a Canadian, Tom Hedley. Even though they had had decades of spoilsport nationalist preaching showered on them, Canadians still had a strong desire to be part of the outrageous bacchanal of American culture. Despite the fact that Irene Cara's song is a simple expression of the let's-make-it ethic of masscult showbiz, it had been all over the Liberal convention and now would become a constant feature of Mulroney's election campaign.

118

No sooner is Manicouagan One in the air than Reid announces in his best housemasterly fashion that the Tories have managed "to pry a few lobsters loose" for the media's eating pleasure that night in Moncton.

With the booze, the eats, and the attractive female press aides, it is immediately apparent that this is the plane for reporters to be on. "Did you see that Broadbent schedule?" one asks as he settles into his drink. "It's just awful. Alberta, Manitoba . . . *by bus!*" As far as the media is concerned, Mulroney's plan seems to be: keep them dozing with plentiful creature comforts and give them such access as is minimally necessary. A couple of weeks before, he had been quoted by a reporter in an off-the-cuff conversation in the back of the plane as remarking vis-à-vis Bryce Mackasey's appointment as ambassador to Portugal that "there's no whore like an old whore." The remark, as I saw it, had been surprisingly down-to-earth.

A prince, in everything, should try to pass as pious, whether he is so or not, wrote Machiavelli four and a half centuries ago. It was a lesson Mulroney, an intuitive student of politics, had well absorbed. The Conservative leader is keenly intent on projecting reverence to a public that has no tolerance for bad language in politicians. (Sometimes it seemed that middle-class America was less shocked at the actual Watergate break-ins than at Richard Nixon's cursing on those tapes.)

The Mackasey quote incident raised the issue of whether remarks made by politicians in casual conversations were on the record. The press corps obeyed an intricate and unwritten code in their relations with politicians, but certain younger and hungrier members of the media, less eager to consider themselves a politician's pal than some of the more established men, considered anything a candidate might utter in any circumstance to be fair game. Politicians liked to court the media by coming back to them on airplanes and buses and making tantalizingly candid comments, which they were then scandalized to see in print. Nonetheless, there were enough reporters eager to delude themselves on the nature of their intimate relationship with the great that they were willing to allow themselves to be manipulated in so transparent a fashion.

The previous day, John Turner, his campaign floundering, had fired Bill Lee, the man who had organized his successful campaign for the leadership. Although Turner had previously promised that his government would be free of "rainmakers and hit men," he had brought back Senator Keith Davey to take charge of his election campaign.

Asked for a comment as he boards Manicouagan One, Mulroney says that Davey's appointment is "an indication that Mr Turner has decided to repudiate the future and stick with the past."

If everything from the art-direction to relations with the press is supremely calculated by Mulroney and his advisors, his discourse above all is designed to ring the changes around the theme of change. It is no accident that both Davey and Norman Atkins come to politics from the world of advertising, an art or sullen craft that has perfected the technique of delivering simple messages to an enormous audience with prodigious force. In an election campaign, a candidate's TV commercials, his appearances on the news, his speeches, his every offhand utterance, are all designed to project one uncomplicated notion to the country. So, as well as being a conflict between contending political messages, it is a contest between the messages of the politicians and those of the media. After more than twenty years of Liberal government, and a decade of economic struggle, "change" was one theme with a lot of potential for effective communication. Brian Mulroney was endeavouring to inhabit that process in the same brute way a character in a medieval morality ploy epitomizes "vice" or "virtue."

The previous week, Mulroney had met Turner in debate. For a few days after, the contest had been judged a draw by the commentators, the paucity of thought on the part of all but Ed Broadbent universally derided. But in fact Mulroney had wiped the floor with Turner so badly that the campaign of the new prime minister was now in full rout. As the election wore on, it would become evident that the debate in English had been as important in this country's history as that between Kennedy and Nixon in 1960 — a watershed in the nation's political life.

Television debates, over the years, had become an unlegislated election institution in Canada and the United States. As an event, they had taken on a sacerdotal and ceremonial character: the candidates, clad in the priestly blue suits of their calling, stood at lecterns in front of their seated inquisitors, spiritually naked before the nation. In Canada the theatrical element was vitiated by the fact that the debate was a three-cornered affair; less like boxing than tag-team wrestling. True to form, the Liberals and John Turner had attempted to finesse the timing of the debate. The Liberals had won the summer elections of 1949 and 1953, and Turner's strategy, characteristically, was based on the party folk-wisdom gleaned in ancient days and passed down through the generations. According to this legend, Canadians were all up at that homely national institution, the family cottage, for the duration of the summer, splashing happily away in the lakes, thinking only of jumping trout and golf scores, politics far removed from their sunstroked minds. In such a mood, not only were they unwilling to tamper with the government, they were reluctant to even entertain the subject.

It was a vision of a happier, more uncomplicated time. The unemployed had no cottages to visit, and those people who did, routinely watched an old TV set there, which, even if it received one local channel, served as diversion for the long country evenings. Given the preliminary of a leadership race, which had dominated the news for months, the election's main event was naturally very much on Canadians' minds. It was Turner's theory that if the debate was held early, when nobody was supposedly paying attention, they would have forgotten all about what had transpired when it came time to vote. The unfavourable reception this ploy had received in the press had prompted Turner to agree to another debate, on women's issues, later in the campaign. (In the event, it transpired that Canadians, in their summer haze, so ignored the debate that more than four million of them watched the encounter in English.)

Turner, however, early on in that portion of the program that pitted him against Ed Broadbent, made the mistake of reminding the television audience of his lame manoeuvrings, saying that he insisted "that Canadians understand as early as possible what this debate is all about." While Mulroney set forth his predesigned campaign themes of change and renewed prosperity, Turner, hunched into his shoulders in the definitive posture of fear, unconvincingly talked of "restoring confidence."

It had long been a platitude of media analysis that television communicated more in the way of the emotion, ambience and general *gestalt* than it did of issues. John Turner, in his roomy suit of unfashionable cut, his hands pleading forward in a gesture intended to be explanatory but which appeared merely defensive — holding off the world at large — communicates little but terror. Hands waving, eyes bulging, he now looks less like Cary Grant than some gothic creature of the nineteenth century in its last moments of defiance.

Ed Broadbent, on the other hand, had made a good impression in the debate in French the previous night because of the greater willingness he had shown to mix it up. But this night, his strong emotional concern for the issues came out with just a hint of a whine. Wide-eyed, Broadbent unfailingly communicated an amazed shock of disbelief at the inhuman monstrosities perpetrated by the leaders of the other two parties. Long years in opposition had made Broadbent a more practiced debater than the others, but at the same time the accustomed familiarity of his presence made him look, in comparison, as Derek de Kerckhove of the University of Toronto's McLuhanite Centre of Technology later propounded on *fifth estate*, like a man "with a great future behind him."

Brian Mulroney, by contrast, better tailored, deeper voiced, projected an unassailable reverent calm. When attacked, he seemed not angry, but just a little sad that a man of his self-evident goodwill could be so unfairly misunderstood. Mulroney comprehended that while Canadians were more intent on respecting their prime minister than the Americans, who had an obsessive compulsion to love their president, it was important that the television audience perceive him as a "nice" man. That is to say, as genteel. A nice guy didn't pick a fight, but only defended himself if he was pushed. A nice guy, no matter what his private contempt for another, always kept a civil tongue. The messianic expectations of purity that the electorate now have of politicians had reached such a fever pitch that it was not only imperative that a candidate not drink, curse, smoke, or womanize, he must not in addition harbour unchristian feelings of malice. But most important of all, Mulroney communicated that unshakeable inner composure.

John Turner was making so many mistakes, he was making Mulroney look awfully good by comparison. When Bruce Phillips of CTV, not troubling much to conceal his Tory bias, queried Turner about "those wretched patronage appointments," the Liberal leader replied that Trudeau had "every right and privilege" to make them, and was prepared to resign if they did not go through, an eventuality that would have resulted in a minority position in the House for Turner and the Governor General refusing him the right to form a government. "So I'm saying to you," Turner insisted, "that I had no option."

It would later transpire that the doubtful constitutional advice tendered to Turner had been made in a private meeting by none other than Pierre Trudeau. Nonetheless, that fatal utterance "I had no option" was quintessentially characteristic of the dilemma Turner found himself in. Unable to either frankly repudiate Trudeau and his policies or to commit himself to their defence, he was drowning in some no-man's-land between. The novelist Stephen Vizinczey has said that in any contest between a politician who is the dutiful servant of interest and a man frankly out for himself, the latter will win since he appears the stronger. In this particular case, John Turner's loyalty to the Liberal imperative of unity had weakened him beyond repair.

No doubt appalled at such a raw sight of self-immolation, Ed Broadbent attempted to let Turner off the hook by discoursing on patronage in general and floating the possibility of taking the whole mess out of the politicians' hands and relegating government appointments to non-partisan panels. But the prime minister just went from bad to worse, the camera catching him looking over his shoulder, making a lame inside joke in the direction of the moderator, the principal of McGill University, David Johnston, who did not seem to find it funny.

Next, Peter Trueman, of that small Canadian network that refers to itself as "Global," asked Turner about his refusal to apologize for "bottom-patting." Early in July in Edmonton, a CTV television crew captured Turner slapping Iona Campagnolo's bottom, laughing, and saying something about "a perfect ass." Ms Campagnolo had responded by patting Turner in the same place. The exchange revealed an undesirable undercurrent of hostility. Then, on 19 July, Turner had done the same thing, slapping the hind quarters of a campaign organizer in Montreal called Lisa St Martin-Tremblay. The portentous solemnity with which these incidents had become a formal campaign issue was truly hilarious. Grave matters of unemployment, the economy, patronage, were all discussed with the identical air of importance as a pat on the bum. Worse than the indignity to women everywhere that was said to be conveyed by Turner's gesture was the impression that it represented the ultimate insincerity. For most men, a caress of such unmistakeable sexual meaning would convey the strong desire to move on to even greater forms of intimacy. For John Turner, it was probably just another handshake on the road.

To compound the mistake, Turner had refused to apologize, insisting that, all evidence to the contrary, he was a "warm, tactile" human being. Then Peter Trueman asked, "Why don't you just pledge to give up bottom-patting here and now, or is it too deeply ingrained a habit to make wild promises about?"

"The gesture meant no disrespect at all," Turner persisted. "I happen to be a warm, outgoing person. People reach out to me; I reach out to them. The gesture was a mark of friendship." Turner once again tried to change the topic to his record on women's issues in general, and Ed Broadbent helped him along by dismissing bottom-patting as "a generational thing and women find it offensive." Looking decidedly uncomfortable with such an embarrassing issue, Broadbent pressed Turner to make "substantive commitments" on certain women's issues. It seemed odd for a socialist, but Broadbent was giving greater importance to these essentially middle-class women's issues than he was to those affecting working-class unemployment. But up against Brian Mulroney, Broadbent scored a telling point when, on the question of the economy, he compared the Mulroney campaign to the one that had elected Bill Bennett in British Columbia: first, Social Credit had made vague promises to the electorate, but once in office, they had set in motion a Draconian policy of curtailing public services and social programs.

Mulroney had a way of implying that the interests of workers and capital were identical. He insisted that Broadbent "not blame the tragedy of the last twenty years" on the United States; in his view, 100,000 Canadian jobs had been lost because of the Foreign Investment Review Agency and the National Energy Program. In other words, what's good for business is good for Canada. Throughout his debate with Broadbent, Mulroney maintained an air of pained reasonableness. But on the issue of tax reform, he promised to close loopholes for the rich and insist that they pay a "handsome tax." It was perhaps a curious bit of psychology, but politicians often projected their own subjective qualities on issues and voters alike. Jean Chrétien liked to tell Canadians that they "had come a long way," just as he had. Mulroney made indiscriminate, self-reflexive use of the adjective "handsome." Nonetheless, Broadbent congratulated the leader of the opposition on his "last-minute conversion to progressivism." After all, Mulroney had been at great pains to state that he didn't support CIA intervention in Nicaragua and that he favoured a clean environment as well, even at a considerable cost to business.

The main event of the evening, Mulroney vs. Turner, got under way. The candidates were asked what it was that in fact distinguished them, since they were agreed on so many of the issues. As far back as the general meeting in Winnipeg that had unhorsed Joe Clark, it had been said that should John Turner ever face Brian Mulroney in a general election, they would be so clone-like as to be identical. Now that they were on view together on split-screen television, large differences became apparent.

It was soon evident that while Turner was thrashing about in a chaos of his own making, Mulroney communicated a perfectly packaged personality. Television, after all, was a medium where political information was masticated and processed for a viewer in a masterpiece of orchestration. News programs were introduced with elaborate animation and portentous electronic fanfares. The formulas of sting, teaser, and kicker were psychologically paralleled by the coherent organization of personality, demonstrated by everybody from Barbara Frum to Ted Koppel. Ronald Reagan had contrived to avoid all responsibility for his acts by assuming the stance of a television commentator analysing events for which he himself was responsible. Any politician would be successful to the extent that his personality was as well-structured as a news program. Mulroney, with his grave announcer's voice, his strong features, his ability to stick to the script, far surpassed Turner in that beautiful unbroken series of gestures that was said to make up the professional personality. Ed Broadbent had been referring to the leaders of the two major parties as "The Bobbsey twins," but Mulroney now concluded that it was the two other guys who were identical in their old-fashioned ways and that *he* was the brand new product.

Turner then tried to skewer Mulroney with John Crosbie's assertion that his leader's election promises would cost somewhere in the neighbourhood of 20 billion dollars. (Crosbie, in typical blundering fashion, had landed his foot in it again, size twelve. It wasn't clear either whether the lapse had been intentional or not. Who knew what bitterness still remained from the Tory leadership race?) Mulroney blinked rapidly when he was struggling to control his feelings. He now assumed the pose of a man unjustly accused. "Why would you say that when you know it to be inaccurate? We're both honourable men. You're the father of public debt in this country and I say this with no malice." There was nothing that Mulroney was more sensitive about than the decency of his character and the uprightness of his intentions. To question his decency was to question his entire rise from the working class of Baie Comeau. The Tory leader still had the working poor's insistence on their own respectability, engendered by honest toil. Often, it was all they had to distinguish them from the hopelessly impoverished and down-and-out.

Then, Turner once again perversely brought up the patronage issue, resurrecting the remark that Mulroney had made during the 1983 leadership race, promising patronage jobs for every living Tory. Mulroney, all starchy indignation, did not now defend his own statement, but went right on the attack. Just as Mulroney almost leaned backwards in his effort to stand erect, he now became overweeningly polite as he launched his assault: "I beg your pardon, sir," he said. "You have done something that's never been done before . . . . I made those statements in the full light of day in a political campaign . . . . I made those statements as someone who has never made a political appointment in my life . . . . I apologized for it."

Peter Trueman then quite rightly pointed out that if neither Turner nor Mulroney had been born with a silver spoon in their mouths, they had since acquired them. He then asked them whether or not they represented "the wealth and privilege of the corporate class." Mulroney trotted out his electrician father with his two jobs, Turner his widowed mother.

Then, Turner allowed as how he had been "recycled a number of times in and out of government." The phrase made him sound as if he was a used car. Worse still, when Bruce Phillips, who had been trying all evening to put a question about the possible eventuality of a minority government, asked Turner what he would do in such a case, the Liberal leader replied smugly that his "blend of freshness and experience will give us a majority."

With his nicest smile, Mulroney returned to the attack. He maintained that Turner represented "the same old bunch: the old boy network is back in town and the Liberal Party doesn't want change." Turner essayed a savage reply, but merely succeeded in looking nasty when he told Mulroney that "the style you've been preaching to your own party reminds me of the Union Nationale and patronage at its best . . . Frankly, I don't see freshness coming out of your choice."

Mulroney had an Irish Catholic's instinct for the value of apology and confession, an especially valuable quality in a country where for twenty years being a Liberal meant never having to say you're sorry. "May I say that if I owed the Canadian people an apology for kidding about it, you should apologize for making those horrible appointments." He then went on to propose unashamedly that with the millions spent on patronage appointments, the Liberals could have given all the country's pensioners a $70 year-end bonus. Mulroney had a patronizing fondness for the idea of year-end, trickle-down gifts. But it played well to the humble mill-town constituency where cash bestowments were well appreciated.

Unwilling to apologize about bum-patting, Turner showed no remorse about patronage either. The strategic retreat, apparently, was not in his repertoire. "I've told you and the Canadian people that I had no option," Turner reiterated. The moderator was already going on to the next question when Mulroney, cutting in, went for the kill: "Well, you had an option, sir. You could have said 'I'm not going to do it. I'm not going to ask Canadians to pay the price.' You had an option to say no and you chose to say yes to the old activities and the old stories of the Liberal Party. That, if I may say so respectfully, is not good enough for Canadians." You had better watch out when Mulroney started calling you "sir". It was an executioner's formality.

All decorum, all *politesse*, Brian Mulroney had just slit John Turner's throat. The Liberal leader was still walking around, but he was as good as dead and didn't know it. It wasn't that Mulroney had been so supremely good. His final sally about Turner's patronage options would hardly go down in the annals of eloquence and wit. One wondered how Mulroney would have fared in debate against Pierre Trudeau's buzzsaw style. In effect, John Turner was like a showboat of a fighter, who had lowered his guard Ali-style, daring his opponent to unload his best shot, and was still dazed with surprise when he woke up a half-hour later in the locker room. He had practically invited Mulroney to decapitate him and the leader of the opposition had, ever so politely, obliged.

So, close to a week later in Moncton, Mulroney's tour has been transformed into a kind of travelling victory celebration. Moncton is a ramshackle town of some 80,000 people. A blood-red sunset is settling over its mudflats when Mulroney comes to address a crowd of supporters at the Beaver Curling Club. With its five lanes, its white concrete walls and its Union Jack, the curling rink is a throwback to a Canada of fifty years ago. It's a steamy August evening and the doors have been left open to let in the cool night air. Mulroney's audience is a touch on the elderly side. A heavy-set guy in late middle age, with white sideburns and foghorn lungs, insists on yelling at every opportunity "I agree with that, I agree with that!!" There is a group of stout, plain young women with heavy freckled arms, and large bosoms encased in blouses done tightly up to the neck, who park themselves in the press section and refuse to budge, despite the efforts of the local organizers. It seems as if they would literally rather die than sacrifice their dignity in front of the whole town.

Up on the platform, before Mulroney arrives, the local candidates are speaking. One of them, Bob Corbett (who distinguished himself the previous year by having his picture taken with Yasser Arafat), in his blue blazer, regimental tie and military moustache looks like a member of the authoritarian British right, circa 1933. Savaging the Grits, Corbett calls Francis Fox "a briberer of judges" and André

127

Ouellet a "substantiator of justice," a pair of slanderous remarks to say the least. If Mulroney wins, there are going to be a lot of strange creatures from the hinterlands surfacing with him in Ottawa. He was a pretty face on an ugly party.

The Scottish sensibility has so penetrated this neck of the woods that it seems that every politician, no matter what his origins, can't make a move without some guy in a highland costume and bagpipes dogging his footsteps. So, Brian Mulroney, having changed from the green suit in which he left Ottawa into a blue one, enters the hall to the swirl of the pipes. Pretty soon, the press is counting who can change their clothes most in a day, Brian or Mila. Most days, Mulroney wins going away.

As the premier of New Brunswick, Richard Hatfield, rises on heavy hams to introduce the Tory leader, the crowd, which had leapt to its feet on Mulroney's arrival, sits back down with a scraping of chairs and enormous relish. Hatfield, one of the most singular personages in Canadian politics, in a severe black suit reminds one of a languorously menacing Sidney Greenstreet. (At the lobster party held afterwards for the press, he cruises through the crowd in a loosely flowing electric blue shirt. Shortly after the election, and in the wake of a Royal Tour, Hatfield is tried on a charge of possession of marijuana and nobody much is surprised.)

Mulroney now gives The Speech. Although most politicians on the stump deliver the same address, with small variations, everyday Mulroney has a knack of making his tired jokes, his long-practiced quips sound newly coined for each new audience. The Tory leader clearly had made a study of platform manners and political personalities in the same way a young writer tries on various literary styles. Far more subtly than Rich Little, Mulroney could put on the manner of everybody from John Kennedy to Jean Chrétien. So, for the small-town crowd in the Maritimes, he is folksy, homespun, his voice taking on the reassuring sound of the television evangelist, as soothing as aural valium, while he lays down a line of pure corn that must date back to the first primeval travelling salesman. It's a shameless return to a style of politics one thought had disappeared with Tammany Hall.

First, Mulroney lets the folks know that he's one of them by telling them how he came to Chatham, New Brunswick, at the age of four-teen to get an education. Next, he lightens them up with a joke straight out of the cracker barrel. ("I was back in Chatham for a medical examination. I got a little worried — the doctor said I was as sound as a dollar.") Then Mulroney informs the crowd what an industrious, thrifty son he is and how he's going to work "sixteen or seventeen hours a day," and "go out and do a tremendous job for Canada."

After that, it's straight into Grit-bashing. However, unlike Joe Clark, Mulroney displays none of that prematurely aged, impotent anger. He is making it stick. Once again Mulroney ridicules the old Liberal troupers like André Ouellet and Herb Gray. Next, in a particularly deft combination of contempt for the government and pious flattery of his audience, Mulroney asks, "Was the first act of the new government to look after fishermen or the elderly — the elderly to whom we owe so much? Did they do something for the youth? The first act of public expenditure was the appointment of all those Liberals. Have you heard about that? Have you heard about that?" It is as if political intelligence still travels by word of mouth in the Maritimes and he can't trust the folks to read the newspapers or watch television. Then, Mulroney punches home his tag line: "The PM said 'I didn't want to do it. I had no option. *The Devil made me do it.*' " The press would get so accustomed to this phrase of Mulroney's, they would begin to hear it in their sleep. But every single time he delivers the line, Mulroney gets big cheers. Now the whole country firmly believed the first item of faith of the man in the street concerning politicians: the Liberals were in politics not to serve the country, but only for what they could grab for themselves.

After dosing Jean Chrétien with some of his own medicine ("Jean, Jean, do not adjust your set. What you see is what you're gonna get,"), Mulroney vows that he has "no hesitation in inflicting prosperity on Atlantic Canada." Evoking just that sense of hope and opportunity the Liberals had patented for so long, Mulroney speaks of "small towns and big dreams." He likes to use himself as his own best example of a man who had gone from small-town obscurity to big-time success. The explicit promise of his candidacy is that he can do the same for everybody else, as if prosperity was uniquely his own to bestow. "You and I were never promised a trip to Miami when we were young," he says, "but always associated our citizenship with a feeling of opportunity. That's what Canada is all about. You knew if you worked hard and contributed to your community, and if you paid attention to social responsibility, that you had an opportunity and that is now gone." Then, reaching his oratorical climax, Mulroney ascends into the ether of the purely sentimental, the rhetorical equivalent of a stage-Irish tenor crooning "Molly Malone": "When I was young and growing up in Baie Comeau, my father held down two jobs to look after a large family, and the reason he went out at night after working a full day at the paper mill was because the benefits of working at night went to my mother and the kids. If he were alive today, he wouldn't do it because those three hours would go to Lalonde in Ottawa and there'd only be one left over for my mother, and that's what's wrong with Canada!" Well, there is Mom and Dad and Canada; all that's missing is the apple pie!

Afterwards, outside, the crowd is well pleased.

"A real good turnout, eh?"

"Jeez, wasn't it, eh?"

(The Mackenzie brothers were no invention. Just simple reportage.)

"Did you see *her*?"' one girl asks another.

"Wasn't she *sweet*!!" they chorus.

The next morning Mulroney's three silver buses, with red-and-blue stylized PC logo and signature, leave for the airport, from where the tour will fly on to Bathurst and Newcastle. The main street in Bathurst is already lined on both sides when Mulroney arrives.

"I'm going to pinch him," vows one elderly woman.

"No, it's the *other* one that pinches 'em on the bum," she is informed by her companion, an old gentleman in a porkpie hat and Bermuda shorts.

The Mulroneys work their way up Main Street, past Zeller's, Central Trust, Dalton's Department Store, the Kent Supermarket, Le Bijouterie, and the Sportsman's Tavern. Mulroney knocks at the window of the Bank of Nova Scotia and waves at the tellers, one door-to-door salesman confident of his appeal to the ladies. Spotting a sullen knot of men standing over by the Esso Station, Mulroney, supremely wise in the ways of small towns, quips, "There's the boys." Mulroney appeared to have every affection for the folkloric ways of small towns. To a city-bred observer, however, the men lurking by the gas station have a decidedly Snopes-like menace.

"Where's Mila?" one woman asks. "I don't want to miss her."

"Oh," says somebody else, "she has her own crowd."

On the other side of the street from her husband, most of Holt Renfrew on her back, spectacularly groomed, cherry red fingernails fully an inch long, Mila works Main Street. In Bathurst, as elsewhere, the folks love Mila. If Mulroney was the Good Son, she was the Perfect Daughter. She could be relied upon not to insist too stridently on her feminist rights like Maureen McTeer; more importantly, she could be trusted not to misbehave as scandalously as that wicked Maggie Trudeau. Mila was a good girl.

On the way to Newcastle, the Mulroney cavalcade travels over some rough road through country that is reminiscent of the American Deep South. Farmhouses that are little more than tar-paper shacks fly the Acadian tricolour with its single white star perched in the corner; old Hudson Hornets decay in the backyards. The campaign crosses the Miramichi River to a huge concrete shopping plaza that stands opposite a Gulf Refinery. "A dull people," wrote Irving Layton about Canada, "but the rivers are wide and beautiful." The shopping plaza seems to have no name, the enormous sign facing the river enigmatically proclaiming BEST FOR LESS.

As Mulroney, looking almost phosphorescently vivid and alive, plunges his way into the plaza beauty parlour and shakes hands with all the stylists, an organ, played by a guy in dime-store orange shirt and scuffed cowboy boots, pounds out a rinky-dink sound usually heard only in hockey arenas. The women, naturally, want to see Mila. "She's here," Mulroney promises. "She's here."

"Is this on TV?" somebody else wants to know.

Newcastle is a pretty little town with one of those renovated "alternative culture" stores on its grassy central square. The "alts," as they were sometimes called, had foregone the corrupt cities where most of them had been raised and had settled in more picturesque small towns, where they restored quaint old buildings, sold antiques, and maintained uneasy relations with the locals.

Mulroney's production team sets up the public address and the portable backdrop, and the candidate delivers a major speech on defence. After the platitudes and flattery that characterize Mulroney's almost oriental sense of *politesse*, he asserts that the Liberals have been cavalier about national defence. Not only does he intend to upgrade the hardware, restore the traditional uniforms of the three services, and reopen the air base at Chatham, he undertakes to increase the armed forces to 90,000 within three years. Mulroney claims that Canada's defence is based on a fourteen-year-old White Paper. He promises that a fixed number of naval vessels will be built in Atlantic Canada over the next ten years, and that Canada's conventional forces will be increased "to reduce the chance of any possible resort to nuclear weapons."

Mulroney reads his speech in a fashion that suggests that he has only a recent familiarity with its contents. Shortly afterwards, there

131

is an ugly scene in a motel near Newcastle, where the campaign is spending an hour before pushing on. Bill Fox, Mulroney's press secretary, comes into the room that has been reserved for the media and explains that although Mulroney is not available for comment, an aide will come out and give details on defence policy, provided that he be unidentified and that the whole thing be treated as background, off the record.

"Well, how am I going to shoot it if it's off the record?" complains a cameraman.

"I do not appreciate this," says Michael Vaughan of CBC radio.

"I tell you what," the cameraman adds, "I'll black out the picture and just use his voice. How about that?"

Fox is short and ruddy, built like a middle linebacker. A shrewd choice of Mulroney's, he is liked by the working press, treated by them as still one of their own, even though their interests are now divergent.

"Are you telling me," he demands of the cameraman, "that you had Mr Mulroney out there and you didn't get any film today?"

There are further grumbles about the off-the-record conference. Fox cuts matters brutally short: "Listen, we're tryin' to help ya. But if you won't go along, we won't do it."

"Why don't we get the leader out and ask him some questions. This is the fourth day and no news conference."

"We're having a major one tomorrow."

"Can we say who the aide is?"

"No."

Then Fox loses patience. "I've only got seventeen years in the business, but I guess I'm breaking new ground here."

"Okay," says a reporter, "bring him out."

Fox then trots out Charles McMillan, a professor of business at York University, Mulroney's one-man Brains Trust. Wearing severe glasses and hair that jumps off his scalp like a cockatoo, McMillan seems less than perfectly briefed on defence. It seems as if he's prepared to discuss the larger question, but the only thing the press wants to consider are the details of the reopening of Chatham Air Force Base. Already in a bad mood, they proceed to put the boots to McMillan. When a reporter asks him whether he's going to bring the base back to its former strength, the good professor says he's not sure of the actual numbers but the intention is to bring it back as "low level flying facilities."

"You're not bringing it back as a fighter base, you're bringing it back as something some day?" asks Vaughan.

"It's now a civilian airstrip," asks another reporter. "Will you return it to the military?"

"He didn't say that, but that's the intention," says McMillan of Mulroney.

"Its role as a fighter base will continue under a Conservative government?"

"That was the intention," says McMillan, his voice growing more quiet by the second.

"You said 'no' a minute ago," insists Vaughan.

"Can you say how much you're willing to go over inflation?"

"I can't say," McMillan confesses. "I'll check the figures."

"Which areas of the country would get the increased development of the armed services?"

"It would have to be checked."

"How much would the military budget increase?"

"Well, it would be hard to cost it . . . ."

Chief among McMillan's tormentors are a couple of young reporters from local New Brunswick papers. There is as much stasis in the newspaper business as in any other. Just as you have Ivy League PhDs teaching in jerkwater colleges, so there are many highly educated young reporters toiling on local rags, minutely informed on issues precisely like the reopening of Chatham's air base and delighted to jump on a touring bigwig unsure of his facts.

Still, the military represents just one more constituency that the Liberals have ignored, and adds to the PC leader's coalition of the disaffected. Although Pierre Trudeau had struck a posture of strong national independence from the United States, he paradoxically remained almost entirely dependent on Washington in most matters of defence. While the citizens of military dictatorships would contend that it was just another blessing bestowed upon ungrateful Canadians, the armed forces did seem to have the low status of a minority group in Canada. With few traditions of military aristocracy, professional soldiers had little standing in Canada and were wont to complain that they were so ill-paid that they couldn't even qualify for bank loans. Mulroney's intentions towards the armed forces appeared more economic than warlike: open a few more bases, recruit some more troops and so bring down youth unemployment. As for the uniforms, the green elevator-man outfits that the forces now wore were — like the introduction of the metric system — another indication of the less attractive aspects of the Liberal mentality. Designed originally to give Canadian troops a distinctive or at least a non-British identity, the uniform had succeeded in giving them no identity at all, wiping out the traditions of two world wars, for another bureaucratic whim.

On the plane to Saint John, Mulroney comes back to the press section to smooth Michael Vaughan's ruffled feathers. He shows the reporter a cartoon he's been presented with back in the Miramichi that depicts Mulroney discovered by old Father McFadden in some adolescent prank, on top of St Thomas's high school in blue jeans and Levis circa 1955. Mulroney, who has an enormous tenderness for his own past, explains how good old Father McFadden has been a Liberal all his life but was now threatening to excommunicate anyone who didn't vote Tory. The man whom Margaret Atwood was later to christen King Stroke is expert at giving the press small attentions on small matters and hardballing all the way on everything else.

The press, undeterred by the story of Father McFadden, attempt to scrum Mulroney as he comes off the plane in Saint John. With Fox running interference, the Tory leader charges right through the crowd of reporters and photographers, his large hands balled in big fists, his mouth clamped tight.

Just as Mulroney has promised to reopen the fighter base in Chatham, he swears to revive the Atlantic portion of Via Rail in St John. His whole candidacy is based on the premise that he can restore the affluence of the go-go sixties, without the inconvenient social turmoil. The French theologian, Jacques Ellul, speaks of what he calls The Political Illusion. Mulroney, the bearer of hope in the form of the American Dream, combining corporate style organization with Irish-style smiles and moonshine, was weaving a chimera in the face of Canadians desperate for the slightest hint of optimism. That night, in Halifax, a couple of lady barflies at the Press Club assert that they can't abide Mulroney's small-town macho style, but they're going to vote for him anyway, in the interests of "change." In part, this disgust with the Liberals, set off by Trudeau's parting appointments, was the distaste with which all government was beginning to be held. The electorate seemed to oscillate between a naive cynicism and an equally naive optimism. They despised the government in power, but always believed the one to come would be pure in heart. That was another part of the illusion that Mulroney, a master dreamweaver, was being quick to exploit. In his pitch to the electorate, he was silent about the cuts in public spending perpetrated by conservative governments from Washington to Victoria; he did not wish to scare away easily frightened voters. But, before a group of Toronto businessmen at a breakfast in the Westin Hotel, unreported by the press, Michael Wilson, referring to a study done under Joe Clark, confides that, under a PC government, there will indeed be cutbacks.

There's caviar in the press room in the Hilton in Saint John but in Halifax relations with the press continue to deteriorate. A large blue paper crepe decoration now physically separates the media from the Mulroney entourage aboard Manicouagan One. During the course of the day, the Arab ambassadors in Ottawa have issued a statement objecting to a throwaway remark of Mulroney's that they have interpreted as one-sided support for Israel. Standing by the elevators of the Hotel Nova Scotian, Joe O'Donnell of *The Toronto Star*, Jeff Sallot of *The Globe and Mail*, and Alan Bass of UPC demand access. As well as a comment about the ambassadors' press release, they feel that it's not too much to ask for a major policy statement. Fox, burly, moustached, looking more like RCMP security than press liaison, tells them to wait for the press conference tomorrow.

In the morning, the reporters converge on Bass's hotel room to work out a strategy for the conference. Mulroney is meeting the premiers of the Atlantic provinces at breakfast; what these correspondents want to do is to get him off the subject of Atlantic Canada and on to some more pressing questions. Bass and O'Donnell are in their late twenties, Sallot in his late thirties. Bass is bearded and likes to tote Stendhal's *The Red and the Black* around in his briefcase. O'Donnell resembles nothing so much as a debauched cherub. He says: "I've been asked to focus on Broadbent's comment that Mulroney wasn't really serious when he said in the debate that he was going to tax the rich. If we're allowed only one question, I have to go with that."

"Naumetz," replies Bass, referring to Tim Naumetz of Canadian Press, "says he'd like to try it, but I don't know where he is."

"What did you want to ask, Jeff?" enquires O'Donnell.

"Along the same lines as you. Are you going to increase taxes?"

"Why don't you ask that and I could follow up with Broadbent's challenge?"

"Why don't we approach Fox beforehand and tell him our questions are related?"

John Crosbie attends the premiers' conference. He looks as if he's lost weight since the leadership conference. Tieless, he seems a much diminished figure. The ebb and flow of political destinies has a physical effect on the human metabolism. Observed at the Lunches with Leaders event in Toronto, Mulroney appeared much larger and more self-assured than he seemed to be even a few months before. Then, with the Liberal leadership campaign keeping him entirely out of the newspapers, his quiet presence in the House of Commons leading many commentators to conclude that he had little to say, he seemed a man of average size and modest demeanour. Just as John Crosbie seems to have actually physically shrunk since his run at the leadership, Mulroney now appears to be of an enlarged dimension. The limelight, over the years, has been observed to occasion curious transformations; these metabolic metamorphoses were just one of them.

The most impressive speaker at the premiers' breakfast is "the best PM we never had" — Robert Stanfield. In his anonymous brown suit, and with his flat nasal tone, Stanfield is weirdly reminiscent, in a spare dry way, of the American Beat novelist, William Burroughs. After a couple of days of Mulroney's smarm, Stanfield is refreshingly straightforward. Nonetheless, he is admiring of his successor: "He has faced the toughest question a Conservative leader can face," Stanfield says, "the language question in Manitoba. Despite enormous pressures and seductive temptations, Brian Mulroney did not seek some fancy formula, some sophistry, that might have allowed him to fudge the issue. It was John Turner that tried that. He almost made me throw up and I have a very strong stomach. But after that test of character and integrity, there are some that say Brian is too smooth. I'm sure that John Turner thinks Brian is much too smooth and far too quick. Well, some thought I wasn't smooth enough or quick enough. It's hard to please everybody."

It is hard not to feel affection for Bob Stanfield. He has a rueful attitude towards his years as Tory leader, but demonstrates no great bitterness. Afterwards, talking to reporters, he also reveals a thoughtful awareness of the historical dimension of current issues, a rarity in the present political environment (the age of computerized mass politics has a memory of about a week and a half). "I was never able to get an unanimous vote in my own caucus on bilingualism," Stanfield remarks, "but bilingualism in Manitoba is a very old and thorny problem. I think Mulroney's achievement was amazing and his courage extraordinary. If I had a hat, I'd take it off to him."

What Stanfield does not say is that it was far more difficult for himself as an English-speaking leader from Nova Scotia to take an admittedly admirable position on bilingualism than it is for the Quebecker Mulroney. Since the latter's main aim as a Tory is to revive his party in French Canada, he could hardly have played to the redneck western wing of his party on language. On the other hand, Turner's primary aim is to appeal to the West. It must have been tempting for him to try to gain some cheap and easy support by appearing less than enthusiastic about the language rights of the French-speaking minority.

Canadians are still trying to decide whether or not they can trust Brian Mulroney. The electorate, that sweet and giddy girl, is making up her mind whether or not to get into the back seat with the travelling salesman, trying to decide whether the temptation of his powerful charms is worth the prospect of being seduced and abandoned. All of Mulroney's overweening piety, finally, is calculated to demonstrate that he won't leave the country in the lurch, holding the baby.

At the press conference later that morning, Mulroney is sporting a pair of bifocals that seem like a prop to make him appear older, more severe. Asked about French-language rights in Ontario, he avers that William Davis "has made extraordinary progress" and that he will be "pressing him in a friendly manner to progress with it further."

Jeff Sallot asks his question about taxes with a certain amount of asperity. "I've asked you this before," he stresses, "and I still don't know whether under Conservative government there'll be a tax increase."

Under even mildly hostile questioning, Mulroney has to use all his powers of self-control to contain what appears to be a formidable temper. The resulting effort causes him (consciously?) to mispronounce the *Globe* reporter's name as "Shallot," as in onion, by which sobriquet he will be referred to by the press corps for the remainder of the tour. Outbursts of temper with press and public were an indulgence that had cost Pierre Trudeau mightily; such an episode would cost Mulroney even more. To the question itself, Mulroney relies on the time-worn refrain of all opposition politicians, that not until he gets into power and takes a "true portrait of the Canadian economy," will he be able to make a correct assessment of what taxes will be.

Alan Bass asks a question about how 46 percent of the respondents queried in one poll asserted that they could see no difference between Mulroney and Turner. Doesn't Mulroney find this "disturbing"?

"I don't find it disturbing at all," replies the Tory leader. There is an eternal struggle between politicians and the press, whereby the politician, no matter what the question, strives to exude confidence and the press tries to shake it. The first requirement of a politician was to banish all sense of doubt from his psyche; that of a reporter to vanquish any sense of belief. Each position led to a caricature of truth. In response to Bass's question, Mulroney argues that the poll the reporter is referring to was taken some time ago, before the debates, and that Canadians have "a much clearer idea of the difference between John Turner and myself now that they've seen us face to face."

Mulroney is next asked by Tim Naumetz whether he's going to wait to announce the cost of his election promises until after 4 September. Mulroney replies that he is going to do his best "within our modest means" to give the cost of his programs. When Naumetz presses him further, Mulroney snaps, "Mr Naumetz, I gave you an answer."

With all the talk about economics, costs, taxes and poll percentages, politics in the 1980s had become a bookkeeper's affair, a matter of arithmetic. Social issues far in the background, the political debate had less intellectual interest. There were personalities, there were polls, and there were a mass of numbers, but seldom an idea in sight. The issues of the economy were no doubt a matter of life or death but paying them close attention was generally as inspiring as spending the afternoon in close consultation with one's accountant.

With Robert Stanfield, John Buchanan, the premier of Nova Scotia, and other miscellaneous dignitaries in tow, Mulroney goes mainstreeting along Halifax's Spring Garden Road at lunchtime. It is remarkable how few Canadians wish to have anything but the most superficial of encounters with their leaders. A walk down Main Street is the closest most of them will come to meeting a major politician, unmediated by the press. Nonetheless, the panoply of aides, security, photographers, reporters and cameramen usually proves too intimidating to a populace distinguished by passivity and diffidence. Most settle for an embarrassed handshake and a smile, although there are a couple of exceptions. A tiny young woman in a McGill T-shirt asks Mulroney forthrightly what he's going to do about unemployed college graduates. He says he has a four-point program; if she wants to see it, he will send it to her within the hour. An aide scrambles to get her name and address. And there is another question about pensions for widows. After eating a French fry at a curbside stand, and plunging as usual into the local beauty parlour, Mulroney heads back to his campaign bus, strategically positioned at the end of the block.

The Mulroney campaign is now beginning to attract correspondents from the big American publications. *Time* magazine is joining the tour, as are *The New York Times,* and the *Los Angeles Times.* Since the debate, they sense that a dramatic change in Canada's government is in the air. Kenneth Freed is the *Los Angeles Times*'s correspondent. Freed had been a combat correspondent in Vietnam, had covered Kissinger in Washington during the Nixon years, had dodged bullets in the Ayatollah's Teheran. What with previous careers as a lawyer and as a symphony musician, he has a far wider intellectual range than the average correspondent. Freed is agreeably impressed with Brian Mulroney as an effective campaigner, but he wonders at the docility of the Canadian media. There is an unwritten agreement between the press and the politicians in Canada that you don't scrum a fellow while he's mainstreeting. According to Freed, there was no such pact in the United States. If a reporter didn't get a satisfactory answer at a news conference, he would continue to ask the question on the street. If a candidate had been dodging the press, as Mulroney had been doing throughout New Brunswick the previous day, there was no way American journalists would have allowed him to walk around unmolested. Instead, he might have found several intransigent reporters blocking his path along the sidewalk. Of course, security in the United States was many times thicker on the ground than in Canada; the secret service took a more active physical role in keeping reporters away from a presidential candidate than did the RCMP.

Later that afternoon, Mulroney's portable telecopiers, his score of Vuitton luggage, and the rest of his chattels are loaded aboard Manicouagan One and the campaign flies to Sydney in Cape Breton. I get a notion of just how well organized Mulroney's campaign is when I run into a man who is a special projects organizer for Bill Davis and Ontario's Big Blue Machine. He has been in Sydney for three days stage-managing Mulroney's visit. The Ontario Machine, although headed by professional planners like Davis's man, was by and large Junior Chamber of Commerce types, who headed for the boondocks and organized halls and crowds out of amateur enthusiasm. Bland, shirtsleeved, bespectacled, cheerfully efficient, these Ontario front-men were working for Mulroney with a zeal they had never accorded Joe Clark. According to the Blue Machine's Man in Cape Breton, Ontario was willing enough to assist, but Clark, diffident, bristling with Alberta's resentment of the East, had never asked for help.

139

While her husband flies by helicopter to Port Hawkesbury, Mila Mulroney visits a Ukrainian community hall outside Sydney and a senior citizens' centre in New Waterford. Mrs Mulroney sweeps into New Waterford in a convoy of three limos, the first containing herself and her personal secretary, the second holding the wives of local PC luminaries. Bringing up the rear in the third car is a solitary correspondent, myself. "Yes," the young driver tells me in his nearly impenetrable Cape Breton burr, just before he asks how to get a job in the media. "They're havin' it pretty quiet in New Waterford."

Leaning up against the rail, outside the senior citizens' centre, stands some gothic Faulknerian specimen of inbreeding. With jug ears, thick glasses, and a thoroughly dazed look, he has never seen anything like the blazing procession bringing Mila Mulroney into New Waterford in all his life. When Mila herself, with shining hair, gleaming clothes and dazzling smile steps out of the limousine, it is all too much for him. The poor guy falls to the ground in an epileptic fit, his eyes rolling in his head, his tongue lolling, the heels of the inevitable cowboy boots scissoring a grotesque tattoo on the pavement. Mrs Mulroney, to her credit, does not just step over the thrashing form and continue on her way into the senior citizens' centre but looks on with concern as a couple of local cops prevent the man from swallowing his tongue.

Inside, Mila Mulroney works the room almost as well as her husband, chatting with the assembled womenfolk of New Waterford about their families. The usual bunch of flowers is presented to her. When her secretary, Bonnie Brownlee, slight, dark-haired, with small, perfect features, is slow to relieve her of the bouquet, Mila Mulroney hisses with a great deal of girlish impatience, "Bonnie, could you take these! Honest to God!" Although there are those wits on board the tour who claim that Ms Brownlee's only job is to dress "almost as well" as Mila Mulroney, there are other small services she performs. When a local radio reporter does an interview, Bonnie Brownlee whips out a tape recorder and records the whole thing, just in case. Turning to me, Mrs Mulroney pleasantly enquires whether I too am based in New Waterford. I restrain an impulse to comment that there aren't really that many news organizations here in town, but content myself with the remark that I'm just one of the mob in the back of Manicouagan One.

Mila Pivnicki Mulroney is a familiar Canadian type. One knew any number of Latvian, Estonian or Yugoslavian girls who might pass as her sister. Their parents arrived in Canada in the 1950s after living through the post-war sufferings of Eastern Europe; they had infused their children with a single-minded ambition to do well out of the new country. These people had inherited an appreciation of Old World *kultur*, they had an undeniable flair, and were unquenchably upbeat and optimistic. While classmates and friends dropped in and out of mainstream society, changed spouses and careers with all the certainty of those who at bottom are sure of their privileged place in society, these girls were seldom swayed by countercultural doubts and rebellions; they were deferential to authority, retained their faith in hard work, and believed that the best times were to be had among "the best" people.

That night, after his speech in Sydney, Mulroney saunters back to the press section of the jet, obviously feeling tiptop. The rumour is that the campaign now has the results of an up-to-the-minute poll and the figures are astoundingly good. Up front, Mila Mulroney is singing the songs of the Beatles and Neil Young, accompanied by the production team guy with the guitar and harmonica. While Mulroney seems to have an unlimited number of blue blazers for his public appearances, he also has a range of expensive casual combinations that are a match for his wife's glossy outfits. Tonight he's wearing a white cotton jersey, with sewn-on geometrical red-and-blue patches. In this getup he looks like a Hollywood studio executive. Full of good news, Mulroney is in a mood to chat with the press. The blue crepe barrier has vanished as mysteriously as it arrived. Mulroney now confides that he's not really running the campaign, but is naturally keeping a close eye on it. A very close eye, one imagines. He also says that back in the spring when the Liberal leadership race was dominating the evening newscasts, he was out by himself on the hustings, perfecting his campaign style, getting it right. Reporters coming off Turner's bus assert that the Liberal campaign is embarrassingly chaotic, with uncertain schedules and small crowds. In one town, the prime minister apparently showed up in a hall ready to speak, only to find no microphone awaiting him on the platform. This scrambling spontaneity had served well enough to win Turner the leadership. He apparently feels it will win him the election too. Everybody in the press is amazed that the Liberals are being so lackadaisical. Where are the big crowds at Maple Leaf Gardens and the Paul Sauvé Arena? Where are the patented attacks that will take Mulroney off at the knees?

Mulroney himself feels that the fact that the big crowds he was drawing during the Liberal leadership contest didn't get into the

141

papers had lulled Turner into a false sense of security. "It worked out great for me," Mulroney crows. When Manicouagan One lands in Chicoutimi late that night, there is a large, enthusiastic crowd waiting at the airport. Mulroney has several personae, all of which he can use at will. If Ronald Reagan is an actor who made a career as a politician, Mulroney is a politician with a thespian future. At a press conference, for instance, he is the formal controlled company president. On Main Street a transformation begins to take place: the hard gs are dropped off the last syllables of his words, and he makes increasing use of the Canadian "eh." Mulroney has one personality for the big city and another for the small town. (In all the halls there are two photos of Mulroney and his wife. In one he wears his blue blazer; in the other a country plaid shirt.) Here in Chicoutimi, the characteristic chocolate smooth sound leaves Mulroney's voice; it suddenly seems as if he's been gargling with broken glass all his life. The cracked, throaty rasp of rural Quebec politics is instantly present, as it's been practiced all the way from Réal Caouette to Jean Chrétien.

Moreover, Mulroney has succeeded in capturing the glamour factor in Canadian politics, previously a major Liberal strength. Canadians were always secretly rather pleased that Pierre Trudeau hung out not only with statesmen but with movie stars as well. If they had tired of other aspects of Trudeau, Canadians never tired of his allure. In the small towns of Canada, Mulroney and his wife are celebrities of the highest order. More important, they are celebrities who convey the impression that they like small-town people, share their values, and are not too unlike them themselves. This was the antithesis of Pierre Trudeau, who almost always conveyed the notion that he'd rather be in some cosmopolitan centre of the world, and only visited this outback of The Great White North under political duress.

The next morning Mulroney holds a press conference in the Hotel Chicoutimi. A story has broken in Calgary that Mulroney's deputy chief of staff for Alberta, Lee Richardson, had been loaned $400,000 for nine years at almost no interest in order to pay off his stockmarket losses. The beginning of Mulroney's Gilded Age seems to have come to pass sooner than anticipated. Jason Moscowitz of CBC television, looking like nobody so much as a young Groucho Marx, asks the Tory leader whether he thinks it right that "people in politics can negotiate deals unavailable to private citizens?"

Mulroney blinks and, just as he had mispronounced Jeff Sallot's name yesterday, he calls the CBC reporter "Mr Moscowich." If Brian

Mulroney has nothing else, he has plenty of what used to be called "front."

"I will be speaking to Mr Richardson," he says. "I know him to be a man of great talent and unsullied honour, and there is no doubt in my mind that everything he has done — I say this without having had the opportunity to speak to him — I have no doubt that everything in his private affairs is beyond reproach."

Moscowitz adds that the bank in this case, the Bank of Montreal, is the identical institution that proffered a controversial loan to Bryce Mackasey. He asks Mulroney for a comment.

"I am not willing," says the leader of the opposition, "to pass judgment on the lending practices of a Canadian chartered bank."

Chicoutimi is a hilly little town whose streets meander down to the Saguenay River. Bells are ringing as Mulroney's procession of buses head out of town towards Jonquière and Roberval. In the latter town, a large receptive crowd in the Collège de Notre Dame is eating hash pie with plastic forks. Mulroney not only goes after Turner but *"son nouveau conseiller spirituel,* M. Ouellet, a man who has come to personify everything about Liberals to Quebeckers." "On September 5th," he tells the crowd, "imagine André Ouellet humbled!" However, when it comes time for Mulroney's invariable line about patronage and "the Devil made me do it," it is notably absent. But then, a smart politician does not joke about the Devil in ardently Catholic, rural Quebec. So, mindful of the many outsize crucifixes dangling from Roberval necks, Mulroney only reports that Turner had said *"Je n'ai de choix."*

As the campaign buses move down Highway 169 towards Quebec City, they are stopped by a spontaneous demonstration of support, two cars blocking the road at a rail junction, a couple of waving girls perched on the top of them. The candidate gets out of his bus and talks to the crowd, even though there's a big red-and-white trailing truck honking angrily behind his calvalcade. The driver doesn't care at all about this conquering hero; he just wants to get his load through.

The reason for Mulroney's good mood becomes apparent as the results of the poll filter through to the press corps. According to CTV, as of 31 July, Mulroney was leading Turner by nine points, the figures reading 45-36-17. The debate has had the effect of turning a volatile electorate right around. Like television, the institution of polling had transformed modern democracy. Allan Gregg and Martin Goldfarb had become superstitiously revered pundits, and polling in general, as that gloomy American cultural historian Christopher Lasch has pointed out, has had the effect of defining a statistical norm of sentiment, deviation from which becomes automatically suspect. Consequently, it is possible to dismiss all unpopular opinion from public debate, on the basis of its demonstrable lack of appeal. Alexis de Tocqueville had long ago warned of the dangers of the rule of the majority. Now in the age of the all-powerful polls, public opinion had degenerated into iron whim. In the backyards and offices of the nation, political judgment is considered to be just one part of general soundness of character. In an era that is increasingly conformist and intolerant, eccentric political belief is held to be the plain mark of the fool. At the beginning of July there were few who would trust a man who believed in the chances of Brian Mulroney. One month later, there weren't many who would bet against him.

Outside Loews Le Concorde in Quebec City, there is a big crowd waiting for the Mulroney party. Unfortunately, one has less than perfect belief in its spontaneous nature because of the staggering presence of a couple of placard-waving winos of the Old Brewery Mission variety, brought in to swell the numbers. As the buses make their way into what must still count as one of the most graceful cities on the continent, Mulroney's French-language press secretary, Michel Gratton, stares at the Plains of Abraham and allows as how when he thinks about that battle, "I still get mad." There was something about Quebec City, its vista of river and sky, that evoked such historical reflection. Perhaps because it was the Canadian city most reminiscent of old Europe, Quebec City seemed to live in present and past simultaneously. There, the Battle of the Plains of Abraham was not a dead event in history, but fresh and alive.

An hour or so later, the media pack is all jammed into the lobby of the hotel, waiting for Mulroney to come down and comment on the CTV poll. A hotel guest, watching the camera jockeys pushing for position, their heavy equipment sitting bulkily on their shoulders, sighs and remarks, "What a sad way to earn a living!"

Mulroney finally comes out to face the press on a grassy boulevard in front of the hotel. The media, punchdrunk and giddy with travel, have been circulating a puerile joke that would shame most ninth-grade locker rooms. As Mulroney comes across the street, Joe O'Donnell, the corps' ringleader, says, "Okay guys, what's the lead question?" In one voice the august gentlemen of the press shout out the joke's moronic punchline and dissolve into shouts of laughter, mystifying the large crowd assembled nearby. "Come on kids," says Ross Reid, "settle down."

After Mulroney informs the press just how pleased he is about the CTV numbers, he turns the corner around the hotel and plunges down the Grande Allée, shaking hands in all the outdoor restaurants while the traffic honks wildly. "*A bas les Liberaux!*" somebody shouts beside him. "*La fin de patronage!*"

"*Nous de Québec*," he had said a few moments ago, "*nous sommes des hommes et des femmes libres capables de dire 'non' à ces anciennes traditions du Parti liberal et 'oui' à un Parti conservateur rajeuni et dirigé pour la première fois dans son histoire par un vrai Québécois.*"

Well, *Vive le Québec libre* indeed. As John A. Macdonald knew more than a century ago, any successful administration in Ottawa must have a strong Quebec component in order to govern. In the modern era, any Canadian prime minister must himself contain both nations, as Joe Clark and John Crosbie discovered to their cost. Like Pierre Trudeau, Brian Mulroney is perceived by English Canadians as English and by French Canadians as French, and thus in some way is seen to embody the nation's fundamental dichotomy. Unlike John Diefenbaker, who owed his Quebec support entirely to the efforts of Maurice Duplessis, Mulroney has a wide spectrum of approval among Quebec politicians like René Lévesque, who had been fighting the Liberal government in Ottawa for years; and unlike Diefenbaker (and R.B. Bennett too, the only other Tory leader to win a substantial number of votes in Quebec in this century), Mulroney is seen by Quebeckers as one of themselves, in a way that John Turner is not. Pierre Trudeau had won the battle of separatism; John Turner would inherit the losers' resentment. There was a disappointment in Quebec that Jean Chrétien had not been chosen leader. Now that Trudeau had gone, for Quebeckers, the Liberal Party meant patronage and André Ouellet. Mulroney was assembling a Conservative coalition in Quebec unknown since the days of Macdonald's Confederation system, and the emergence of an authentic Quebec voice among the Progressive Conservatives was a phenomenon of historical proportions.

While it was far too early to start comparing the frequently glib and empty boy from Baie Comeau to an historic figure like Macdonald, there are some provoking resemblances to the historic situation in which each politician found himself. The decades of the 1850s, according to the historian Donald Creighton, represented a rapid decline and discredit of the Liberal creed, brought on by the revolution of 1848, the decline of the Second French Republic and the rise of Louis Napoléon, all of which had a strong influence on Quebec. The 1980s have seen a similar decline in the fortunes of liberalism, as exemplified in the fates of the Democratic Party in the United States and the Labour Party in Britain, the consequences of which are felt throughout Canada. Except for the bad judgment of Joe Clark, it seems safe to say that this country would also have had a Conservative government since 1979. Furthermore, as Creighton notes, many of Macdonald's contemporaries felt that he could have as easily been a Liberal as a Conservative; the same thing has been said about Mulroney. If John Turner gives the impression that he still goes around dropping dimes in pay-phones, Brian Mulroney makes one feel that he is at one with the times. Just as Pierre Trudeau represented the onrush of historical forces such as the Quiet Revolution in Quebec, post-war affluence and the development of the welfare state, Mulroney is a perfect example of how history itself brings men to prominence. If Trudeau's glamour recalled that of the Kennedys, Mulroney can easily pass for Ronald Reagan's nephew. There is a similar actorish quality, a lack of depths.

Since Manicouagan One has developed mechanical troubles, Mulroney flies home to Baie Comeau in another plane. When it is announced that there will be no drinks served on the flight, the media pack starts chanting, "Tur-ner, Tur-ner, Tur-ner." Nonetheless, the success of the Mulroney campaign is contagious; only the worst of churls could resist such onrushing good fortune. The "William Tell Overture" comes galloping over the plane's speakers as it takes off. Mulroney, seemingly growing larger by the minute, swaggers by to chat. "I'm going to start changing some of the lines next week," he confides. "I know you guys are tired of them, but Jack Kennedy said never throw away a good line." Any politician who, like Mulroney, has named his daughter Caroline, we can be sure has studied the Kennedy career closely. For any politician of Mulroney's age, despite the current assaults on the reputation, Kennedy still remained the exemplary model. As the plane lands in Baie Comeau, the speakers blast out "Land of Hope and Glory." To the crowd at the airport, Mulroney shouts "Bye-bye *les Rouges!*" His aides are now beginning to refer to him as "The Chief." It's cold in August up here on the North Shore; summer is a brief interlude of two months. When Mulroney visits the Centre Récréatif, they are playing hockey on the artificial surface, a pick-up game nevertheless played in full pads. Hockey! In August!

Saturday morning, there is a better opportunity to investigate Mulroney's home town. Baie Comeau is the quintessential company town, where license plates often display the mill's logo rather than the fleur-de-lys, and Brian Mulroney is its definitive product. It's a small settlement, precariously perched on the edge of a wilderness that stretches uninterrupted all the way to the Arctic. Forty years ago it was just bush. Baie Comeau is not one of George Grant's idyllic nineteenth-century Ontario towns; it is a raw, frontier sort of a place. One which owes its very existence to an American corporation.

On the main drag there is a Bay department store, two taverns, one bookshop, two banks, one pharmacy and a boarded-up movie theatre. Outside of town there is a characteristic highway strip with a number of motels, a McDonalds and a shopping plaza. Most of all there is the huge Quebec North Shore paper mill, an enormous grey building with a dozen smokestacks belching out pollution, an edifice that William Blake might well have had in mind when he wrote of the "dark satanic mills."

In front of the mill is a statue of the man who brought both the QNS and Baie Comeau to life and for whom Brian Mulroney sang "Dearie" at the age of eight, Col. Robert McCormick, of *The Chicago Tribune*. The bronze sculpture portrays McCormick seated in a bronze canoe with bronze rifle, knapsack and map, his noble visage peering up into the future. If that is how Baie Comeau saw the man, it is not how he is remembered in Chicago, where a contemporary observer recalls spotting him pulling up to the *Tribune* building in his bulletproof car, surrounded by pistol-packing bodyguards, the style of the Chicago tycoon interchangeable with that of the Chicago gangster.

If John Diefenbaker had been a proponent of small-town enterprise, growing up in Baie Comeau with his father working at the QNS had no doubt taught Brian Mulroney that the biggest man in town was the loyal servant of the company, the mine manager. In a town like Baie Comeau, the most important social dynamic lies between the management of the mill and the people of the town; and Brian Mulroney's entire career from settling longshoremen's strikes on the docks of Montreal to the Cliche Commission into violence in the construction industry in Quebec to his presidency of the Iron Ore Company of Canada can be understood in terms of his ability to travel back and forth between millworkers and management. It should be kept in mind, though, that while Mulroney was never known as a union-buster, he always worked for the company. As a lawyer Mulroney was far from being a legal scholar. Instead, he was, as one prominent Quebec politician calls him, "God's little fixer."

Mulroney's local campaign headquarters are out on the highway, in the shopping plaza. Mulroney's grade school essays are tacked up on the wall, examples of the best that was thought and written by the Young Pen Wielders of 1948. Joe Lachance was born on the same street as Mulroney; indeed, the leader had been the best man at his wedding. Lachance works for the town of Baie Comeau and, though paunchier and less well-groomed, doesn't appear too different from what Mulroney might have looked like if he had stayed home. Asked whether he considers that Mulroney was an extraordinary sort of fellow when he was growing up in Baie Comeau, he replies that he was "an ordinary man." But then, Lachance asserts that the ordinary inhabitants of Baie Comeau are possessed of unusual qualities of determination. If you're born in a little town in the far north, he claims, you have to be a fighter to stay alive. That sounded like a familiar notion. In the tough times of the 1980s "survival" was a word on everybody's lips. The whole country was beginning to live its life according to the hard-pressed ethic of the wilderness town.

When Mulroney comes to address the hometown folks at his campaign office, he is clearly aware that he has put the place on the map. If image politics lends a touch of magic to people, it has the same effect on places. Baie Comeau, this unexceptional company town on the north shore of the St Lawrence, is in the process of becoming the Plains, Georgia of Canadian politics. Mulroney, holding one of his children in his arms, imagines that it is election night. "I can hear Knowlton Nash saying to Barbara Frum, 'Barbara where are you?' and Barbara saying 'I'm in Baie Comeau with everybody else.' . . . Unlike somebody else I know, I don't have eighteen home towns. I only have one."

Surely there can be fewer greater pleasures in life than returning to the scene of one's origins in such complete triumph. But the next day, Mulroney's caravan of three silver buses, weighted with an ever-growing contingent of press, loads up and is gone.

It was, of course, the result of television's increased focus on the leaders, but it was no secret that Canadian politics were becoming more presidential. As the political scientist Arthur Kroker points out, the House of Commons was a nineteenth-century theatre, designed as a gothic palace; there was something quaint about it in the age of the instant transmission of information. The member of parliament, in effect, was a human medium of communication between the centre and the margins. In a system of government by cabinet, the back-bencher had less and less significance. At election time, the leader became the party.

Suddenly, the Progressive Conservatives were no longer the right-wing Sinclair Stevens and the maladroit Joe Clark. Brian Mulroney was now the sum of the party. If the Tory leader promised change, he was doing his best to assure a congenitally cautious people that it would be not so much of a change after all. Canadians were guaranteed to reject an honestly Conservative approach such as that of Margaret Thatcher or Ronald Reagan. Instead, they had to be convinced that Brian Mulroney represented a soft landing. The country would be delivered from the vanities and transgressions of the Liberals, but there would be no hard Tory discipline to face after election day. Change that was, in effect, no change at all was an attractive notion to a people that treasured the status quo. All that and the illusion of prosperity too was a prospect difficult to resist. And Brian Mulroney looked like being one travelling salesman who would have no trouble closing a deal.

CHAPTER 7

RUNNING ON EMPTY

For Keith Davey, John Turner's summer election campaign had been a mistake from the outset. When he had been asked by the new prime minister to take over from Bill Lee, Davey had little hope that the election could be won, but he felt that he would have been an awful jerk not to help. Even though his enthusiasm for election campaigns had become somewhat dimmed in the course of thirty years, Davey, close to sixty, silver-haired and stooped, was one of the few Canadian senators who managed to carry off the associations of authority usually attributed to those more powerful members of the American Senate. The most respected of Liberal organizers through five general elections, he was attributed almost supernatural and sometimes sinister powers by the party's opponents.

Davey had been very much of the opinion that Pierre Trudeau could have won the election, and had been one of the few dwindling voices in the Liberal establishment urging him to cling to office. Davey believed that Trudeau would retain his overwhelming support in French Canada, that he would safeguard the traditional Liberal coalition; that, most of all, despite his waning popularity, he was still the most formidable campaigner in Canadian history.

In Davey's view, Turner had made a bad mistake in calling an early election. If Trudeau stayed on, the election would not have taken place before 1985, for sure. Davey felt that Turner should have gone on tour with the Queen in July, should have escorted the Pope across the land in September, and then convened parliament in the fall. But, despite Turner's scepticism about Trudeau's record in office, like the rest of the country he was mesmerized by the myth. The former prime minister had called an election in 1968, taking advantage of the heat and momentum of Trudeaumania. There was little you could cite as evidence for an equivalent enthusiasm for John Turner; more a sense of resignation at the drearily inevitable.

Keith Davey believed that Turner's attempt to take the party to the right was a political disaster; what Turner, and his advisors like Lee, John Payne and David Smith, had done was asinine. First of all, there were an awful lot of Liberals in the country who enjoyed and liked the Trudeau era. That, the Constitution, the National Energy Program and other measures were sound pieces of legislation, and there was a long record of achievement that John Turner should have been talking about on the hustings. What's more, for Davey, one of the problems a reformist party like the Liberals had to guard against was its tendency to be tugged further and further to the right, the longer it stayed in office.

To cap it all, Davey felt that the Turner camp had played the patronage issue foolishly, that the campaign organization was too large and chaotic. It hadn't taken him too long to realize that Lee's strategy was backfiring. Davey had gone south for the first couple of weeks of the campaign, but he kept on getting these, well, *distressing* calls. He was troubled by the appointment of the Winnipeg businessman, Izzy Asper, as co-chairman of the Liberal campaign, and felt that Turner's claim that he was taking "the high road" was turning the prime minister into Little Lord Fauntleroy. Returning to the fray, he set out to make John Turner into a politician again.

But Davey made few organizational changes. His one significant move was to replace Dennis Baxter on the campaign plane with Ralph Coleman, a former Trudeau aide and an officer in the armed forces. So Davey flew to Toronto to meet the Ontario campaign committee and the Toronto area candidates; he told them the numbers, showed them what kind of jackpot they were really in, almost twenty points behind Mulroney. Keith Davey found himself striving to reverse the entire thrust of John Turner's return to public life. He had three weeks to help the Liberal leader convince the Canadian public that he was in fact a liberal.

On 9 August, John Turner's campaign finds itself in Sudbury, Ontario, headed west, trailing fresh gaffes from the East. In the Maritimes, the prime minister had conveyed his best wishes to Miss Prince Edward Island by asserting that he certainly hoped she went all the way. In Quebec, when a nervous waiter had spilled coffee on Turner's trousers, he had repaired to a washroom with André Ouellet, while the trousers were passed out to Geills Turner for her to get out the stains. (In the Mulroney campaign, six aides would have dived into ten pieces of Vuitton luggage and come up with ten pairs of trousers. The idea of Mila Mulroney actually condescending to such homely ministrations was unthinkable.) Outside of Sherbrooke, not for the first time, the Turner campaign bus had got lost. Out in the ridings, party workers were discovering that the Liberal vote had vanished. "We're dead in the water," one man says. "It's 1957 all over again."

Nonetheless, this Friday morning, gingered up by his regular morning call from Senator Davey, John Turner comes to address the local believers at Cassio's Motor Hotel, a name, for anyone on the lookout for omens, that communicated unhappy overtones of Shakespearean treachery.

Located on a highway strip on the outskirts of town, the motel, a masterpiece of pseudo-Italianate kitsch, is perched at the very edge of the mining-town landscape. At the end of the parking lot, there's a sheer cliff of black rock, on top of which stands a ten-foot-high Canadian nickel. Close by, an Inco stack belches out an unceasing tail of dirty industrial waste. Across the highway, there is another chimney: this time, iron ore. It's a sunny morning. Men with big bellies, women carrying infants in their arms are waiting for John Turner; they are all dressed in their Sunday best. The Liberal leader, who is often far from sparkling early in the morning, arrives looking as if he needs another hour's sleep, that odd, crumpled smile fixed to his face. Although John Turner is officially prime minister of Canada, it is difficult to fully accept him in the role Pierre Trudeau inhabited for most of one's adult life. There seems something provisional and insubstantial about Turner's grasp on the office.

If Brian Mulroney's campaign is the last word in high-tech, John Turner's can only be characterized as low-rent. The press room is not a suite at the prime minister's hotel, but is hidden away in the seedy basement of Cassio's Motor Hotel. There is no lobster and caviar to keep the pack in mild humour, just coffee and triangle sandwiches. The women press aides do not radiate the groomed-to-the-eyeballs glamour of the women working on Mulroney's campaign, but have a style that is more in the vein of gee-whiz camp counsellors. Ralph Coleman lacks the inclination of Bill Fox and Michel Gratton to pass as one of the boys. Instead, he is left over from the *noli me tangere* days of Trudeau's front-running campaigns. Coleman is indeed marvellously adept at keeping the press away from his candidate, but what Turner desperately needs is some sympathetic coverage. Consequently, the atmosphere among the reporters travelling with Turner is one of blackest gallows humour. Where Mulroney's campaign gave off a sense of hardworking hunger for power, John Turner is straining to recover from the fast-dissolving notion that the people of Canada have spent ten years just panting for him to assume his rightful place.

In the ballroom of Cassio's Motor Hotel, the Liberal leader is introduced by Sudbury's own Judy Erola, the minister of both consumer and corporate affairs and social development. With her small, flat features, indestructible blonde hairdo, and nickel-plated smile, Erola is as brassy as a truckload of trombones. Although she displays all the self-willed enthusiasm for the cause that seems to be an inevitable component of every woman politician's personality, her introduction of John Turner is remarkably ambiguous. In the Davey-inspired effort to portray their leader as something more than the corporate number-cruncher of recent reputation, Erola asserts that Turner is "warm, understanding and compassionate." Then, she adds that she's "bloody glad" that the "myths" around John Turner have dissipated. Consciously or not, in Cassio's Motor Hotel, Judy Erola has just called her leader a loser. After all, the hallmark of the myth about John Turner was that he was the golden boy, the unvanquished winner, the man untarnished by the recent Liberal past. If this is gone, what can be left?

(There is, of course, the possibility that John Turner is even now, three weeks before the election, being transformed into that curious Canadian figure, the National Loser, the leader of the opposition. Unlike the United States, where a defeated presidential candidate usually bows out of public life, in Canada's parliamentary democracy, the National Loser sticks around to be alternately ridiculed and encouraged. Canadians had a fondness for a political loser like Clark or Stanfield, and were always claiming that he was getting a raw deal and folks should be nicer to him. It was just possible that Brian Mulroney had remained so very quiet as leader of the opposition because he had no wish to be identified with such an unrewarding role.)

Up on the platform, Turner attempts to convey his warmth, understanding and compassion. Still fighting the bad impression that the bum-patting incidents have made, he tells the Sudbury Liberals not only that his party has a record number of women candidates, but also that Erola is "the most powerful woman in the history of the country."

Endeavouring to pass as a social reformer, Turner lists off a number of new programs — not only for women but for youth and small business. Concerning his government's youth employment program,

First Chance, Turner uses a line that, with daily repetition, will become even more banal than Mulroney's "The Devil made me do it." Wielding the catchphrase that the good Joseph Heller contributed to the vernacular, Turner maintains that young people are caught in a Catch-22: "No experience, no job. No job, no experience." It isn't a great line to begin with, but heard every day it becomes positively vacuous.

Next, Turner reminds the audience of a recently announced program where that notoriously harassed individual, the small business-man, can discover in one place what the government intends to do for him about taxes, regulation, and so on — "one-stop shopping" in the prime minister's phrase. Along with women and youth, small business is thought to be a grateful beneficiary of Turner's newfound compassion. "The government," he cries out, "is making it easier for you for a change." Yet there was no group less likely to be wooed away from the Tories than small business. Where corporate exec-utives had any number of layers of management between themselves and their industrial workers, and could thus afford "enlightened" relations, small business lived right at the cutting edge of one of the more fraught varieties of human intercourse — that between em-ployee and boss. For small business, the availability of unemployment insurance meant that it was tougher to keep staff — minimum wage just cut into one's profits; these people were appalled when somebody working for low wages didn't show the same dedication to the job as they did themselves. The people who ran small businesses all too often represented the nastier side of conservatism, the one that inched out into the far shore of reaction.

After enumerating these various social measures, Turner an-nounces yet another program, "shelter assistance for single-parent households." Where Mulroney held out the tantalizing promise of new prosperity, Turner, now attempting to outflank the Tory leader on the left, is offering a new series of federal social programs. To an electorate recently entranced by the romance of capitalism and Mulroney's vision of new riches, the programs must seem like mere handouts. Nonetheless, Turner assures his Sudbury audience that he's going to tightly cost his programs and "give a clear picture of the financing." Where Mulroney is campaigning on a jewelled vision of coming wealth, Turner is running on "fiscal responsibility." Com-pared to the notion of fresh booty, accurate accounting is not, com-paratively speaking, a theme calculated to plumb anyone's depths.

Finally, contriving to leave his Little Lord Fauntleroy image behind,

Turner lays into Brian Mulroney. But the assault comes nowhere near the jugular. He starts out bravely enough: "This election is becoming an election of trust — who's levelling with you, who's frank, who's telling you the story." It is not Turner's style, however, to submerge his opponent in the same vat of humorous ridicule employed by a Jean Chrétien. Instead of portraying Mulroney as contemptible and fatuous, he represents him as spendthrift, a bad manager. If John Turner's greatest motivating engine was a sense of duty, correspondingly his idea of the greatest sin was irresponsible mismanagement. So he represents Mulroney as a bad administrator, claiming that his opponent's promises would leave the Tory leader with "only three options." According to Turner, Mulroney, if elected, would be compelled to either "renege on his promises, raise taxes, or cut social programs." If Mulroney is selling hope, Turner's only chance is to sell fear.

The Tories, after all, are very sensitive about Mulroney's inveterate ability to evoke instant mistrust. Their television commercials now feature, right off the top, a wide-eyed, virginal young woman who straightforwardly testifies that "I trust Brian." In the early days of the campaign, Turner had been waiting around for Mulroney to commit the traditional Conservative rite of self-immolation. Since the debate, however, it has become clear that the Tory leader could not be counted on to trip over his own shoes. And so the issue was no longer Mulroney's competence, but his sincerity. Turner was relying on the discrepancies in Mulroney's accounting to prove his case. But untrustworthy or not, Mulroney was communicating good news, while Turner was hopelessly stuck with the bad.

As a kind of postscript, in an effort to get the Sudbury Liberals out on the streets and canvassing, perhaps with Mulroney's campaign in mind, Turner stresses that "this is not a presidential election, despite all the television cameras here that concentrate on the leaders. This is a parliamentary democracy and we elect members of parliament to 282 constituencies. There's no secret to politics, even in the television age. In the instant information age, politics is still one-on-one, and you know it."

This is a familiar Canadian lament, last heard from the apologists for Joe Clark, whenever the issue arose of their man's lack of television presence. When in trouble with the voters, blame television, blame modern times, blame the Americans. Opposed to this damnable modern age was some vague British parliamentary past. The British parliamentary present of Margaret Thatcher was just as dominated by polls and television as was the America of Ronald Reagan; the Iron Maiden did not make decisions about elections without first consulting the advertising firm of Saatchi & Saatchi. The institution of the British prime minister, as well as the Canadian one, increasingly had presidential overtones. Previously, this form of nostalgic complaint had been a Conservative preserve; it was significant that John Turner was now making it his own. (As for politics still being a one-on-one proposition, it seemed far more likely that the voters were going one-on-one with the apparitions of Barbara Frum or Knowlton Nash on their television screens than with some annoyance of a canvasser at the door.)

At the Sudbury Science Centre, Turner welcomes home the Olympic Gold medalist, Alex Baumann. The Science Centre's geometrical architecture is supposed to represent "the snowflake of the North." One is more vividly reminded of a flying saucer come to rest amidst the Sudbury moonscape. The Olympic swimmer's audience is dotted with young guys with blonde surfer hair, padding around in bare feet as if they had just this minute come from the pool: an oddly Californian touch for a northern Ontario mining town. The crowd is there solely to welcome the hometown hero. "John Turner, who's he?" one kid wonders.

According to Turner, however, Baumann is "one of the superheroes of the century," and "that performance was just solid gold, heugh, heugh, heugh." One reporter speculates that Turner must feel strange standing on a stage with Baumann since he had always wanted to win a gold medal as an Olympic sprinter. "Yeah," agrees the toughest-talking of all the reporters, a young woman, of course; "he probably wanted it on his CV."

Unlike Manicouagan One, John Turner's campaign aircraft is a very ordinary DC-9. There is no customized signature on the nose, no musical fanfares blaring from the speakers. Instead, a large computer terminal sits in the middle of the plane; two phones are built into the back of a seat; the hotline, one supposes, in case all hell breaks loose in Ottawa or Washington. As I walk down the aisle, I bump right into a bulky figure bent over and scrambling under the seats. At first all I can see is a pair of grey flannel trousers. Then the man straightens up, apologizing profusely. It is John Turner. Unlike Mulroney, Turner is not separated from the media, but can be seen wearing his black horn rims, nursing a Scotch and Perrier and a cigar, immersed in paper. Still, after a couple of incidents early in this campaign, he isn't really talking much to reporters; not even engaging in the kind of meaningless banter that Mulroney employs to keep selected members of the press well stroked.

This plane, like Mulroney's, has its token campaign joke. It concerns the unhappy fate a crowd of sexually aroused natives, not unlike the press corps themselves, visit on a pair of British missionaries. It is only marginally funnier than the one on Mulroney's tour, but the joke's punchline becomes a constant refrain, in both official languages, in the course of the trip. When Turner's eyes bulge with characteristic intensity, he's said to have "booga-booga eyes"; when Geills Turner is clonked on the head by a TV camera during a particularly rough scrum at the Calgary Airport, it is known as "the booga-booga scrum." In the self-enclosed bubble of the tour, what with too many drinks, too many tasteless sandwiches, too many cigarettes, too many early starts, too many days of life lived in each others' pockets, "booga-booga" begins to take over with the boys on the plane. Whatever statement is made by a politician, an aide or a reporter, somebody is sure to say: "But first, *mais d'abord* — booga-booga." While John Turner tries to convey a clear and solemn message to the voters, the press can only stay halfway close to sane by babbling a bit of nonsense.

There is a cruel edge to the relationship the press has with John Turner. Making reference to Turner's college nickname, to the tune of John Lennon's "Give Peace A Chance," they incessantly sing their own version of "Give Chick a Chance." Two French-language reporters sing a parodic version of Turner's Quebec jingle, *"Passons vite à l'action."* The song was never an unforgettable peak of intelligence and wit, but when sung by this pair, in close to the accents of the mentally retarded, it sounds positively moronic.

Geills Turner, unlike Mila Mulroney, is not accompanied by a lady-in-waiting. When there is a brief stop in Winnipeg as the tour heads West, Mrs Turner leaves the plane alone, lines up with everybody else at the newsstand in the airport, buys some stamps, a magazine, and a couple of sticks of licorice and gets back on the plane. Compared to the *arriviste* dazzle of the Mulroneys, the Turners' air was that of any well-established, fundamentally decent upper-middle-class couple. Unlike the Mulroneys, who clearly relished all the things that money could buy and the perks of high office, the Turners were clearly long accustomed to the comfortable, stolid life of the high bourgeoisie of Rockliffe, Forest Hill and Westmount. While Geills Turner was an attractive enough resident of those parts, Mila Mulroney was a starlet.

157

As the booga-booga scrum unwinds at Calgary Airport, Mrs Turner, to the great displeasure of her son David, receives a bonk on the head from a television camera wildly jockeying for a good spot in the scrum. Ken Becker, a transplanted New Yorker working as the Toronto bureau chief of UPC, watches a close-mouthed Turner being pursued the entire length of the airport by the yapping pack and reflects with no small amusement that "the last time I saw a scene like that was with some Mafia guy outside a courthouse in New Jersey."

Outside the airport, the tour buses are late.

"*Les autobuses sont perdus,*" one Quebec reporter informs another.

"*Encore?*" his colleague murmurs in disbelief.

But then, the Quebec press never travel West with great enthusiasm. By and large the French-language reporters are more cultivated than their Anglo counterparts, passing back and forth tapes of Mahler and Schumann for their Walkmans on the plane, while the English-speakers are immersed in Bruce Springsteen and Waylon Jennings; they also seriously doubt that an edible meal can be had west of Montreal. When Turner eventually alights in Calgary East to do a little mainstreeting, Michel Auger of *La Presse Canadienne* says to a friend, "Don't speak French when you get off the bus or they'll lynch us." He's only half-kidding.

There's a small, indifferent crowd at 36th and 17th as Turner works his way up the block at his infinitesimal pace. There are mountains in the distance, but this part of Calgary is far from being the most scenic part of Alberta, a block of boarded-up shops and offices — just another honky-tonk strip. When Turner announced that he was going to run in a British Columbia riding and Mulroney that he was standing for election in Quebec, it seemed that the historic regionalism affecting the two main parties might be at an end. But where Mulroney is an indisputable son of Quebec, the West was far from claiming John Turner as its own. As Turner makes his way along the street, as if in slow motion, one woman in a gift shop doesn't even bother to interrupt her telephone conversation when her prime minister comes calling; she just cradles the receiver on her shoulder, unenthusiastically holds out her hand for Turner's shake and then goes right on talking.

Realistically, the Liberals have only once chance in Alberta and it's here in Calgary East, where the ex-mayor, Rod Sykes, is their candidate. It's an immigrant riding and there are East Indian dancers in a strange combination with the inevitable C & W band to welcome Turner at the Marlborough Inn, which is oddly situated in a shopping plaza. After the big whooping "Calgary welcome," Sykes — a skinny, thin-haired man with an undeniable resemblance to a chicken — says that Alberta has had "nothing but Tories and nothing but trouble." He blames the various battles between the province and Ottawa on the Lougheed Tories, and claims that Turner is a "prime minister who speaks our language and understands us"; under his leadership, Alberta is "ready to come back into Canada and play its full part in our government much more."

Identity in English Canada was to a great extent a negative phenomenon. Canadian nationalists defined themselves by discovering and hanging on to everything that separated them from Americans. Western Canadians generally found the standard brand of nationalism to be just Ontario imperialism. Most often, a westerner defined himself politically as somebody who disliked and distrusted the East. Other differences were over-magnified, except those that perennially divided rural people from city folk. Outside Quebec, except for geography, regional differences in Canada were too often a matter of exaggeration.

At the Marlborough, later that afternoon, Turner attempts to win the audience's loyalty by pointing out that he is the third Canadian in history to run in three provinces, and the first prime minister since Macdonald to run in British Columbia. He claims that the Liberals have the strongest slate ever in southern Alberta. In general, there was a disappointment among senior Liberals about the quality of candidates Turner had been able to recruit across the country. It was assumed that he would be able to convince potential superstars like Paul E. Martin, Ken Dryden or John Rae to run, and thus provide the party with a genuine invigoration. John Turner had promised to inaugurate a new Liberal era. Instead, it was looking sadly like the same old faces.

Eyebrows arching, neck bullishly thrust forward, Turner continues to fire volleys at Mulroney, asserting that the whole reason he himself had returned to politics was to prevent "another party of another political stripe from dismantling social services." This is revisionist history with a vengeance. The man who spent ten years fulminating in Winston's about Trudeau's socialist drift is now presenting himself as the knight errant of social welfare! Then he charges Mulroney with being soft on separatism, accusing him of running at least three separatist candidates in Quebec under the Conservative banner. "I will only negotiate," Turner thunders, "with a government in Quebec that believes in Canada." It is a stance badly calculated to appeal to the anti-Quebec feelings of the West. "If this election is going to be decided on trust," Turner concludes, "we're going to win going away."

Where Mulroney has put together a coalition of those in Quebec who are disaffected with Liberal governments over the last decade and more, Turner is finding no contrary constituency in the West. His accusation that the Tories are confused about their election promises does not have the punch of Mulroney's blitz on the patronage appointments. Unconvincing as the defender of social welfare, unpersuasive as a true westerner, failing in his unlikely attempts to portray Mulroney as a closet separatist, Turner is cutting no ice out here.

Unlike Mulroney, with his multiple changes of outfit, his unceasing stream of freshly pressed blue blazers, Turner frequently looks rumpled at the end of the day. As the plane travels on to British Columbia, and Turner dives into his Scotch and Perrier, the media pack is unmerciful in its raillery. "All we are saying," they sing in chorus, "is give us a scrum. All we are saying is don't read the polls."

The next morning, across the border in Cranbrook, there is talk of a new Southam poll that has Mulroney leading Turner and Broadbent 51-32-17. Looking on as Turner's campaign buses load up are three Tory organizers. They are in Cranbrook working on a Mulroney event that is still weeks away. This morning, in an outdoor gathering, surrounded by the green forests of the Kootenays, despite the fact that every breath of air is like a hit of champagne, Turner delivers one of his most sleepy speeches yet. Addressing a small crowd seated on wooden bleachers, the prime minister seems barely awake, stammering and slipping, and swallowing his words. "When I graduated from the University of British Columbia in 1949," he says, careful to work in the regional reference, "we were told that the future is limitless. The BC Chamber of Commerce used to have those signs 'We have men to match our mountains'." Then he adds, in an effort to make an equal opportunity joke, "I don't know if we really want to get bisexual about that." *Bisexual!* Sure, bisexual is to the relations of the sexes as bilingual is to the relations of French and English. Or is it?

Noticing the plentiful Ban-the-Bomb signs in the crowd, Turner pays lip service to nuclear disarmament, provided that Canada first live up to "our international obligations." Both Turner and Mulroney make ritual nods towards this issue, having realized through Pierre

Trudeau's efforts just how widespread is anti-nuclear sentiment. However, one could imagine that, had Trudeau stayed on, his campaign would have centred almost entirely on the search for disarmament.

Endeavouring to stretch out his reign to a quarter-century, what could have served Trudeau better than the prospect of nuclear apocalypse? After all, jobs were important, but surely not more important than the possibility of annihilation. Where Turner presented his concerns about nuclear disarmament as a kind of afterthought to the economy, you could be sure that Pierre Trudeau would have made the issue a central plank of his platform. Mulroney, already close to Ronald Reagan, would then be forced to run either as an apologist for nuclear apocalypse or as a me-too proponent of disarmament. The economy was in its essence a Tory issue; but it would have taken a Liberal as fond of fearless surprise as Trudeau to run flat out on anti-nuke.

Clearly, Turner is not a man for the bold stroke. His speech in Kootenay East is pedestrian and rambling. He fails to hold their attention and people start drifting away. A man in a plaid shirt, on his way out, resignedly remarks to his wife, "Same old rhetoric."

No matter how badly a politician is doing, there are always those who believe such a powerful man must possess magical powers. As Turner shakes hands in the crowd after his speech, a drab middle-aged woman keeps tugging at his elbow. She wants to introduce the prime minister to her deaf son. Finally capturing Turner's attention, she informs him that the boy can read lips. Turner, trying to be compassionate, tells him about his wife's first cousin who reads lips too. Then he wishes the boy, who is almost in tears, a lot of luck. On some primitive level, there was still a belief that a great man, by his very presence, could confer healing powers. Whenever Turner is confronted with a potentially emotional situation, he almost always deals with it indirectly, mentioning either his mother or his wife.

Leaving Cranbrook, Roger Smith of CTV asks Turner to comment on the Southam poll. "I don't comment on polls," replies Turner emptily, "I only comment on people." As Geills Turner waits for her limo to pull away, she spots two reporters in dark glasses and asks "Why are you looking so jaded?" "Because it's all so terribly interesting, Mrs Turner," says Mr Shades. Up rolls the window.

On the way to Vancouver, Geills Turner gets on the plane's public address system and graciously thanks everyone from the aides to the baggage handlers. "Even the press hasn't been too bad," she

161

bravely adds, "even though they knocked me down a couple of times."
From the back of the plane, the boys sing out, "All we are saying is
give Geills a chance."

That afternoon, John Turner campaigns in his own chosen riding of
Quadra. With the mountains, the ocean, and the balmy climate, it is
hard to dislike Vancouver. After all, British Columbia was what Canadians had instead of California. The rest of the country always held
it out as the home of the second chance. If things didn't work out in
Toronto, Ottawa or Montreal, you could always move to Vancouver
and try again.

At a coffee-klatch in a white stucco house on 41st Ave., Turner
continues to make an issue of how much Mulroney's promises will
cost. Wearing his summer issue uniform of Lacoste shirt, tan slacks
and blazer, Turner tells the press that, contrary to his protestations,
Mulroney has access to the same figures and forecasts as everybody
else. After his remarks, an older woman rushes up to Turner and
says, "Hello, Mr President."

"No," Turner assures her, "I'm Prime Minister."

Watching Turner in the crowd is a young woman with a new baby.
Unlike the great masses who are forming their impressions of the
leaders solely from television, she's one of those rare Canadians
who's actually doing a lot of reading about the issues and, even rarer,
coming out to hear what the politicians have to say. She has, she
confides, "a lot of criticism" of Brian Mulroney.

As he takes to the streets of Quadra, the Liberal leader runs into
an old classmate from UBC. This man has clearly not risen to the
same station in life as John Turner; he looks a trifle ragged about
the edges. Turner's old UBC confrère tells a couple of reporters that
he's not going to vote Liberal because of the 80,000 "Pakis" they let
into Quadra and because of "metric." Racism and opposition to the
metric system often go strangely hand-in-hand out here. But then,
East Asian immigrants and centimetres and Celsius were just two
more disagreeable new facts of life to the near-elderly and disappointed. There's one guy in jogging shorts with a placard deprecating
corruption in the Catholic Church in Quebec. There's a woman lawyer, out Saturday shopping with her family, who says it's time for a
change but doesn't want to be quoted to that effect because "I have
to do business with Liberals." Another man says Turner "should
have stayed in Toronto." Talk about a low, dishonest decade. Walking

162

through Quadra in 1984 with John Turner gives one the sensation of being many hundreds of miles to the south, in the purlieus of Orange County.

Also watching John Turner is a woman who surely must symbolize the entire age. She is young, attractive . . . and a Tory. For a living, she works as a bill collector. Asked if she subscribes to her sex's mistrust of Mulroney — the so-called "gender gap" — she acknowledges that "Turner would seduce me a lot faster than Mulroney if it's based on looks. I think a prime minister should be smooth."

Although the commentators were forever telling us that women distrusted Mulroney's oleaginous suavity, it is just possible that they were almost entirely wrong. For years, the shaggy, textured style of John F. Kennedy had been what politicians, or their media advisors, had tried to emulate. Things had changed. If the sixties were the age of shaggy dense texture, the eighties are the age of shiny, flawless polish. The middle class appreciated the gloss of a highly finished manner; to them, it was evidence of much hard work. Even though the current appetite for lustrous surfaces started out in the coke-sniffing recesses of show-biz, it had by now percolated into the mass consciousness sufficiently that it had become attractive to find in a politician. Women like the Tory bill collector apparently approved of the fact that someone like Mulroney had taken the trouble — with what degree of effort and will we would never know — to work on that voice, work on that appearance, until the whole ensemble gleams so phosphorescently that he is forced to damp down the aggregate wattage.

All the Saturday afternoon crowds here in Quadra seem to be coming from playing some sport or other — tennis, field hockey, jogging. They don't seem overwhelmed with enthusiasm for Turner. There is little of the proud home-town sympathy that Baie Comeau felt about Mulroney.

That night at the Commodore Ballroom, Turner dances to the music of Doug and the Slugs — just takes off his jacket and gets down. "Not bad for a white guy," says Ken Becker. "Makin' it work takes a little longer," sing Doug and the Slugs. "Makin' it work, John, takes a little time." What with all the time that Pierre Trudeau had put in on the dance floors of the nation, being able to shake one's ass with perfect aplomb had become as necessary to a Liberal prime minister as the ability to give a good speech. While Mila Mulroney listened to the Beatles and Willie Nelson on her headset up front in Manicouagan One, there were no scenes of her and Brian doing the

163

monkey in the airplane's aisles. In general, it was an axiom of Canadian politics that, as far as their leaders went, Tories don't dance.

Well, if Turner can dance, so can the press. And there they go, out on the floor. While an election is designed to determine many grave issues, it is also a kind of national celebration. One Quebec journalist doesn't see it that way, though, and carefully notes down the names of all his colleagues, male and female, out there moving to the music; he later writes a story wherein all concerned are accused of frivolity and insufficient amounts of *sérieux*. But it's a steamy Saturday night on the edge of the continent and the revels continue long into the dawn. Far less puritanical than Toronto, Vancouver was one raunchy town; the media help themselves to all the pleasures of the harbour.

Next morning, despite many hangovers, the party continues as Turner flies back to Ottawa. There is a sense that Davey's salvage operation has stabilized the campaign. There is little sense of panic that Turner had reached bottom and is inching his way back up. All the same, somebody tapes up a photo of Mulroney in the back of the plane, under which is scrawled "Go with a winner."

On the long flight, the camp counsellors serve wine and cheese. Everybody stands in the aisles, parodying Beatle songs: "I Wanna Hold Your Bum." There is the sensation that, for the press, what with the exhaustion, the giddiness, the quick love affairs, this is as close as any of them come to the no-tomorrow ambience of wartime. Except, in this case, there was the pleasant bonus that nobody but the politicians got killed.

At a brief stopover in Winnipeg, Turner has his picture taken with the crew, his arms around the stewardesses. Somebody in the press asks, "Where are his hands?"

Ken Becker shows Turner a tabloid headline that reads, "Two-headed turtles battle for life." "Sounds like Mulroney," says Turner.

When Becker flips over to the sports scores, he asks Turner who he roots for, the Blue Jays or the Expos. Turner's answer is depressingly non-committal. "I root for both our country's teams," he says. "And we're going to get one for Vancouver." I mean, what if he had said that he cheered for the Blue Jays? How many votes would that have cost him in Montreal?

On Monday, Turner holds a press conference in Ottawa's Westin Hotel. The occasion ostensibly has to do with women's issues, since the debate on that subject is two days away. All the Liberal women candidates are present, seated four abreast just in front of Turner's dais. With Turner is Judy Erola, in blue suit and pearls. There seems to be some question about just who is in charge. She instructs the press to ask only questions about women's issues; Turner says it's an *open* conference. The press then ignore women's issues entirely. They ask him what he's going to have to do to catch up to Mulroney in the polls; they ask him about interest rates. When finally Marguerite McDonald of CBC TV asks a question about equal pay for equal work, Erola jumps in to tell her what Turner *really* means. Then, she tries to wrap up the conference. No more questions.

"Well," says Turner, "I'll take two more."

Naturally, he is asked if the women candidates interrogated him on the solemn question of bum-patting. Possibly humbled by the events of the last few weeks, Turner offers a half-apology: "I told them," he says, "that the media very much overplayed those two isolated incidents. They were gestures of friendship with two friends politically and certainly meant no disrespect, and if I've offended anyone, I'm sorry. It hasn't happened again. Nor will it."

Sitting in the audience are most of the Ottawa columnists from Fotheringham to Sears. Also present is Senator Jerry Grafstein. With him is a small, grey Irish jockey of a man named Paddy Sampson. Together they are studying John Turner. Sampson is a veteran CBC variety producer, who had long advised Pierre Trudeau on the use of television. The winner of any number of awards, Sampson had a deft touch; there was little that could happen on a stage of any sort about which he was not expert. Sampson's favourite political maxim was "It's all show business." There was no doubt that a considerable portion of Trudeau's political flair was deeply calculated for theatrical effect. Sampson had since spent some time with John Turner. Now the senator and the veteran showman are peering at their man with expressions that say "What the hell can we do with *this* guy?"

In any event, Turner does not seem to have done anything to prepare for the women's debate. A couple of days later, heading once more into the dungeons of the Royal York in Toronto, I run into a woman working as one of the debate's producers. An elegant sort, she is socially situated at that top of the media pyramid that is contingent upon the upper levels of business and politics. The producer is unimpressed with Turner's approach to television. Brian Mulroney had sent Tom Gould, a veteran TV executive, down to the Royal York and he had been all over the set like a hawk. John Turner had sent some unknown, who took one glance and left. Mulroney, it's expected, will arrive with his own make-up man and plenty of time to prepare. Turner, it is anticipated, will rush in ten minutes before showtime.

The Canadian Ballroom, previously the site of the Liberal policy session, has now been transformed into a television studio. There's a huge squad of women, all wearing their very best, waiting outside the doors chanting both "We want in!" and "We want Ed!" Ed Broadbent is the favourite, in agreement with practically all the positions taken by the women of the National Action Committee on the Status of Women, the event's sponsor. However, a representative of a radical lesbian group sneers "I don't trust any of them."

Mulroney seldom attends any of these official women's gatherings without bringing Flora MacDonald along as a bodyguard. MacDonald, who was more and more beginning to resemble her illustrious predecessor from Kingston, Sir John A., fulfilled the same sort of role for Mulroney as Judy Erola did for Turner. They both served as a kind of Designated Woman, who was able to confront the professional outrage of the more militant sorts in a way that their leaders never could. In the 1980s, to appear to be hostile in the slightest to the women's lobby was to commit political suicide.

At 7:35 p.m. Mulroney is ushered in by Tom Gould and Bill Fox; since Baie Comeau, his glamour quotient seems to have multiplied by a factor of six. The Tory leader has a strategy as far as women are concerned. Knowing that the type represented by the bill collector in Quadra is in the minority, and that there still remains a certain lingering mistrust among women, Mulroney does his damndest to repress his natural animal spirits. He seems to be impersonating an ambulatory corpse. Always endeavouring to appear all things to all people, Mulroney here assumes a hangdog, penitent expression, careful not to communicate excessive male assertion. He speaks in the quietest of voices, hoping that the assembled women will forgive him for his membership in the hopeless sex.

Because Mulroney is so subdued, the debate is far more somnolent than the previous one. The moderator, Caroline Andrew, demands beforehand that "things must be kept calm, collected, and very pleasurable for everyone." At this stage, the women's movement was very desirous of respectability, anxious to forget its bra-burning past. Motivated by the ubiquitous careerism of the 1980s, the women's movement seemed eager to forget its origins in the radical styles of the sixties and keen to meet the conventional standards of the worlds of politics and business.

The panel of interrogators runs down the ritual list of women's issues. Broadbent maintains that women must be given proportional representation in job-retraining programs. Mulroney says women should be given increased access to bank credit. Broadbent favours freedom of choice on abortion. Turner says that the two opposed camps on the issue are irreconcilable and that the country is best served by the present state of the law. Everybody, natch, is opposed to pornography. It would take a brave man indeed to plead in these circumstances that freedom of expression is indivisible: ban pornography and you ban Art.

As the debate idles along, with few fireworks, Mulroney continues to lie low. Turner seems to recover some of the ground he had lost in the previous debate. Broadbent is in favour of every possible women's program; there is nothing they want that he doesn't want too. Somebody could propose a program for a free Volvo for every woman in the country and Broadbent would probably go along with it. There was still an unfortunate tendency of the women's lobby, deplored by intelligent men and women alike, to view government and leaders as not some extension of all of us, but as Daddy. Turner and Mulroney were contaminated by the original patriarchal sin of male authority, which was always seen as denying and forbidding. Broadbent seemed like a good bet for househusband, for Permissive Pa.

At long last, the nub of the matter is resolved by one of the panelists, who asks, given their dismal record on women's issues, why should any of the leaders be trusted at all? Turner is adamant that nothing is higher on his agenda than economic equality for women. But before Brian Mulroney can give his answer, Caroline Andrew cuts in and says that time is up. Now the question of why Mulroney should be trusted has become the prime issue of the election; the audience has suffered through almost two hours of uneventful debate and the moment that the single most germane question has been asked, the plug is pulled!

But Mulroney, looking his most corpse-like, merely applies one more touch of flattery: "Your question is dead on," he says. "I can't give you an answer. I'm going to have to ask you to believe."

It is characteristic of Mulroney, when confronted with doubts about himself, merely to insist on his sincerity. He is so abundantly infused with goodwill, the implication is, that any reasonable person must believe. As for sceptics, well, how can he account for the manifestly bad intentions of others?

In any event, Mulroney must feel sufficiently in front that he does not have to risk any further broadside against Turner. But just before the debate ends, in his closing statement, Turner delivers his most telling attack so far. "You know and I know," he tells the women's audience, "that Mr Broadbent will not form the next government." There comes back a chorus of boos. "Face facts," insists Turner. "Face facts." Then he bores in for the kill. "Mr Mulroney sat in the House of Commons for ten months. He only asked thirty-nine questions. In 1982, at their national policy conference, the Conservatives took a poll. Seventy-four percent of Conservatives were opposed to increased funding for daycare facilities, 75 percent were against affirmative action for women and minority groups, 72 percent wanted to reduce spending on Family Allowances. That's their record. Today the Conservatives are let's-pretend liberals. Now they say they support these policies." Turner finishes up by saying that he's a Liberal by choice; recalling his party's commitment to fairness, progress and equality, he says that "men and women together should work for a better Canada."

It is the best the prime minister has sounded since the Liberal convention. Just as the economy is naturally a Tory issue, minorities, including women, are natural Liberal ground. Forced back onto the party's traditional turf, in the hands of experienced Liberal strategists, Turner is beginning to run a coherent campaign. With two-and-a-half weeks to go, he is making his last stand on the issue of trust, especially as regards the cost of Mulroney's programs. It is Keith Davey's theory that 40 percent of the voters make up their mind in the first week and another 40 percent in the last. It is his hope that John Turner would now come hammering down the stretch and close some of that 20-point gap.

CHAPTER 8

THE SOUL OF MAN UNDER SOCIALISM

In the third week of August, Ed Broadbent, the leader of the New Democratic Party, is travelling through his party's strongholds in the West. Last spring, when a poll had shown that the NDP had declined to 11 percent of the popular vote, there had been speculation that it would fail to win the twelve seats necessary for major party status in the House of Commons. Now, with Liberal support collapsing from the centre, both to the left and to the right, the Gallup poll of 17 August had the NDP back up at 18 percent. Any other Canadian political leader who stood well in the estimation of only eighteen out of every hundred voters might well find himself with a suicidal case of the glooms, but such was the curious role played in the country's political life by its third party that its leader is now in the best of spirits.

The previous Tuesday, in Vancouver, Broadbent had visited CKVV, a small independent television station, to tape an interview. The NDP leader, who loves to take the sun, sports a deep, leathery tan that gives him a faint air of the reptilian. Ed Broadbent has little of the professor about him, even though that was his vocation in the long-ago days before he entered politics. Now, he has a grey, anonymous presence, which well suits his campaign theme of "Ordinary Canadians." Far from communicating that flavour of the working class that invariably attends trade union leaders, Broadbent's manner could easily belong to a high-school principal, an office manager or a sales executive. A low parting covering thinning hair, he exudes little of Mulroney's surface charm or Turner's regal good looks. Nonetheless, Ed Broadbent is an experienced, disciplined, formidable campaigner; long practice has made him entirely at ease in the public eye.

In the yellow bleachers of the CKVV studio sit that typical game show audience of the elderly and eccentric — the promiscuous votaries of celebrity in our time. Although Broadbent is far more willing to take a combative stance than his two opponents, he has never been a controversial figure in Canadian public life. If leaders of the opposition from Diefenbaker to Stanfield to Clark played National

Loser, the head of the NDP (as the CCF before it) has eternally been The Last Angry Man, raging and ranting about the world's injustice. Like the National Loser, the Designated Ranter seemed to satisfy some deep therapeutic need in the Canadian psyche. Few became enraged when Broadbent did; a perennial state of choler was expected of him.

Notwithstanding, a lone RCMP security man is present. Where there is a whole squad surrounding the prime minister and a good-sized contingent attending the leader of the opposition, two amiable sorts accompanied Broadbent; Broadbent's aides and the campaign press dubbed them "Smith and Wesson," or else "Burly I and Burly II." Whichever leader they were protecting, the Mounties all seemed to have a weakness for expensive jewellery. If their defensive tackle size wasn't enough to identify them, you could always tell who the RCMP man was: he was the guy with the gold bracelet on one hand, the gold watch on the other, and several gold rings on each chunky finger. While the RCMP assigned to the other leaders kept a discreet distance, Smith and Wesson would go drinking at night with both Broadbent's staff and the reporters.

The other guest on *The Vancouver Show* is "The Strongest Man in Canada." This guy, a weightlifter, has arrived with his bodybuilding entourage, who are hugely striding around the small studio in warm-up suits and loincloths, organizing their equipment, preparing to pump iron. What with the *Day of the Locust* crowd in the bleachers, the bejewelled Mr Burly I, and the assembled aides and newshounds, there is an oddly assorted circus atmosphere on the television set.

Since the regular host of *The Vancouver Show*, Laurier LaPierre, is well known for views espoused by the NDP, Broadbent is interviewed by a man named Mike Winlaw. The stand-in host commences by remarking on the most salient point concerning Broadbent's campaign: that the NDP has defied predictions of imminent obliteration by taking advantage of the Liberal collapse.

"Well," Broadbent interjects, "it couldn't happen to a nicer bunch."

How great was the general satisfaction at the Liberals' misfortunes! There was an almost palpable anticipation of Liberal defeat throughout the land. Canadians couldn't wait to be rid of the crew who had governed them for so long.

Winlaw then enquires whether or not Broadbent feels he is adding to the fortunes of the Tories by draining away Liberal support. "No," he replies. It is his predictable opinion that Canadians are looking for progress as well as change. For the NDP, change was synonymous

with social progress. History was a straight line reaching ever upwards. It was inconceivable to them that its course could well be far
more mysterious, irrational and dark-hued than had been accounted
for in their optimistic diagnosis. Asked whether he conceded that a
Tory majority looked likely, Broadbent, demonstrating that Brian
Mulroney isn't the only Canadian political leader who's quick with a
platitude, trots out that hoary Yogi Berra quote, beloved of hockey
coaches and politicians alike: "It ain't over till it's over."

After a commercial break Broadbent is shown an interview between Laurier LaPierre and Michael Walker, head of the Fraser
Institute, a right-wing think tank. Walker rattles off the usual cant
about cutting the deficit, reducing government spending, and the utter
necessity of "short-term pain" for the populace at large.

Asked to comment on all this, Broadbent punches shrewd holes
in Walker's argument. As far as he's concerned, Walker's prognostications are "laughable." "The relevant question," Broadbent ob-
serves, "is who bears the pain. He is talking as if all economists
agree with him."

Since the first OPEC oil price increases had taken effect in 1973,
the subject of the economy has dominated all public discourse in the
West. Before then the subject had been characterized in the general
mind as MEGO or My Eyes Glaze Over. In the last decade, however,
the public has been forced to unglaze its eyes and take instruction
from the experts. But the innocent who would venture among such
economic pundits soon begins to feel like a dewy-eyed teenager at
his first Moonie session. Always present, one way or another, is the
uncomfortable sensation that you are being hustled. Listening to the
pontifications of "experts" eager to assure a credulous public that all
economists think as they do, one soon realizes that "the economy"
and "jobs" have replaced the flag as the supreme object of dubious
piety. You begin to suspect that Karl Marx had things precisely upside
down; to a large degree political ideology determines economics.
Financial philosophy seems, in the end, only to serve as a fiscal vehicle
for differing visions of society.

"Mr Walker," continues Broadbent, "is the architect of a program
that has produced here in BC less private investment in the private
sector. Instead of more jobs, unemployment in this province has
increased to the level of Newfoundland. He talked about Reaganomics
without mentioning that President Reagan has produced the most
massive deficit in US history. Average Canadians are prepared to
bear some burdens, but what Mr Walker wants is that the average

person in the country bear all the burden. You didn't hear him talk about removing tax loopholes for the rich."

In British Columbia, the Social Credit government of Bill Bennett, under the guise of resuscitating the economy, had introduced measures of "restraint," whose barb-edged political intent was transparent. In an effort to transform the province into a social backwater that would resemble a cross between Hong Kong and Alabama, the Socreds, guided by thinking such as Walker's, had introduced legislation that attacked the entrenched rights of labour, minorities, health services, housing and education. In every case, the social security net had been pulled out from under public employees, tenants and teachers, leaving a looming chasm underneath. Bennett's government appeared determined to restore to the rich and strong every possible advantage over the poor and the weak, all in the name of "restraint." The word itself had disturbingly totalitarian overtones. In addition to the notion of curbing fiscal extravagances, the restraint program was designed to subordinate workers to owners, tenants to landlords, teachers to the government. In the name of prosperity, Social Credit, assisted by theoreticians like Walker, was endeavouring to overturn the entire social consensus of the past half-century. In the cause of economizing, a new social hierarchy, consciously designed to increase the gap between rich and poor, was being smuggled past the voters.

Of course, huge rallies had been held in protest. A Solidarity Coalition had organized demonstrations of up to 60,000 to denounce the "restraint package," and the same body had called a series of strikes. The teachers had walked off the job, the crown agency employees had downed tools; there had been no comparable sense of social unrest in Canada since the Winnipeg general strike of 1919. From California to British Columbia, the west coast of North America had a tendency to anticipate what would happen in the rest of the continent. The experience of the Bennett government suggested that, if elected, Brian Mulroney would not be able to institute a Thatcherite program of restraint, without risking the most serious social disturbances in nearly a century.

To further questions by Winlaw about the economy, Broadbent cites Japan's success in deficit financing, asserting that it has a much greater deficit compared to GNP than Canada. Deficit spending, he avers, can be used to create jobs; it makes little sense to reduce the deficit by throwing people out of work, further curtailing their spending power, and putting even more jobs in danger.

Then comes the cruncher. Winlaw asks Broadbent the inevitable question. If the NDP has no chance to win power, what are its prospects? Well, replies Broadbent, the NDP forces the other parties to come to grips with issues like tax reform. Yes, counters Winlaw, but is that enough? What with the swing in NDP fortunes, Broadbent responds, they are now building to the position where they will some day be able to do nationally what they have done in the provinces of British Columbia, Saskatchewan and Manitoba; that is, form a government. This was the curious role the New Democrats had carved for themselves: good influence on the other parties, tribune of the people, existing on an everlasting diet of hope.

The next day, Broadbent's campaign sets out for Nelson and Kimberley in the province's interior. His Air Canada DC-9 is being fuelled some distance away from the main airport building in Vancouver. The Broadbent plane is serviced by a resourceful Air Canada purser named Denis Langlois; it has the reputation among the press as the "four-star" flight. There is Heidseck champagne and orange juice as soon as you come on board "Air Ordinair," and a selection of fresh fruit, including kiwi. Better still, there is no howling band of media apes such as those accompanying Mulroney, no sardonic mockers like those harassing Turner. Broadbent's campaign, when he isn't relying overly on buses, is regarded by the press as a little bit of R&R. There's no crush of rivals; lots of empty seats to stretch out on. Best of all, there is less pressure; unless the NDP leader strips naked and commits hara-kiri, there is little chance that what they write about will reach page one. Unlike Mulroney, who sets a killing pace around the country, Broadbent does not work savage hours, but proceeds at a more dignified and restful rhythm, sounding the high-minded note of humanity, speaking up for social justice.

What's more, Broadbent's aides and the media share a common culture. Unlike the corporate neophytes around Mulroney, Broadbent's cronies tend to beards and spectacles. As for the women; well, if the women press attachés with Mulroney are like stewardesses and those with Turner resemble camp counsellors, the women with Ed Broadbent would not seem out of place at a daycare centre. What with the yogurt and fruit for breakfast, you can feel well at ease on Air Ordinair. The only things missing are house plants.

Yet, for all this, columnists like Richard Gwyn and Jeffrey Simpson were claiming that Broadbent was enjoying a free ride from the press, that his statements and policies were not being challenged as rigorously as those of the other two leaders. It was a charge that Broadbent denied indignantly. However, one sensed a certain community of purpose, if not belief, between Canada's third party and the reporters. In their separate ways, each served to check the power of the major parties by dictating what the issues were and by criticizing the Liberal and Tory platforms. Like the media, the federal NDP was spared the functional burdens and responsibilities of office.

Air Ordinair flies over the astonishing river and mountain landscape of interior British Columbia. Up front, Broadbent is working on the speech he is to deliver in Nelson. His bearded press secretary, Rob Mingay, says it is to be a major one. The approach to the Castlegar Airport is difficult: the jet banks low along a river, weaves its way between two mountain peaks, turns sharply and lands. It's a neat manoeuvre, duly applauded by everyone aboard.

Nelson's economy is severely depressed: much of the logging industry has been shut down; all the town has left in the way of jobs come from the railway repair yards. Broadbent is greeted by a noisy crowd of six hundred at the David Thompson University Centre. A huddle of buildings on a hillside, this small college has been shut down by the Socreds and the town is angry. Greeting Broadbent are many handpainted signs protesting the provincial cutbacks. "Beware," reads one, "Reagan = Bennett = Mulroney."

Outside, the mountains reach to a blue sky; Lake Kootenay stretches out below. There are no end of beards in the audience, lots of sandals. Numerous women stand with children slung in backpacks. Even more than with the Liberals, NDP politics are a family affair. There are always small children present and every speech is heard against a backdrop of wails. Nonetheless, where the legions of the vegetarian, the bearded and sandalled frequently looked ridiculous, they were now full of dignity: their cause was just.

The hall's cafeteria looks as if it could serve as a nursery, but its food is no match for what is served on the plane. Ed Broadbent and his wife Lucille, after being inevitably ushered in by another band of pipers, sit down to a lunch of cabbage soup in a styrofoam bowl, followed by hotdogs. Unlike Mulroney, Broadbent has no production team, no portable sound system; he is at the mercy of whatever the local organization can rig up. More often than not, what they provide isn't all that great: plenty of electronic beeps and chirrups are a feature of Broadbent's speeches, as are speakers that suddenly fail, leaving one part of the audience in the dark about what he is saying up there.

But even though his sound system occasionally folds up, Broadbent seldom is less than loud and strident when he addresses a public gathering. One hand in his pocket, the other forefinger stabbing and pointing, his face reddening as if he is on the verge of some species of fit, the NDP leader just ups and whales away at the ancestral enemy, "Bay Street."

Broadbent recalls how he launched his campaign in Toronto, in Spadina riding, among the bank towers. One part of the constituency, he says, is Bay Street, and the other end is Main Street "and I tell you, we're going to be holding that seat."

Well, Spadina riding could be described as many things, but homely "Main Street" is surely not one of them. That jumble of ethnics, academics, mediamen and yuppies had long been a Liberal bastion until Peter Stollery ascended to the Senate to help further the parliamentary ambitions of Jim Coutts. While Coutts in 1981 had feverishly courted the "ethnic" vote, it had been the riding's middle class that had installed an uninspiring, dogmatic socialist named Dan Heap as a kind of protest against what it regarded as Coutts's indecent lust for power. But rather than any populist "Main Street" uprising, the battle for Spadina was a contest between elites; the intelligentsia of downtown Toronto confronting what it regarded as the high-handedness of mandarin Ottawa in trying to direct its local affairs.

"I say to you," continues Broadbent, "that we have two voices speaking to Canadians. One voice, with two different faces, represents what I have described as the corporate voice of Bay Street. That voice has been presented in two different forms: that of Mr Mulroney and that of Mr Turner. *They're* not speaking out for Main Street, Canada."

In his typically aggrieved tone, Broadbent asserts his political credo. Ordinary Canadians — "miners, loggers, farmers" — are very special and have made the country what it is today. "Any political party that wants to run a democracy should not be putting the ordinary Canadian in second place in terms of its priorities, but in top place. Throughout the campaign, I have not been content just to speak in vague generalities, make fine-sounding phrases, and hope that the Canadian public will respond to some kind of image. Instead, I have proposed policies to make the country a better place, to change Canada from a country with so many privileges for the minority, to a country which is open much more to the priorities of the democratic majority."

For Broadbent, "ordinary" did not mean commonplace. Citing John Stuart Mill and Jean Jacques Rousseau, he liked to claim that there was something, after all, special and extraordinary about the common man. What was most important about Broadbent's idea of the common people was a sense of solidarity, a common sense of fate for the people who go to make up a nation. "Ordinary" did not imply that the common people did not possess divergent talents, unusual capacities. For Broadbent, what Canadians had in common, from the point of view of morality, was more important than their individual differences, skills and talents.

The problem was that, as a piece of rhetoric, "Ordinary Canadians" seemed so drab. The white collar middle class was not eager to classify itself among blue collar miners and loggers. Neither, increasingly, were white collar professionals. Since the onset of the economic freeze, the sentiments of equality were in short supply. To young people pouring into business schools and law faculties, economic guilt and feelings of social solidarity, were becoming an inconvenient burden. Clearly, for the four-fifths of the country who did not support the NDP, the "ordinary Canadian" was somebody else.

Next, Broadbent talks briefly about what his party is proposing to do about jobs, young people, taxes, women, nuclear disarmament, and health services. Long inured to opposition, he is eager to get on the assault. "What," he asks, his voice taking on an edge of profound scepticism, "what about the other voices?"

Mulroney and Turner, according to the New Democrat leader, have been doing a contemptible dance around the issues he has christened "The Bay Street Shuffle."

There is no possible way that John Turner, despite his Davey-inspired move to the left, can appear as genuine and convinced a spokesman for social issues as Ed Broadbent. Turner's job-creation program for young people is great in principle, the NDP leader says, until you read the fine print. Then you discover, he thunders, that Mr Turner is willing to provide jobs for fewer than one-half of one percent of unemployed youth. What's more, according to Broadbent, Turner wavers in his support for affirmative action for women.

Then he turns to his favourite issue, taxation, and churns up a storm of purple rhetoric: "I have talked to men and women all over Canada. I have talked to them in parks, I have talked to them at clambakes, I have talked to women and children. Working families are paying lots of taxes, pensioners are paying lots of taxes, and it's time the rich in Canada pay their fair share." There's large applause. Broadbent moves in for the kill: "Mr Turner had nothing to say about that issue until this morning, and just as they duplicate what we're saying on jobs, John Turner says he supports our tax proposals. But

I say to you and through you to the people of Canada, this will not gain credibility for Mr Turner and the Liberal Party. This will show ordinary Canadians just how cynical and desperate the Liberal Party of Canada has become."

It is difficult to discern whether Broadbent's audience in Nelson has any injured feelings about being "talked through," as he, through the media, addresses the rest of Canada, but their applause remains loud. Next, he turns his attention to Mulroney. The Conservative leader, he says, has learned all the right phrases. Broadbent almost fell out of his seat, he claims, when during the first television debate Mulroney supported the NDP's tax proposals. Two days later, however, according to Broadbent, a Conservative spokesman came forth to state that Mulroney's position was not party policy.

Mulroney, says Broadbent, maintains he's in favour of equal pay for equal work for women, but has acknowledged that equality for women will have to wait for a new boom in the economy. The NDP leader intimates that, come Monday, Mulroney will state that the deficit is his first priority. The next day in another part of Canada, Mulroney will promise four or five million dollars to try to do whatever he thinks is necessary to win some votes on that particular day.

Broadbent now moves to the crux of the matter: "The NDP," he cries, "is dedicated to the maintenance of all social programs. Brian Mulroney has indicated that Bill Bennett was moving in the right direction. And we are meeting today in a facility that was once proudly serving a community. And this facility was destroyed by the Bennett government, and Mr Mulroney says this is moving in the right direction. Canada take note. If you believe in social programs for health services, for education, don't rely on Conservatives!"

There is little doubt that Broadbent has a sharp eye for the contradictions of his two adversaries. His campaign tactics are effective in returning the NDP its customary share of the popular vote. He had moved shrewdly into the vacuum on the left created by the replacement of Pierre Trudeau by John Turner. Yet, in the larger sense of party philosophy, there was little doubt that these were the identical policies that had made the NDP a perennial afterthought.

James Laxer, the political scientist who had so well described the Liberal formula for sustained rule, had a similarly gimlet eye for the ideological failings of the NDP. As the party's research director, he had once published a penetrating report on the NDP's policies and in so doing had earned Ed Broadbent's enmity. (When asked to comment on Laxer and his ideas, Broadbent resorted to the worst insult he could conceive; he called Laxer a Liberal. The epithet was not without its truth. While John Roberts had paraded as the first Canadian paragon of neo-liberalism, Laxer's ideas were far closer than Roberts's to those of Gary Hart and Robert Reich.)

It was Laxer's argument that there had been little new thinking in the NDP since its formation as the CCF in 1933. The Keynesian universe, he contended, was now extinct, and huge deficit financing was far from being in the interests of ordinary people. As far as Jim Laxer was concerned, if buying people with their own money was the key to electoral success, the NDP would win every election.

Keynesian economics, according to Laxer, was chiefly concerned with the redistribution of wealth in an affluent society. In the altered reality of the 1980s, economic scarcity changed everything; the NDP would be better advised to concern itself with problems of production rather than with redistribution. The NDP, which had started as the party of ideas with J.S. Woodsworth and Frank Underhill, had long since ceased to think. There had been few new thoughts about these altered conditions.

The CCF was founded for two reasons, Laxer argued. In those days, the Liberal and the Conservative parties were, in effect, closed shops — exclusive gentlemen's clubs, scarcely amenable to new members or to change. Now, it seemed clear that both these parties were floating crap games, open to the strongest comer; they could be changed in almost any direction one wished. The rise to power of both Pierre Trudeau and Brian Mulroney was a perfect example of the relative malleability and contemporary openness of the two older parties.

More important, the men who founded the CCF in the 1930s, children of their time, were convinced that capitalism was coming to an end and that socialism represented the future. But, in the 1980s, after the Gulags of Soviet Russia, after Cuba, socialism no longer seemed to represent the promise of an unstained future; Ed Broadbent was far from campaigning on a socialist platform.

There was, however, a variety of left-wing thought in Canada that went unmentioned by Laxer. It existed mainly in the universities and was mostly distinguished by a vein of ideas best described as Mannerist Marxist. The influence of European thinkers like Adorno, Benjamin and Althusser had resulted in a left philosophy that examined culture and thought in a poetical, reflective fashion that was oddly divorced from the practical problems of how the left was to attain power.

Because of the influence of the prophets of Euro-Communism, the leftist thinking to be found in Canadian universities, rather than any working program of political action, had become a kind of mandarin ideology, which helped distinguish the modern clerisy from the mere mob. Accordingly, the traditional left critique of the injustices of capitalism had degenerated into mere snobbism: pedantic disgust at those who soil their hands with trade, fumbling with greasy thumbs at the till. Where Karl Marx contemplated the dynamics of society in order to change the world, Mannerist Marxism had declined into paltry public relations for an occupational group.

In the 1980s, as far as Jim Laxer was concerned, socialism was no longer the issue. The role of a Canadian third party was to ascertain whether it could be an effective force in getting the country through the difficult technological transition that lay before it. The real issue was exactly where Canadians would end up in the new international division of labour. In his opinion, the NDP was making a bad mistake by continually presenting itself as the opponent of the producers of wealth, as the opponent of technology. Although New Democrats liked to appear as the proponents of progress, they were unwilling for any technological change to occur if it happened to conflict with the entrenched interests of trade unionists. In Laxer's estimation, the NDP had not come to terms with the fact that the great issue of the time was to get the economy working again, and the greatest desire of the Canadian people was cooperation in achieving this goal.

Just as George Perlin had well assessed the problems of the Progressive Conservatives, Laxer had a good sense of the NDP's chronic disabilities. The party had never been able to make itself appealing to the genuinely poor. It had become a kind of alliance between well-off unionists, like the autoworkers and the steelworkers, and the Volvo-driving social workers and high school teachers who had a direct economic interest in the continued maintenance of the institutions of education and welfare. The very poor, in places like Atlantic Canada, had a political culture that the NDP had never really cracked. Neither had the party ever been a strong presence in Quebec. It was Laxer's contention that the NDP had to risk offending the core of their traditional constituency and risk creating some disharmony in the party, in order to attract a larger segment of the electorate.

Ed Broadbent angrily dismissed Laxer's diagnosis of his party's ills as "comic book analysis." Continually, he used the policies of the Swedish and other European social democratic parties as touchstones for his own policy. He would not be unhappy if the NDP was to

179

change its name to the Social Democratic Party. As far as he was concerned, the chief strategical priority of the NDP was to estimate the positions of the other two parties and take a stance that was far enough to the left as to be different, while still striving to build a democratic, socialist society.

Broadbent denied that he had moved his party closer to the centre than it had been under Tommy Douglas and David Lewis. Still, it seemed that as the Liberals had drifted right, so had the NDP. It could now be argued that there were in fact three centrist parties in Canada. With Mulroney coming left and Broadbent coming right, it was little wonder that the Liberal vote was disappearing. Because of what he perceived as a change in mood in Canada since 1980, Broadbent talked less about direct state intervention in the economy, especially on energy matters; in his estimation, he had merely shifted the emphasis onto other things, such as taxation and the status of women.

Broadbent adamantly dismissed Laxer's notion that the NDP was a social worker's party as a "pejorative stereotype." To the accusation that his attack on a mythical, bully-boy Bay Street was hopelessly out-of-date, Broadbent countered that he was not attacking the private sector in and of itself; he wasn't even saying there had to be equality of personal income. But he did insist that tax handouts to corporations should not be equated with the public good, but must be seen to produce public benefit through employment, research, and retraining. As far as he could see, the corporations had finessed the dismal state of the economy into an argument to get more out of government in an unaccountable way. Once society had been re-composed to the liking of the corporations, they would proceed to restore prosperity.

Insisting that his own ideas for industrial strategy compared well with those of European social democrats, Broadbent charged that Laxer practiced little in the way of "intellectual integrity" and that his own strategies for a mixed economy went well beyond Keynesianism. Broadbent still believed, though, that Keynes was one of the great creative economists of the century and that many of his short-run measures were still relevant for a mixed economy. In many of its particulars, the argument between Broadbent and Laxer was reminiscent of that between Walter Mondale and Gary Hart. In the present campaign, Broadbent had tapped a pure vein of working-class resentment. Both Turner and Mulroney did remind the hardhats at the factory gates of every management type they'd ever loathed on sight. In the long run, however, Laxer had set the terms of debate for the party's future.

The campaign moves on from Nelson to Cranbrook, where Broadbent is met by a small crowd at the airport. There are a lot of older people in the group; Broadbent appeals to senior citizens who are worried about holding onto their hardwon benefits. Kimberley, a small mining town to the northwest, has been turned into an alpine style village with plenty of mock Bavarian architecture. The sign at the edge of town says "Wilkommen Kimberley." The thoroughly Teutonic atmosphere was more than slightly unsettling. Where were you in '42? one felt like asking the inhabitants.

There are old bearded sourdoughs in baseball hats and plaid western shirts in the crowd, as Broadbent gives them "The Bay Street Shuffle" one more time. He gets a warm response when he mentions pensions. An elderly woman presents Lucille Broadbent with the ritual bunch of flowers. "They say," the donor intones into the microphone, "that an honest man is the noblest work of God."

As his plane makes ready to leave British Columbia for Saskatchewan, omitting Alberta as everlasting Tory country, Broadbent's good mood is unabated. He loves elections, loves to fight. It was a quality that played well against the other two candidates' corporatist attitudes; the result of a business culture that considered scrappiness to be undignified. "What a slack-looking bunch," he comments good-humouredly as he surveys the newshounds. Broadbent is consistently available and friendly; there's no sense of the beleaguered relations one finds on the other two aircraft. Spotting a placard carried by one of the crowd outside, Broadbent jokes " 'Make the rich pay more.' Yes, it's time the Marxist-Leninists took over this campaign."

Despite the friendly atmosphere on Air Ordinair, it is not a rowdy plane. The press tend to read a lot, or engage in quiet and serious conversation. But as the jet comes closer to Saskatchewan, the irrepressible Québécois begin to sing "O, Regina." The plane lands in the dusk, and the airfield is bathed in an electric blue prairie sunset.

That night, there is an opportunity to watch the other campaigns on hotel room television. The Tory commercials are all continuing to make Mulroney appear prime ministerial. He is portrayed against a backdrop of glossy black lawbooks, blond mahogany and dignified panelling. The Liberal commercials all close in on the theme of Mulroney's untrustworthiness, just stopping short of saying "Would you buy a used car from Brian Mulroney?" On the news, Turner was

181

looking more sweatily desperate, a hank of hair dangling from his forehead. National leadership politics, evidently, demanded much more of body and soul than the leisurely boardroom ethos of Winston's Restaurant.

The next morning, Broadbent tapes a television interview and then has another working-man's lunch of sauerkraut and sausage at the German-Canadian Club in Regina. Saskatchewan in the summer is so hot and dry it reminds you of something out of the Oklahoma dustbowl days. On the sidewalks outside the club, the grasshoppers are thick on the ground, almost as big as pullets. The club is a modest, slightly down-at-the-heels structure. The walls are cinderblocks painted yellow, and are hung with large travel posters of Deutschland. Up on the platform with Broadbent is the former NDP premier of Saskatchewan, Allan Blakeney, as well as two New Democrat MPs from Regina, Simon de Jong and Les Benjamin.

Blakeney, in a rumpled grey suit, looks like a bureaucrat's bureaucrat, bearing something of a resemblance to a more elderly and less personable version of football's Ron Lancaster. But once he is launched upon his speech, it proves to be one of the best of the entire election campaign. The art of rhetoric was largely lost in the television age, but Blakeney under full sail brought back the memory of every prairie populist from Bible Bill Aberhart to John Diefenbaker and Tommy Douglas. The provincial NDP leader is dull on television, but in a small hall like the German-Canadian Club, he brings to life a grand speech-making tradition that has its roots in circuit-riding Methodist preachers shouting hellfire and the social gospel. Just as Hank Williams or George Jones could make you shed an undeniable tear for the pathos of lives eked out in trailer camps and honkytonks, a prairie fire-eater like Blakeney can deliver a speech that inspires you to put down your pen and notebook in sheer admiration and mutter, "Go, baby."

The former premier warms up by taking a few tribal swipes at those familiar devils, the eastern media; then he turns his attention to the primordially satanic CPR. Next, it's Mulroney's turn. Blakeney pumps considerable air into the cathedral organ of his rhetoric by comparing the federal Conservative leader to the premier of Saskatchewan, Grant Devine:

"I say," he bellows, "we know what a Mulroney government will be like because we know what a Devine government has done. In Regina we've had an avalanche of promises, a cascade of commitments. We've already seen that."

182

Then, his voice envenomed with sarcasm, Blakeney ridicules the Tory campaign slogans: " 'Prosperity for all,' 'There's so much more we can be.' Mr Mulroney says it in the same tone of voice with slightly different words. Now that's the promise by Devine, by Mulroney. And they'll deliver prosperity, if you happen to be an oil company. But ordinary people are seeing the toughest times in decades. 'Jobs for all.' So says Mulroney. 'Bring the young people home. There'll be jobs for them.' So says Devine. And Devine has delivered jobs for some dozens of PCs. But in two years, unemployment is up in this province by 70 percent, for young people by almost 20 percent. 'Fiscal responsibility,' 'good management' — that's another Devine promise, another Mulroney promise. What about staggering deficits to pay for even bigger tax breaks for oil companies and trucking companies?"

It is the most stinging attack on Mulroney one has heard so far. Blakeney has a clear sense of how the current Tory slogans were larded with euphemism, designed to gloss over the ugly face of class warfare. As well as "fiscal responsibility" and "good management," terms like "economic reality" and "business confidence" were being uncritically swallowed by the voters. When Blakeney goes on to speak of "slashes in social services," he puts such bite and edge into his language that you can almost feel the gaping wounds in the body politic:

"You might recall Mr Devine promising no cuts in social services and hear Mr Mulroney promising the same thing, but here in Saskatchewan they've delivered a steady barrage of cuts and [have] chipped away at social service programs. University programs have been closed for lack of repair; there have been deep cuts in social aid payments to the unemployed, and there has not been one cent of increase in daycare rates. Just as Devine has slashed social programs, so indeed will Mulroney."

Canadians were deeply attached to their social welfare system and would not give it up lightly. There was no way Mulroney could get elected on a declared program of cuts in social spending; after all, he had gone so far as to call social welfare programs "a sacred trust." Les Benjamin follows Blakeney, and Broadbent delivers such an impassioned version of The Bobbsey Twins of Bay Street that he knocks his microphone clear off the lectern as his hands rip and tear at the air. But after Blakeney, it's anti-climactic. Where Broadbent, used to decades of Liberal rule, gives equal time to Turner and Mulroney, Blakeney has a better appreciation of who is the main opponent.

Broadbent always takes on the enemy in traditional NDP order: first the Liberals, then the Conservatives. Blakeney is immeasurably more effective; he just forgets Turner and sets his sights on Mulroney.

Late that afternoon, Air Ordinair flies on to Winnipeg. Burly I and Burly II, expiring with boredom, take turns acting as wine steward. They remove the pistols from their holsters and walk up and down the aisles, linen napkins wrapped over their arms, pouring out the Côte de Beaune Villages Labourie Roi for the Broadbent entourage and the press. Denis Langlois has made the four-star flight a kind of airborne gourmet shop, and there are always surprising hors d'oeuvres, cheese plates, little snacks, just to give everyone a little respite from all that workers' food they're getting down on the ground.

One has the sensation that having achieved his 18 percent, Broadbent has got what he wants — he's the leader of a respectable third party, a major public figure; that looking out for the interests of ordinary Canadians constitutes quite a comfortable life. Back in Nelson, a reporter had asked him about a story that had Gerry Caplan, the party's national director, conceding what everybody knew to be the truth, that Mulroney was so out in front that he had the election won. No, Broadbent had insisted, that statement had been premature. The NDP vote was growing; he was raising important issues. Once the election was over, Caplan would resign his position. From Stephen Lewis to Jim Laxer and Gerry Caplan, the NDP was hard-pressed to retain the loyalty of its best talent. Those men who became frustrated with 18 percent and raising important issues invariably came into conflict with the party establishment. It wasn't an original observation, but it was nonetheless true: there was a certain moral satisfaction in never contaminating yourself with power.

In the hotel in Winnipeg, I'm riding in the elevator up to my room when the doors slide open and there's Ed Broadbent, naked except for swimming trunks and a towel. For a second it's a moment of dizzy speculation: what is the Ordinary People's candidate doing prowling the halls of the Delta Inn in a towel? The world settles: Broadbent is commenting that he's been taking the sun: he likes to campaign in the summer — he finds ten minutes in the sun very refreshing. I nod sagely.

That night in Vimy Park, there is old-fashioned socialist folk music — Bring back the Travellers! — and a gathering of supporters from many Winnipeg ridings that are still solidly NDP. A message is read from Stanley Knowles, who, for the first time in decades, is not running in Winnipeg North Centre. If there was any romance in the

184

CCF-NDP, it emanated out of North Winnipeg: the site of the 1919 general strike, the seat of Knowles and of J.S. Woodsworth before him. Now just another depressed area of town, during the thirties and forties, the North End, with its large Jewish and Ukrainian populations, and its socialism, had been a kind of exotic enclave in the Canadian West, a little Moscow on the Assiniboine.

There are union officials in the audience and bearded house-husbands pointing out to their young charges, "There's Ed"; balloons coloured an NDP orange flutter over the blue-and-white striped tent. "We're sick and tired of being conned," Broadbent tells the crowd in Vimy Park. Tonight he's using that curious NDP accent, which overcarefully enunciates every syllable as in "the New Dem-o-crat-ic Par-ty." This painstaking pronunciation stemmed from the days when David Lewis, concerned to jettison any immigrant nuances, overcompensated by articulating his words ever so clearly. Now, it had become a New Democrat idiosyncrasy.

The next morning, Air Ordinair flies up to Churchill on Hudson Bay, above the 59th parallel. If there ever comes such an unfortunate time that the Canadian government institutes a Siberian-style Gulag, Churchill would provide the perfect location. Even though the town has a population of just over a thousand, there is little sign of habitation. It's muskeg country; the vegetation is sparse on the ground, except for dwarf pines. Although it's still summer, there is an air of desolation. The plane lands at a ramshackle tin shack belonging to the Department of Transport and Broadbent's entourage travels into town in two decrepit school buses. The Arctic landscape presents a scene of Nordic isolation that should be scored for solo piano by Sibelius.

Churchill is a raggy assortment of tin sheds, bad roads, and prefab housing. In the port are a number of immense slate-coloured grain elevators and a rail spur with a few freight cars; a ship flying the Greek flag is loading. The wind, even in August, is howling; it carries a light rain of grain with it that gets caught in the hair. Workers in hardhats, steel-toed boots and denims are lined up, patiently waiting to meet Broadbent, in the administrative offices that crouch under the massive elevators. They are mostly Indian and Métis; small, bow-legged, poor looking. In western Canada, the NDP is a far more accepted part of the community than it is anywhere else. Rod Murphy, the local NDP member, is there. The workers have the air of attending on a personage of some consequence.

Broadbent shakes hands all round; two girls say they're going to run up and pinch his bum. Just as Trudeau's upraised middle finger was the best remembered aspect on the streets of his two decades in office, Turner's lapse seemed to have the entire female working class believing that all Canadian politicians pinched bottoms.

Broadbent crosses the railway tracks to visit the Greek freighter. A local organizer strives to explain to the Greek sailor lounging on deck just who Broadbent is. The sailor is amiable but uncomprehending.

Outside the Arctic Hotel, an old-fashioned wooden platform is set up for Broadbent's speech. It is the first such object I have ever encountered outside of tintypes of the nineteenth century. When Broadbent comes out to address the crowd of a dozen or so, he takes one look at the rickety structure and decides not even to try to mount it. He addresses the faithful few without benefit of a microphone. There is a housing problem in Churchill and Broadbent is presented with a petition. He accepts it, saying that he's been critical of the government's housing programs; he's going to read the petition later, but he needs the address of the woman who gave it to him, so that he can get back to her. She uses the New Democratic leader's back as a writing board; he smiles, the cameras click, and this is the picture that appears on the front pages the next day.

From Churchill, we fly on to Ottawa. Broadbent comes back to chat with the press in his stocking feet, gin and tonic in one hand, cigar in the other. Like John Turner, Ed Broadbent appreciated a good cigar; no politician in the media age, however, was going to appear in public with a stogey clamped in his jaw: the image would evoke too much of backroom deals in the public mind.

As Air Ordinair approaches the capital, soul music percolates through the sound system and there's even dancing in the aisles. Lucille Broadbent asks her husband for a dance. Broadbent wiggles his eyebrows. "Yes," he leers. "We haven't had a dance in a while."

Yet, despite the self-congratulatory air on board, the political environment was changing around the NDP. As Jim Laxer liked to point out, the CCF-NDP had always had the luxury of living in a political system where the Liberal Party had been in power. Since the party was founded, there had never been two majority PC governments in a row. With the Liberals in almost permanent office, the NDP had been assured of a centrist consensus that took some notice of their own concerns. But now the situation was changing; there were eight provincial Tory governments; there was Reagan in the United States and Thatcher in Britain. The NDP position as the country's R&D

laboratory of social welfare policy was no longer assured. Inevitably, there was going to be a reaction against what amounted to a revolutionary conservative endeavour to remodel society. The question was whether the party was going to stick with its old, comfortable verities and fight a mere rearguard action against ever-eroding social programs, or whether it was going to seize the opportunity to serve as a focus for the opposition and become a truly national party at last.

CHAPTER 9

THE CHANGING OF THE GUARD

The Ritz-Carlton in Montreal is the closest Canada comes to possessing a Grand Hotel. Although other hotels may display more extravagantly modern forms of comfort and elegance, none of them evokes an equivalent sense of historical resonance. The Windsor Arms in Toronto offers a similar social arena, where the local shooters can rub shoulders with visiting glamourosi from the worlds of professional sport, showbiz, business, politics, the media, and God save us, literature. Where the Windsor Arms had relatively humble beginnings, and its current status is of comparatively recent provenance, the traditions of the Ritz-Carlton stretch well back in the century. The hotel's decor, general ambience, even its name, evoke Scott Fitzgerald and the Jazz Age. The novelist's Princeton friend and posthumous collaborator, Edmund Wilson, had stayed there while he was researching *O Canada*, a book that is still probably the best study of the country's culture written by a foreign observer. More importantly, the Ritz could still keenly summon up, even in the most jaundiced of souls, a hint of Fitzgerald's naive sense of wonder at the magic to be found at the top.

A few days before the 1984 general election, Brian Mulroney, finishing a swing through rural Quebec, arrives at the Ritz-Carlton Hotel. Three sleek silver buses are now travelling with him, just for the media. CBS is there and *Time* and *Newsweek* and *Business Week*. *The New York Times* is present and the *Los Angeles Times*; there are television crews from as far away as Sweden and Finland, reporters from West Germany, as well as the full panoply of Canada's national press corps. It is The Big Time in the flesh.

If Baie Comeau is the site of Mulroney's roots, the Ritz is a fit symbol of his ultimate destination — his true spiritual home. Tales are told in Westmount of Mulroney, in the first flush of his prosperity at Howard, Cate, Ogilvy, flashing *arriviste* wads of cash around the hotel as he respectfully squired the daughters and wives of the senior partners from tennis court to country club and back. Now he was on the hotel's board of directors. ("Where are you living now, Brian?"

a reporter had asked in the late 1970s. "You know the Mountain?" Mulroney replied. "Right at the fuckin' top." "Are you ambitious?" a scribe had asked on another occasion. "Well, I ain't no shrinkin' violet," was Mulroney's thoughtful response.) Now, as far as anybody can see, there is nothing that is going to stop Brian Mulroney from becoming the first man born in the Canadian working class to be elected prime minister.

For John Turner, the absolute capper, the knockout blow, had arrived a few days previously in the shape of the battle of the book-keepers. On 28 September, as promised, in a speech in Toronto, Mulroney had costed his promises at $4.3 billion dollars. It was Keith Davey's tactic to let the media struggle with Mulroney's numbers for a few days, then release the Liberal figures at the end of the week. Instead, on the plane from Saskatoon to Montreal, Turner's aides, under pressure from reporters, revealed that Liberal programs would run up a bill of $5.1 billion. As far as Davey was concerned, the premature disclosure of the Liberal numbers was the act of amateurs, unable to withstand a little press arm-twisting.

That night, at a Holiday Inn in Pointe Claire on the West Island of Montreal, Turner delivered his best speech of the campaign, telling a noisy audience of bedrock Liberal supporters that "the only job Brian Mulroney has given the Canadian people is a snow job," and that the Tory leader's figures "show conclusively that he doesn't understand the economy." Canadians wouldn't support Mulroney, said Turner, when they realized "just how shallow his programs and policies really were." According to Turner, his rival's figures were just "a hodge-podge of numbers." The PC leader had failed on the one pledge he had promised to deliver.

But John Turner's best speech went all for naught. The next morning, *The Globe and Mail*, which had previously run a photo portraying the prime minister with the upright fork logo of the Lunches with Leaders group sprouting like devil's horns from his head, ran "Liberals outbid PCs in price of promises" as a headline. Underneath, side by side, ran stories sub-headlined "$5 billion for Grits," and "Tories top $4 billion." As far as Keith Davey was concerned, that front page on Canada's national newspaper completed the Liberal disaster. The next day, Turner had flown from Montreal to Sarnia and Toronto. At the end of the day, sitting at the very front of his airplane, wearing his black horn rims, he seemed poleaxed, his face pale, lips fixed tight in a grim rictus.

Now, two days later in Ville St Laurent, in anglo suburban Montreal, Mulroney is enveloped in a Felliniesque carnival atmosphere. In a blue-and-white tent pitched near a shopping plaza, Mulroney addresses a rabidly partisan crowd. At every possible interval, loudspeakers blare out the party's tinny Quebec jingle, a tune that sounds like something out of AM radio in the ratlands of Mexico, promising that *"avec nous ça va changer."* (It is a slogan amended by Quebec wits to *"avec nous ça va chômer."* "With us there'll be lots of unemployment.") A rowdy bunch of guys in white hoods are running around brandishing straw brooms and chanting "Tory sweep, Tory sweep!" When it starts to rain, the crowd surges under the tent. Mulroney is in ebullient spirits. "Ah, let it rain," he booms. "Each drop that falls is another Conservative vote!"

Seated on the platform with Mulroney are the Conservative candidates of English-speaking Montreal like Gerry Weiner and Nick Auf Der Maur. The latter is a kind of *boulevardier* journalist and politician who had co-written a skimpy biography of his leader. During the 1970s Auf Der Maur had made that familiar contemporary journey from New Left to New Conservative and is now running against Warren Allmand in Notre-Dame-de-Grâce.

English Montreal is an embattled enclave and its journalists seem without exception to be on good terms with Mulroney, more than willing to take his part against a sceptical outsider, especially one from Toronto. Mulroney had been a public figure in Montreal since the days of the Cliche Commission into the construction industry. Toronto did not have an overwhelming interest in what it regarded as the tainted, parochial politics of Quebec; it was grudging in its recognition of Mulroney as a national figure. *The Toronto Star* would do almost anything to avoid putting Mulroney's picture on its front page. *The Globe and Mail* had endorsed the Progressive Conservatives, but not their leader. As the novelist Hugh Hood has argued, a national reputation is like a new proposition in formal theology: condemnation of the first proponents, eventual withdrawal of the condemnation, the slow winning of acceptance, and finally the triumphant definition of the proposition as dogma. Mulroney was a proposition that had long since carried off the journalists of English Montreal.

"Mr Chairman," intones Mulroney, sending up his own solemnity, "the question that arises just now is 'Can the House of Commons survive Nick Auf Der Maur?' And the answer is 'Yes'. It'll be a lot better off with Nick."

Mulroney is letting himself go, allowing the pious mask to slip a

190

bit, relaxing the 'let's-pretend Liberal' stance and permitting his conservative temperament to show through. There's going to be a brand new Conservative government, he says, and you don't have to take it just from him. He had been reading a newspaper today, one that was not on strike, and "even the ones that are on strike are endorsing us." Montreal papers did seem to go on strike with some frequency; Mulroney had made his reputation by settling one of these disputes. When a union struck, the public only thought of the inconvenience to itself. There is nothing to be lost in some Tory union-bashing.

Reading from the newspaper, Mulroney quotes Jean Chrétien, who has said that imminent defeat was not going to make him panic, that he was a hard worker, and that besides his work as an MP he was going to start practicing law again. "Jean," Mulroney laughs, "is an outstanding lawyer, and anybody who has legal business on Wednesday morning can bring it right to his office."

Mulroney is strutting now, his hands perched on his hips, the big jaw out-thrust, positively bloated with triumph.

"Know who he looks like now?" an American reporter asks his Canadian buddy.

"No, who?"

"Look at that jaw. Look at the way he's strutting up there. Doesn't he remind you, just at the moment, of another great leader . . .?"

That night, after the speech, two Americans and a Canadian are having a drink at the Ritz bar. Sitting across from them at the bar is Allan Fotheringham and a woman in a red dress. She is, as they say, of a certain age, but still attractive. In loud, carrying tones, impossible not to overhear, she conveys her desire to accompany Fotheringham to his room. The columnist protests that he's got an early curfew.

"Oh Allan," she whines, "you only come to Montreal when there's a referendum or an election. You don't care about my body."

The three men who have been overhearing all this come to the conclusion that it is a decidedly private conversation. Embarrassed, they pick up their drinks and retreat from the barstools to a table far across the room.

"Ohh," exclaims the lady, "did I drive them away?"

The next day the press scolds Mulroney for his cockiness. So the chameleon characteristically tones himself down for a tour of rural Ontario, a double date with Bill and Kathy Davis.

If Mulroney sounds like Jean Chrétien in rural Quebec, Davis is without doubt his model in Ontario. The soon-to-retire premier has a similar capacity to appeal to both rural and urban voters, as well as an unparalleled ability to walk straight down the centre line on any conceivable issue and never to get mud on his shoes. Leaving Montreal, Mulroney picks up Davis in Toronto, travels on to London, Kenora, Thunder Bay, North Bay and returns to Montreal via Ottawa, all in the space of one killer of a day.

The purpose of the trip is to try to make a difference in some marginal ridings. It is Davis's role to assure the folks that, Turner, Broadbent and portions of the press to the contrary, Brian is a man you can depend upon. If there is one man trusted by rural Ontario it is Brampton Bill. And if *he* trusts Brian, why shouldn't you?

The essence of Davis's style of politics is never to make an unnecessary enemy. So, throughout the trip he says he doesn't have to be critical of the Liberals, "they're doing it to themselves." Davis cracks his folksy jokes about Brampton and says how much he and Kathy have come to like Brian and Mila and how nice it is to see a federal leader who understands that Canadians are looking for "something positive," who understands the importance of agriculture, who is sensitive to the needs of senior citizens. Davis acknowledges what an asset Mila is; Mulroney returns the compliment and so the two men do-si-do, curtsy and bow, square-dancing their way across the province.

You might as well call the trip Yogi Berra Day. Although the outcome of the election is beyond dispute, it's bad form to boast the fact before the electorate has indeed spoken. So, joining Broadbent, both Davis and Mulroney keep saying "It ain't over till it's over." Everybody knows it's over.

In Kenora, Mulroney speaks, not as a director of the Ritz, but as a guy from a paper mill town in northeastern Quebec, talking to a paper mill town in northwestern Ontario. He trots out all his familiar lines, including the one about his electrician father and the two jobs and how all the money would now go to "Leaky Lalonde" in Ottawa. He talks about "a new dimension of prosperity" and how "what this country needs is somebody from a paper mill town in Quebec with somebody from a paper mill town in northwestern Ontario down in Ottawa." He tells the joke about the dollar, and talks about "small towns and big dreams," but, what the hell, the folks here haven't heard it before.

In Thunder Bay, Mulroney doesn't bother to get off the plane, just talks to the crowd from the steps that have been wheeled up — a real whistle-stop. "Sincerely, genuinely," he says without benefit of a mike, "we need your help. We're just a little late." The locals on the tarmac say, no they're not disappointed, they understand he has a tough schedule. One woman looks at the huge entourage of aides, production and press and wonders plaintively, "Why is he travelling with *all those people*?" One wave from the top of the stairs and he's gone.

In North Bay, Mulroney's meeting is held in the Memorial Gardens; the North Bay Centennials have given up their practice time so Mulroney and Davis can speak. Here is Canadian culture at its finest: there is a hockey scoreboard advertising Export "A", a big portrait of Queen Elizabeth taken about thirty years ago, and an Indian youth group doing their tribal dances in buckskin baseball caps and razor-cut hairstyles. There's a depressingly clean-cut band in blue polo shirts and white ducks, singing mercilessly upbeat songs about "On-tari-ari-ario." Once again Davis introduces Mulroney. As the day wears on, the premier is sounding more and more like a beer commercial: "I trust him," he says. "He will bring out the best in all of us."

In the course of his own speech, Mulroney launches an attack on the Canadian film industry. It might play well in a hockey rink in North Bay, but it does not augur well for the arts in Canada. Talking about the need for research and development to create jobs, Mulroney says that the Liberals spent less on R&D than any country in the world. "Why weren't we part of this new wave that created jobs and prosperity in places like North Bay and elsewhere? Why? We were busy making movies. Remember that? Nothing for R&D, but we were making movies. We were going to become the Hollywood of the North." In the small-town hockey arena, there's a wave of appreciative laughter at such folly. "Remember the great Academy Award winners? *Elmer, Wonder Dog of the North*; never seen by a Canadian, but real big in Albania."

This disgraceful little passage is a flat-out appeal to the philistinism of the Canuck boondocks. Ignoring acknowledged successes like *The Apprenticeship of Duddy Kravitz, Lies My Father Told Me, Scanners*, and *The Grey Fox*, Mulroney is telling the people of North Bay that government money invested in the Canadian film industry is costing them jobs. Jobs in the paper mills were going to be more important than jobs in the film labs or soundstages or editing rooms.

Back in Montreal, Pierre Trudeau has given a speech attacking Mulroney's Quebec coalition as an "unholy alliance of malcontents." As

193

always, Trudeau is following a personal agenda. The patronage appointments were a last *"je m'en fou"* gesture, rewarding loyal friends, and devil take the consequences. He had campaigned for his old friend Jim Coutts in a carefully chosen riding where no NDP graduate student with purple hair could come up and force yet another confrontation. Questioned by a TV interviewer about the appointments, Trudeau, defiant to the last, challenged the man to prove they were bad for the country. It was a possible line of defence that had been ignored by Turner. These are good, experienced men; what's wrong with them? For a second, on television, Trudeau had you believing him. Still, it was an argument that only Pierre Trudeau had the effrontery to pull off. The former prime minister had not appeared on any platform with John Turner, and this effort had only been meant to help Sheila Finestone in Trudeau's old riding of Mount Royal.

Boarding Manicouagan One, Mulroney is asked to comment on Trudeau's remark. At this stage, the last thing Mulroney wants to do is arouse Trudeau's wrath. "I think it's a free country," he says, "and I think Mr Trudeau's a fine gentleman and he can say whatever he wants. I think Quebeckers realize that Mr Trudeau has resigned; he's gone now and he's been replaced by Mr Turner."

"Does his statement bother you?"

"Do I look bothered?"

Back on the plane, Mulroney tells the boys in the back one of his patented Irish jokes. The story concerns The Father and Timothy and The Raffle, but the tone is exactly the same as when he's talking about the Liberals and patronage and "The Devil made me do it." Both the joke and the campaign speech contain a similar rueful, knowing sense of corruption in high places. As the plane descends into Montreal after the long day, the press start chanting "Tur-ner, Tur-ner" and singing "Give Chick a chance." Mulroney pops back from his first-class compartment, a big smile on his face, and gives them the finger; nonetheless, he's fastidiously careful to flash a euphemistic first finger, not the vulgar middle.

Travelling that day with Mulroney and Davis was the link between the Big Blue Machine and the federal campaign — Norman Atkins. Mulroney's campaign manager was moon-faced, curly-haired and amiable. Atkins did not have the same sort of power and influence Keith Davey did among Liberals. He was a campaign guru, the veteran of more than forty provincial and federal elections. With his brother-in-law Dalton Camp, Atkins ran an agency that specialized in government advertising, especially tourism. The Canadian government was the

194

biggest advertiser in the country. Atkins liked to say that advertising was his business and organizing was his hobby. Beginning in the fall of 1983, he had designed and staffed the organizational structure that had become a state-of-the-art election machine. Although the federal Tories had been dogged for years with various forms of incompetence, organization had never been one of them. Part of their legacy from the world of the corporation was an unsurpassed ability to coordinate committees, meetings and organizational flow-charts. Not surprisingly, Atkins talked in the corporate language of "timeframes" and "critical paths."

Organizational structures aside, Atkins was like a general manager in a sports franchise; his most important job was to make sure that the most competent people were appointed to the most decisive jobs. The corporate technique of advertising campaigns and the corporate technique of election campaigns had much in common. Market research and voter polling were practically identical sciences, carried out by many of the same people.

As well as being the lead hands of the campaign organization, Atkins acted like a fighter manager in the solicitude he lavished on Mulroney. He had to keep tabs on the candidate's physical and mental state. A campaign manager had to worry about just how tired his charge was getting. In the long haul across Ontario today, Mulroney had had to get himself up for every event, wind down afterwards, and then get himself up for the next one. It was part of Atkins's job to make sure his man could relax in between events, remind himself of what is important to the people he's going to address at the next one.

Atkins was amazed that the Liberals had been so disorganized; astonished that Turner had called an election so soon. He knew there was no way you could put an organization together in eight weeks. Atkins had believed that John Turner would have been a more formidable opponent than he in fact turned out to be; he had just not lived up to expectations. It was one thing to be minister of finance and a candidate for the Liberal Party leadership; it was altogether another to be leader and the prime minister.

For Atkins, the most difficult obstacle his party had to overcome was what he called "the incumbency barrier." He had always believed that his party was going to win the election, even though the polls did not always confirm it. All through the winter of 1983–84, the Tories had been leading in the polls; and although they were trailing after the Liberal convention, Atkins thought they were seriously in contention. What's more, while he thought little of Broadbent's charge that Turner and Mulroney were corporate clones, he didn't believe the accusation had hurt his party.

As for the future, Atkins asserted that Mulroney would be most successful not by emulating Reagan, Thatcher or Bennett, but by impersonating Bill Davis and charting a course right down the centre.

The trick, of course, was going to be how to discern, in a rightward-moving political environment, where the centre was going to be.

Also travelling with Mulroney is his chief policy advisor, Charles McMillan, last seen doing battle with the press in New Brunswick. If the Tory surge represented the revenge of "small towns and big dreams" over more cosmopolitan concerns, McMillan typified all those who had stayed at Canada's smaller universities, rather than going off to the Sorbonne and LSE. He had studied economic history in Charlottetown, got his MBA at Alberta, received his doctorate and was now teaching business at York University in Toronto. The brother of Tory MP Tom McMillan, he had worked as a pollster on Brian Mulroney's first leadership campaign in 1976.

McMillan had just published a book on Japan and was brimming with the lessons Canadians could learn from the Japanese. In his estimation, Japan was going to be a lot more important to Canadians than were France or Britain. For McMillan, the traditional model of Britain was a bad one to follow because it kept imposing the labour-management models of the vanishing smokestack industries of the nineteenth century. Japan was now Canada's second largest trading partner. Canadians were going to have to understand what the Japanese were doing in management, technology and market structure if they were going to compete with them in the US market.

MacMillan brushed away all objections that Canadians were culturally different from the Japanese; he believed we could apply 90 percent of their methods. What was required was more cooperation between labour and business, less intervention in the economy, less power for the trade unions. Instead, the worker needed thorough on-the-job training. There had to be more technological links between business and the universities. But on how much Brian Mulroney was willing to turn the country into another Japan or what his own role in a Mulroney government will be, McMillan is vague. Like the rest of the PC leader's entourage, he is in the best of moods. Just before he gets off Manicouagan One at Thunder Bay, referring to Joe Clark's election gaffe of 1980, McMillan quips, "Do we make the announcement about the embassy here or at the next stop?"

On Saturday, 1 September, Mulroney addresses an enthusiastic crowd in the east end of Montreal, right in the heart of traditional Liberal territory. *"C'est un prince comme Jack Kennedy,"* says one of the onlookers. On Sunday, though, in Wabush, on the Quebec-Newfoundland border, Mulroney runs into a crowd of chanting trade unionists, who want to run him right out of town. Wabush is close to Labrador City, where many jobs were lost when Mulroney, as the president of the Iron Ore Company of Canada, closed down the town of Schefferville on the instructions of the company's American owners. The Steelworkers Union are demonstrating at the airport; they're an angry crowd, carrying signs that say "Brian helps the rich, God help the poor," and "You got your home for one dollar. I lost mine."

"Mulroney's an arsehole," stoutly maintains a unionist named Nelson Larson. "He's not wanted here."

The small Tory greeting party and the demonstrators trade cheers and boos. The Tory organizers try to play the jingle "We're voting PC now." A journalist says, "They oughta change that to 'We're cloning BC now.'" And a union rep is quick to talk about how many steelworkers in Labrador City have been deunionized.

A nervous PC worker vainly tries to appeal to the traditional Canadian sense of order. "Air Canada Express asks you not to step on the baggage carousels," he pleads.

"They don't even come here!" shouts one of the steelworkers.

"Well, who is it? EPA then."

The PC organizers consult hastily and there's a long wait before Mulroney leaves Manicouagan One.

"He's not going to stay on the plane?" worries one of the demonstrators.

Finally, Mulroney is ushered in with a phalanx of security. He endeavours to cool down the situation with his standard line for hecklers: "I tell you," he begins, "the NDP knows where to come to find a crowd."

It doesn't work; there's just a steady chorus of jeers. Every time Mulroney tries to open his mouth, the steelworkers try to boo him down. "Go home," they shout. "Go home." Finally, microphone power wins out over massed lung power.

"There are some people who don't want to hear the truth because the truth hurts," Mulroney shouts hoarsely. "But I'll tell you this: it's going to take more than a couple of malcontents to shout me down, that's for sure!"

Usually, Mulroney blandly assures the crowds that there's nothing at all wrong with Canada, except for the Liberal Party. Here, he points at one of the more irate protestors and says "I have a grown man that's conducting himself like a child, and that's what's wrong with this country. If you think I have any lessons to learn about treating workers with justice, you've got the wrong guy. And you go home because I'm home in Labrador and I'm home everywhere in Canada, and I can tell you that prosperity and new hope will come with cooperation and not with shouting people down as some NDPers and Liberals would like to do. The Canadian people want people who listen, they want cooperation, and they're not going to be impressed with a bunch of people who deny others free speech! It's because of people who speak in the night and hide behind signs that the Canadian people want the sunshine of new hope and new promise and that's what the Conservative government is going to bring."

This sort of conduct, Mulroney says, has never been the Newfoundland way, has never been the Labrador way; it's not the way the new Conservative government is going to bring hope, he adds, even though, naturally, "we're taking over a country in bad shape."

"I see a sign," Mulroney shouts, "that says Brian Mulroney supports the corporate shareholder and not the worker; we put together the most generous package in Canadian history and you should be proud of it, because everybody else is! And I'll tell you that when the United Steelworkers laid off permanent personnel, they never treated their employees as generously as the Iron Ore Company of Canada did."

Well, there it is. After weeks of placid crowds and pseudo-events, the campaign, in its last days, finally witnessed a moment of truth. Cooperation between business and labour was a marvellous thing, but it seemed as if it would be just a little while before the United Steelworkers would be singing hymns to the Iron Ore Company, as the Japanese workers did at Sony.

In a political environment that was universally Conservative, there was something ominous now about the term "cooperation." Strikes and demonstrations were the only weapons organized labour had left to ensure a modicum of social justice in a changing technological landscape. The kindly intentions of business were always taken for granted; those of labour seemed permanently in doubt. Just as in North Bay Mulroney opposed "jobs" to Canadian movies, he was all "prosperity and new hope" to a union protest in Wabush. Did the Canadian people want "people who listen," or just docile workers who didn't talk back when they were laid off? The insistence on

198

"cooperation" in the new political dispensation had some unhappy authoritarian overtones for those who chose to dissent from the dictates of Canada, Inc. Everybody was in favour of cooperation. The only issue was on whose terms it was to be found.

"Well," says one steelworker, full of the salt of Newfoundland motherwit, as he watches the Mulroney entourage board the buses that will take them to Fermont on the other side of the Quebec border, "if he wants the job, he's got to take the shit that comes with it."

As Manicouagan One flies from Labrador to Sept-Iles, Mulroney comes back to talk to the press, more upset about the incident than he's letting on. The demonstration at Wabush, he says, wasn't composed of unemployed steelworkers; they were professional hecklers. But he's happy with the way things turned out; better than if he had arranged things himself.

Since the election is now over bar the shouting, the incident at Wabush makes the headlines. That night at the Auberge des Gouverneurs in Sept-Iles, Mulroney throws a party for the press. The entire evening is nicely calculated. There is good booze, good eats. Few newspapers were published on Labour Day, the election was as good as over; even an unguarded quote, if some rogue reporter were unpleasant enough to use it, could do little damage. This evening of stroking was an investment for the future.

Mulroney, in casual clothes, accompanied by his wife, circulates through the room, careful not to omit a single table. Anybody who wants to learn how to work a room should spend an evening watching Brian and Mila Mulroney. They know to the second how much time to devote to each person there, according to precedence; just how much time to devote to each individual, so that satisfying communication can be felt to have taken place; they never get caught too long in a single conversation. You leave with the impression that Mulroney is a genuinely likeable man; that his wife is really very easy to talk to.

At one table, Mulroney says that the man interviewed as an unemployed steelworker was really a trouble-making union leader. The package each worker got at Labrador City, he says, amounted to some $21,000. One reporter asks the Tory leader about the integration of his French and English caucus. Mulroney replies that he's going to lay down the law, just as he did about minority language rights in Manitoba: this is our policy; if you don't like it, you're welcome to leave and sit with Bill Yurko, the maverick from Edmonton. He told his caucus, there's only one way to get power. And he re-enacts the scene. Opposition is for losers; I'm going over there (pointing to the government benches). You can stay here all your life and write letters to *The Globe and Mail*, but not me. Needless to say, the informal and tough-talking Mulroney is preferable by a factor of about 100 percent to the guy who oozes vaporous pieties and platitudes on the campaign trail. But then Mulroney can never be accused of not having an intuitive sense of any audience. If Mulroney is Jean Chrétien in Quebec, Bill Davis in Ontario, for the media he is the hard-bitten realist, bursting with the privileged information of the insider. To every group in society Mulroney the chameleon gives back its own image. Few groups, especially the media, were sufficiently free of *amour propre* to resist falling in love.

After they have circulated at each and every table, Mulroney and his wife leave. There's a three-piece band playing for the dancing pleasure of the ladies and gentlemen of the press.

"Don't ask me to dance, honey," Mulroney tells his wife, " 'cause I'm all danced out."

It's grey and rainy when Brian Mulroney arrives in Baie Comeau the day before the election. There's a chill in the air; the long winter is on its way. Abandoning the stance of the straight-talking political insider, he lays down some vintage corn for the hometown folks, about the son of the electrician, making his long journey home. Baie Comeau is already celebrating; in the crowd they're drinking beer straight from the bottle.

At the Centre Récréatif the ice has been removed from the two hockey rinks. The practice rink has been set up with tables and telephones for the press; the arena itself will house the celebration. There is no room to be had at the town's hotels and motels. Some of the correspondents find themselves billeted with local residents, sleeping in rec rooms where stuffed snowy owls and other sub-arctic hunting trophies look down at their camp beds, hired for $40 a night. Mulroney appreciates the value of cash money to a small town: the locals appreciate the windfall.

On Election Day, Mulroney votes at the local school, at the Edifice Ste Amélie where he attended grades 1 through 7. The day before, he had taken the media for a stroll on Champlain Street where he had grown up, pointing out Number 99, which didn't look much like a log cabin, rather a standard Canadian middle-class house on a tree-lined street. Now he regales the press with tales about how he and his buddy Jimmy Green terrorized the school. Mind you, with harmless pranks.

"I went to this school right here," he twinkles, "and I want you to know that I was a model student."

Since he is about to become prime minister, Mulroney's unexceptional childhood now becomes pregnant with significance, to be pored over by biographers for hidden portents. If fate is character, clues to the nation's future were now to be read in its leader's destiny.

Mulroney casts his vote in the school gymnasium. The gym is covered with photos of the class of '84: Sandra, Alex, James, Cindy, Laura and Lee. As the PC leader drops his ballot paper in the box, the photographers and cameramen swarm around him. "Stay behind the red line," warns Mulroney's media bullyboy, Bill Fox, "or I'll clear the room."

As evening falls, a heavy fog starts to gather along the North Shore. There's not much in the way of suspense. The polls are right on the money. At 7:45 Radio-Canada projects a Conservative majority. The night is over before the vote is counted beyond the Manitoba border. For the Liberals, it's a total wipe-out, worse than what Diefenbaker handed them in 1958. Cabinet ministers go down like ducks in a shooting gallery: Fox, Erola, Roberts and Joyal are all defeated, as are Iona Campagnolo and Jim Coutts. But Turner, saving himself from total humiliation, wins in Quadra; despite Mulroney's best efforts, Chrétien, Ouellet and Garneau survive in Quebec; nor does the PC win that seat in Labrador. When it was all over, the Tories had won 211 seats to the Liberals' 40, and the NDP's 30. They had won 50 percent of the popular vote, to 28 percent for the Liberals and 19 percent for the New Democrats. It is the biggest Liberal loss in Canadian history; one would be hard-pressed to say they didn't deserve it.

On television, John Crosbie twirls a rose — ever since Trudeau, the symbol of power in Canada. Jean Chrétien is generous in defeat, although he says it was a mistake to run a summer election. One remains curious about what kind of campaign Chrétien would have run. He would surely have been able to stop Mulroney from getting the astounding 59 seats he won in Quebec; he would not have been put on the defensive as easily as Turner. But even the lion-hearted Chrétien would have had difficulties in refusing Pierre Trudeau his parting appointments.

Marc Lalonde speaks bravely through his obvious pain, saying that every quarter of a century the country tries the Tories for four years and then returns to the Liberal fold for another quarter-century. Ed Broadbent claims that the NDP are going to be the real opposition. Turner, speaking from Quadra, allows as how "the people are always right," vows to offer constructive criticism in opposition and dutifully offers to effect "an orderly and speedy transition". "Tomorrow," he says, "I start the task of rebuilding the Liberal Party." What he doesn't say is that Liberalism itself is in critical need of redefinition if it is going to survive. Although the Tories are victorious everywhere, two of their more quirky candidates, Nick Auf Der Maur and Peter Worthington, lose; it's a bad night for journalists endeavouring to become politicians.

The Mulroney entourage are rushing around congratulating each other. Mulroney's college friend, Sam Wakim, big and burly with a cigar clenched in his mouth, is enfolding everybody in a bear hug. L. Ian MacDonald, Mulroney's biographer, congratulates Charles McMillan on his prognostications. "Charley," he says, bursting with boyish admiration, "you're a genius, as always." A few minutes before, MacDonald had appeared on national television. He had been the only journalist present in the Manoir Comeau, where Mulroney was watching the election returns. "What was going on there?" CBC's Peter Mansbridge had asked. "Read my book," MacDonald replied, endearing himself to the nation, "and find out." Mulroney arrives at 8.53 pm, his hair damp from the rain outside. When he takes the stage with Mila, the crowd won't let him speak, so tumultuous is its applause. Baie Comeau has won the Stanley Cup. Mila claps, as one more time the Tory anthem plays:

> We're going to get this country working
> That's a promise, that's a vow.
> We're going to do this all together
> And we're voting PC now.

As they sway back and forth to the music and the cheers, hand-in-hand, for a second it seems as if they might break into a dance. The Canadian voters had bought Mulroney's dream of prosperity, his example of affluence; he obviously made the country feel good.

(On the campaign bus there had been a young German reporter. He was blond, solitary, silent. It was his first time on the North American continent and he had the habitual European's impression of unparalleled affluence. In his shrewd estimation, the most salient feature of the election was the Canadian determination to hold on to the country's affluence, whatever the social cost.)

Mulroney's first words to the nation are in French. Without doubt he has achieved a historic turnaround in Quebec. He thanks the voters of Manicouagan, he thanks the voters of Central Nova, where he won his first seat. Mulroney speaks of his high personal regard for Turner and Broadbent. He thanks the voters for their sweeping expression of confidence, talks of the enormous responsibility, speaks of unity, reconciliation and hard work. One is reminded of the speeches of generals after battles. Noble-sounding generalities hide the carnage. The congratulatory call from Ronald Reagan comes the next morning at half-past nine. The newspapers are predicting a Tory dynasty lasting until the end of the century. In Canada, the Conservative era is at hand.

In the crowd, they are just beginning to celebrate. There's 18 percent unemployment in Manicouagan. Among the crowd in the Centre Récréatif there are these strange rink rats; they have pinched, feral faces. One of them wears a sleeveless undershirt, his shoulders are specked with acne; he has an open beer in his hand. Drunkenly, he keeps peering over a reporter's shoulders, to see what the guy has written in his notebook. First of all, the writer tells the bush rat to get lost. It doesn't work; the guy keeps prying. The writer resorts to the only incantatory spell he knows. "Fuck off," he intones, feeble magic. The face of the bush rat splits open in a horrible, beatific and toothless grin. It's his country now.

LAMENT FOR A NATION

In the first few months of Conservative rule, it became clear that the new government was making changes that went to the fundamental heart of the nation, and that Brian Mulroney represented the sugar on what was going to be a bitter pill. He started generously enough by appointing Stephen Lewis, a man too talented to stand indefinitely on the sidelines of the country's public life, as ambassador to the United Nations. Still, there were sceptical observers who claimed that the Lewis appointment was just a typical Mulroney bit of soft soap, preparing for the thrust of patronage to come. The campaign had shown Mulroney to be a man of considerable abilities; for the span of the election, television put a presidential cast on the country's politics and the Progressive Conservatives were perceived as Brian Mulroney alone. Back in parliament, day after day, the ground shook under the PC leader, as Tories acted as Tories always did. Joe Clark, the new minister of external affairs, heedlessly sent a tape to a radio station in St Catharines that contained eight minutes of Clark's dictation concerning matters Nicaraguan. An aide of the new finance minister, Michael Wilson, inadvertently taped a private meeting with the NDP finance minister of Manitoba. As mentioned earlier, the Conservative premier of New Brunswick, Richard Hatfield, was charged with possession of marijuana. In the course of the scandal, a fey young student came forward to report an incident where he claimed the premier had plied him with cocaine. "There was the premier," he informed the newspapers, "with white powder all over his nose." The scandal threatened to reach right into the federal Tory government when it came to light that the new solicitor general, Elmer MacKay, had had consultations with Hatfield on the conduct of his trial. The premier of New Brunswick was soon joined in the headlines by Robert Coates, the right-wing minister of defence, who resigned his portfolio after he was reported to have enjoyed several drinks with a bar girl in a seedy nightclub in West Germany. It was revealed that the new minister of the environment, Suzanne Blais Grenier, who wasted no time in applying a Reaganite policy to the country's wildlife, had been reportedly fired from her previous job for incompetence. If during the campaign Brian Mulroney's favourite word was "handsome," during his first few months in office, it became "honourable." Coates was honourable, Mackay was honourable, Wilson was honourable.

All of this was comic enough. Not so amusing were some of the new government's measures. In his first mini-budget, Michael Wilson, just as he had promised in that unreported speech in Toronto, cut government spending and help for the unemployed, to the tune of $286 million. Mulroney made a pass at universal social programs, but backed down when he was reminded on all sides that, on 18 August, he had called universality "a sacred trust not to be tampered with." As the speech in North Bay hinted, Mulroney was no particular friend of Canadian culture. The budget for the CBC was cut by some 85 million dollars; there was a bloody purge in the Corporation's Toronto office and scores of producers lost their jobs. Neither Ed Broadbent or John Turner came to the defence of the CBC; there appeared to be little political mileage in doing so. Arts groups were forming to protest the government's policies. Another million dollars was cut from the budget of the Canada Council. The Tories, who in opposition had fought for the traditional arm's-length relation between arts organizations and government, in office, under the new minister of communications, Marcel Masse, held no such belief. Spending on the environment was also out. As far as other patronage was concerned, the new group that won the contract to manage the federal government's $60 million advertising account was accused of being forced to kick back part of its fees to the PC party machine in Quebec. Norman Atkins's ad agency received the tourism account of the federal government. Amongst other Tory appointees, the general manager of the Ritz-Carlton hotel, Fernand Roberge, was appointed to the board of Air Canada. The New Gilded Age was truly at hand. The Canadian dollar, which Mulroney had had such sport with during the campaign, under his government fell below 72¢ American, its lowest ever. Although Mulroney was continuing to steer a course down the centre, Big Business was not nearly satisfied with Mulroney's cuts; they wanted even fewer social services. Having promised prosperity, it seemed to be Mulroney's role to let Canada's quality of life slip as gently as possible. The prime minister had gone down to New York and announced that Canada was "open for business," that the Foreign Investment Review Agency was now Investment Canada. The announcement was greeted with a thunderous silence in the United States; nobody seemed anxious to buy. "Prosperity" and "new hope" seemed somewhere in the future. The optimism generated by the elation of Mulroney's exhilarating election campaign now looked to be the anxious optimism of despair. The Progressive Conservatives had campaigned on the Liberals' lack of political morality and the bad state of the economy. After six months, neither have seemed much improved in a Tory government. After twenty-one years, the Liberals deserved their defeat. But going into the spring of 1985 it seemed that Canadians had traded a bad government for one that was different, but little better; in some ways, considerably worse.